THE CATHOLIC UNIVERSITY OF AMERICA

GALAHAD IN ENGLISH LITERATURE

A Dissertation

SUBMITTED TO THE FACULTY OF THE GRADUATE SCHOOL OF ARTS AND SCIENCES
OF THE CATHOLIC UNIVERSITY OF AMERICA IN PARTIAL FULFILLMENT OF
THE REQUIREMENTS FOR THE DEGREE OF DOCTOR OF PHILOSOPHY

BY

SISTER MARY LOUIS MORGAN, O. S. U., A. M.

THE CATHOLIC UNIVERSITY OF AMERICA
WASHINGTON, D. C.
1932

TO THE

URSULINE NUNS

OF

LOUISVILLE, KENTUCKY

TABLE OF CONTENTS

PREFACE

M. Albert Pauphilet in his *Études sur la Queste del Saint Graal* [1] concludes that the Galahad character, as a definite literary creation, came from the pen of a twelfth century Cistercian monk, whose motive was to convert the existing Arthurian legends into a hortatory allegory designed to turn men's minds from the chivalry of earth to the chivalry of heaven.

The purpose of the present investigation has been to trace the character of Galahad through the pages of English and American literature, and to show how, from Malory in the fifteenth century to E. A. Robinson in our own day, Galahad has reminded the apotheosis of knightly virtue, the ideal of purity and singleness of purpose. Wordsworth, Tennyson, Westwood, Hawker, Hovey, Hamilton, and Robinson, all treat him as a more or less constant quantity, a fact, which in a literature of ever shifting ideals, must appear curious if not indeed phenomenal.

The writer wishes to acknowledge her indebtedness and gratitude to Professor Patrick J. Lennox, Head of the Department of English, for his kindly encouragement and helpful and constructive criticism, and especially for his valuable assistance in the field of Celtic folklore; to Dr. Francis J. Hemelt, Associate Professor of English, the author wishes to express her appreciation for his kind assistance in the general direction of the dissertation. Her thanks also are due to Dr. Paul G. Gleis, Head of the Department of German, for many valuable suggestions.

S. M. L.

CATHOLIC UNIVERSITY,
January 21, 1932.

[1] Paris, Champion, 1921.

GALAHAD IN ENGLISH LITERATURE

CHAPTER I: INTRODUCTORY

FORERUNNERS OF GALAHAD

More than thirty years ago Jessie L. Weston laboring in behalf of Arthurian scholarship made an eloquent plea for the further elucidation of Arthurian romance through a careful study of the stories connected with the individual knights. By means of separating as far as possible the threads of the fabric, Miss Weston thought to discover the nature of the groundwork, and perhaps thereby to arrive at what may have been the original Arthur saga. She adds that such an undertaking is " only practicable, and indeed only serviceable in the case of the leading figures of the legend— such characters as Gawain, Perceval, Kay, Tristan, Lancelot, and Galahad." [1]

Herein the present investigation finds its justification and argument, but an argument with a difference. Instead of proceeding as Miss Weston suggests by attempting at the outset to discover what was the original form of the Galahad story, the writer purposes rather to begin with the outer strands, the *known* Galahad material, and examine Galahad's position and importance in only one, but its greatest field of development, the literature of the English-speaking world. For there are two ways of unweaving a fabric: one is to start at the very center and dexterously to disengage the tightly woven threads from their close-fitting position; the other is to begin from the outside, and to work on parallel lines towards the center. By the first method there is no little danger of breaking the fragile threads and of pulling the whole fabric hopelessly awry; by the second method, there is a greater facility in separating the loose strands and scarcely any possibility of interfering with the general pattern.

In the school of origins, so many and such complicated problems present themselves—problems for which veteran Arthurian scholars

---

[1] Weston, J. L., *Legend of Sir Gawain*, p. 4.

1

have never found solutions—that the most enthusiastic tyro must perforce throw down his arms in despair. The second method mentioned above appeals by reason of its simplicity. Working backward from a mass of particular examples to their prototypes, one has the advantage of observing the natural literary evolution of the character, and at the same time of opening countless doors of research through which one may eventually be led to the hidden mysteries of origins. Indeed, if the following dissertation does nothing more than to inspire a more experienced Arthurian scholar with the idea of undertaking a complete and exhaustive study of Galahad origins, a study which has yet to be made, the writer will feel eminently repaid for the labor spent on the outworks.

The purpose of the present investigation, then, has been to collect all the Galahad material available in English literature, to note something of the historical, philosophical, literary, and social backgrounds both of the period of the writer and of the writer himself who took Galahad for his theme, and to give a brief estimate of the literary character of those works in which Galahad appears either as the hero or as a subordinate character with a quasi-stellar role. While making no pretense at a study of origins, the writer has attempted in the third chapter to advance some hypotheses of her own as to the possible genesis of the Galahad character, these hypotheses being but the outgrowth of her necessarily extensive reading in Arthurian source material, accompanied by an examination of medieval backgrounds.

That a study of this nature has never been done will be readily admitted by those familiar with the literature. M. Albert Pauphilet in his *Études sur la Queste del St. Graal*[2] has given us an excellent critical study of the first extant literary work in which Galahad appears, but he confines his study exclusively to the twelfth century romance which is the parent source of the later Galahad romances. The present writer, accepting for the most part Pauphilet's conclusions, takes up the study where he leaves off, and attempts to follow the *boine chevalier* through the pages of English and American literature.

The desirability of such a study appears among other reasons

---

[2] Paris, Champion, 1921.

from the fact that through several centuries Galahad has been the inspiration of some of our noblest literary creations. No literature, no work of any \art, in fact, ever surpassed in greatness the ideals which inspired them; and if Malory found in Galahad the necessary hero for his immortal Grail quest; if Tennyson saw in him the solution to the mystery of sense and soul enveloping the Table Round; if Wordsworth, Westwood, Hawker, Hovey, and Robinson, hailed him as a light to guide the sense-darkened souls of men, then surely there is ample justification for the present attempt to seek out Galahad from his several hiding places in English literature, and to discover where, and by whom, and under what circumstances, this ideal of purity and singleness of purpose, this boy-knight of the Middle Ages, came to be the vital force he is in our literary thought and history.

Galahad, the son of Lancelot du Lac, is probably a comparatively late addition to the world of Arthurian romance as seems to be the case also with his famous father. Geoffrey of Monmouth in his *Historia Regum Brittanniae* (1137) makes no mention of him, nor is his name found in the writings of the other early chroniclers, Gildas, Nennius, and William of Malmesbury. The *Annales Cambriae*, which like Nennius carries the story of Arthur back as far as the sixth century, knows nothing of Galahad, and Wace's *Roman le Brut* (1155), though mentioning for the first time the historic Round Table, is silent concerning the *boine chevalier* who was destined to occupy the most important place at that table.

As far as can be determined, the name of Galahad, the son of Lancelot, appears for the first time in extant literature in the vast body of late twelfth century prose tales now popularly known as the *Vulgate Cycle of Arthurian Romance*.[3] True, as Dr. Loomis points out,[4] there is mention of a King Galahal in the *Lai du Cor* (1150-1175), a work which he claims to be one of the oldest pieces of

---

[3] Edited in seven volumes by Oskar H. Sommer, The Carnegie Institute, Washington, D. C. Vol. I, *L'Estoire del Saint Graal* (1909); Vol. II, *L'Estoire de Merlin* (1908); Vol. III (1910), Vol. IV (1911), V (1912), *Le Livre de Lancelot del Lac*; Vol. VI, *Les Aventures ou La Queste del Saint Graal, La Mort le Roi Artus* (1913); Vol. VII, *Supplement: Le Livre d'Artus* (1913); Index of Names and Places to Volumes I-II (1916).

[4] Loomis, Roger Sherman, *Celtic Myth and Arthurian Romance*, p. 28, 155.

romantic French Arthurian literature extant; still, no evidence can be found to prove that this Galahal is in any way identified with the Galahad of the fully developed Grail quest, the Good Knight of medieval romance. Moreover, the name *Galahad* with its variant spellings [5] is not an uncommon one in medieval romance; in the Vulgate Cycle alone there are, besides Lancelot's son, three bearing the same name, Galahad *le roy des Pastures,* Galahad *le Sires de la Terre des Pastures,* and Galahad the son of Joseph of Arimathea from whom Gales (Wales) is supposed to have received its name. Our interest in the present study is confined exclusively to Galahad the son of Lancelot and *la belle fille au roy Pelles de Listenois,* to Galahad who in medieval parlance was known as *li boine chevalier, le millor chevalier del monde,* the ninth descendant of Nascien d' Orberique.

Whatever connection may ultimately exist in a source way between this and the other Galahads, or between him and the Galahal to whom Dr. Loomis refers, the fact remains that the Galahad, whom the writer identifies specifically as the son of Lancelot, has developed in literature generally, and more particularly in English literature, as a character distinct as, let us say, the Hamlet of Shakespeare. Whatever may be thought of the origin of the melancholy Dane, whether he be an actual son of the King of Denmark, or find his genetic roots in Geronimo, the Hamlet of Shakespeare is as distinct a personage as our next door

---

[5] The *Galahads* mentioned in the *Vulgate Cycle* are thus set down by Dr. Sommer. The numbers refer to the respective divisions in the Vulgate Cycle:

(1) *Galaad* le roy des Pastures (sometimes called *Glaalant*);

(2) *Galaad* le Sires de la Terre des Pastures, II, 237; 238; 243;

(3) *Galaad,* Galahad, the son of Joseph of Arimathea and Helyap his wife, I, 209; 226; 281; 283; 284. He was king of Hocelice, named after him Gales (Wales). He married 'la fille al roy des Lantaines Illes'; his son Lienor was the ancestor in the direct line of Urien the father of Ywain. Galahad the son of Lancelot found his tomb. III, 117; IV, 175; 177; 179; 181; 221; VI, 185; VII, 140;

(4) *Galaad, Galahos, Galahad,* the baptismal name of Lancelot del Lac, III, 3; IV, 176; V, 243; VII, 140;

(5) *Galaad, Galaat, Galahad, Galaas,* the son of Lancelot and 'la belle fille au roy Pelles de Listenois'; 'li boins chevaliers' 'le millor chevalier del monde,' the ninth descendant of Nascien d'Orberique.

neighbor, and we discuss his propensities, his virtues, his faults with the same assurance as we do the vices, virtues, and general characteristics of any definite historical personage or of any of our contemporaries in the flesh. Just as well defined a character in literary history is Galahad, the son of Lancelot, from the old French Queste down to E. A. Robinson, and it is of this Galahad in English literature that the present dissertation proposes to treat.

In like manner, with the question of ultimate origins as to character, the writer wishes to set aside the whole controversy over the name of the Grail hero. Whether the name be Celtic in origin, as Dr. Loomis [6] and Miss Weston [7] contend, or whether Galahad's relationship with one of the biblical Galahads [8] be responsible for his bearing that name, as Heinzel,[9] Lot,[10] and Pauphilet,[11] suggest or whether assonance with Wales (Gales) may have determined its selection, as Newell moderately accepts [12] and Bruce [13] maintains, is all beside the present question. What the present writer wishes to show is how that character whom the medieval writers recognize as Galahad the *boine chevalier,* the *millor chevalier del monde,* how that Galahad who was at once the son of Lancelot and a scion of the race of Joseph of Arimathea [14] came to occupy his present position in English literature.

The *Vulgate Cycle of Arthurian Romance* is the earliest literary document of that definitely identified Galahad. The exact dates of the five enormously long romances comprising the *Vulgate Cycle,* namely, *L'Estoire del Saint Graal* (or *Grand Saint Graal*),

[6] Loomis, R. S., *Celtic Myth and Arthurian Romance*, p. 155.

[7] Weston, J. L., *Legend of Sir Perceval*, p. 340.

[8] There are three Galahads or Galaads mentioned in the Bible: Galaad, a great grandson of Joseph (*Numbers*, XXVI, 29; XXVII, 1); Galaad, Jephthah's father (*Judges*, XL, 1, 2); and Galaad, a chief of a family of Gad (I *Chronicles*, V, 14). It is to the first of the three Galahads that Heinzel and the other two scholars refer. Galahad also occurs quite frequently as the name of a district.

[9] Heinzel, *Über die französischen Gralromane*, pp. 134 ff.

[10] Lot, F., *Lancelot*, p. 120.

[11] Pauphilet, A., *Études sur la Queste*, p. 137.

[12] Newell, W. W., *Legend of the Holy Grail*, p. 59.

[13] Bruce, J. D., *Evolution of Arthurian Romance*, I, p. 423.

[14] Newell, W. W., *ibid.*, p. 52.

L'Estoire del Merlin, Li Livres de Lancelot, La Queste del Saint Graal, and *La Mort Artu,* have never been determined, and until this is done it is impossible to say in which of these romances Galahad was mentioned first.   Arthurian scholarship, arguing from internal evidence, appears to have now fairly well established the priority of the *Queste* over the *Estoire del Saint Graal,*[15] and of the Lancelot over the *Queste.*[16]   Until the question of authorship and priority of texts and manuscripts has been definitely settled, however, we must be content with taking Galahad as he appears in each of the Vulgate romances.   For, whether the Galahad of the Vulgate Cycle sprang fully armed from the mind of a Cistercian monk, as Pauphilet maintains,[17] or whether he evolved gradually from an original Lancelot-Grail corpus, as Lot suggests,[18] or whether he was derived from a preexisting Galahad legend, as Heinzel would have us believe,[19] is not imperative for the compass of the present study to decide.   Nor, indeed, can the question be satisfactorily settled until the assumed original Lancelot-Grail corpus of which Lot speaks is brought to light, until the lost original Galahad legend of which Heinzel tells us is discovered, until, indeed, as Miss Weston says, *all* the evidence gathered from *all* these manuscripts has been carefully sifted and tested and weighed.[20]

[15] Bruce, *Evolution,* I, 374 ff., and 374, note 1.
[16] Bruce, *Evolution,* I, 398 f.
[17] Pauphilet, A., *Études sur la Queste,* p. 135.
[18] Lot, F., *Lancelot,* p. 122 ff.
[19] Heinzel, *Gralromane,* p. 134.
[20] " We are, so far, only on the threshold of a satisfactory and scientific criticism of the Arthurian cycle," wrote Miss Weston, " and I doubt whether all who are engaged in this study recognize sufficiently either the extent or the complexity of the questions involved, or the absolute futility of, at this early stage, enunciating dogmatic decisions on any of the various points at issue.   Is there any one living scholar who is perfectly aware of *all* the evidence at our disposal for any of the great stories of the cycle?   If there be, he will know, better than any other, that till critical editions place us in a position to determine the characteristic readings of the MSS representing not one alone, but *all* those stories, their inter-relation, their points of contact with, or variance from each other, the very best work that can be done will be liable to bear the impress of a temporary character—it will not, it cannot be final."—*Sir Lancelot du Lac,* Introduction, p. vi.

Before launching into an analysis of the various romances of the *Vulgate Cycle* in which Galahad actually appears, it would seem only consistent with the present study to give as succinctly as possible the history of two earlier literary works, the *Conte del Graal* of Chrétien de Troyes, and the *Joseph* of Robert de Borron, in which, though Galahad does not appear, he is foreshadowed; for literary tradition and popular view correctly associate Galahad with the Grail and the idea of the Quest; so intimately, indeed, that a Galahad, as literature records him, without the Grail and the Quest *motif* is unthinkable. Moreover, had there been no development of the Christian Grail idea,[21] or no religious motivation of an original pagan Arthurian material, Galahad would never have been the Galahad of our literary traditions.

The *Conte del Graal* (or Perceval) of Chrétien de Troyes (1174-1190) and the *Joseph* of Robert de Borron, placed by scholars at the end of the twelfth or the beginning of the thirteenth century,[22] are apparently the earliest extant works in which the Grail story appears. Robert de Borron's *Joseph* is, so to speak, to Chrétien's *Conte del Graal* what the prologue is to a play. Chrétien's poem merely notes the existence of the Grail; Robert's poem attempts to amplify and explain it by telling its early history and the exploits of the ancestors of him who was to become the Grail hero.[23] " Just as in the *chansons de geste*," says Bruce,

[21] The designation here employed is a present concession to those who think that a Galahad, admittedly quite other than the traditional Galahad, might have entered the cycle of Arthur from other folklore sources. (See Chapter III.)

[22] Geoffrey of Monmouth knew nothing of the Grail, nor of course did Wace who followed Geoffrey. Skeat believes that the true explanation of Geoffrey's failure to mention the Grail was due to the fact that the fabulous portions of the narrative (the story of Joseph and the early history of the cup) were not invented till after Geoffrey's death in 1154, although, says Skeat, " the legendary portion of this narrative was probably known centuries earlier." For this latter statement, he cites Bede's story of the quarrel between St. Augustine and the Britons " who preferred their own traditions before all the churches in the world." (Bede's *Ecl. Hist.*, Bk. II, Ch. 2.)—Skeat, *Introduction to Joseph of Arimathie*, E. E. T. S., 43, p. xxix.

[23] The definite relation between these first two literary sources of the Grail legend has never thus far been definitely determined. Heinzel, one of the most eminent advocates of the Christian origin of the Grail, believes

" the poets naturally began by celebrating the great deeds of their heroes, performed in the full vigor of maturity . . . and only later . . . if occasion arose, exploited the curiosity which the narration of such feats of arms may have awakened . . . by presenting the story of the *enfances* . . . of the heroes in question, so, doubtless, it was with the Grail." [24]

From their very inception the extant Grail romances are practically divided into two groups: those dealing with the early history of the Grail, and the others dealing with the " search " for the Grail, the " quest." The latter portion is again likewise divided into two sections differentiated from each other by the person of the hero.

Perceval is Chrétien's hero, but in order to compare the earliest Galahad-Perceval romances, it may be well to outline his story:

The youthful Perceval hunting in the forest in the springtime is suddenly confronted by a company of Arthur's knights in glittering armor. They so fascinate him that, instead of regarding them as devils, as his mother had admonished him, he mistakes them for angels, and hastens home to beg his mother's permission to join them. The poor lady, remembering the tragic death that had befallen his father and brother in the service of knighthood, swoons from fear. Perceval, however, persists in his plea, and finally wins her reluctant consent to let him seek his adventures at Camelot. Arrayed in the garb of a Welsh peasant, *à la guise des Galois*, and armed with a single dart and much good advice from his mother concerning prayer and the courtesy due to ladies, he sets out for Arthur's court.

In spite of his rustic appearance, the youth is kindly received by the king, but when he clumsily knocks off Arthur's hat, a damsel of the court who for many years was never been known to laugh, and who, report had it, would never laugh until she should see the flower of chivalry, laughs

---

that both Chrétien and Robert were drawing independently from lost sources. (Cf. *Über die französischen Gralromane*, p. 92.) Birch-Hirschfeld is of the opinion that Chrétien borrowed from a lost poem of Robert. (*Die Sage vom Gral*, p. 195 ff.) See also W. A. Nitze's edition of *Robert de Boron, Le Roman de l'Estoire dou Graal*, Paris, Champion, 1927; and G. Cohen: *Chrétien de Troyes et son oevre*, Paris, 1931, p. 446 ff.; and Maurice Wilmotte: *Le Roman du Graal*, Paris, La Renaissance du Livre, 1930, (Introduction, p. 15) ; and M. Wilmotte: *Le Poème du Gral et ses auteurs*, Paris, 1930.

[24] Bruce, J. D., *Evolution of Arthurian Romance*, I, 378.

heartily, whereat the rude Kay strikes her on the cheek. Perceval observes the insult, but, being unarmed, is unable to avenge it. Suddenly a knight in red armor snatches a golden goblet from the royal table and rushes from the banquet hall. Perceval, eager to win his armor, dashes forth in pursuit of him, overtakes the knight, slays him and dons his armor. For some time he sojourns with Gournemant, a kindly old knight, who instructs him in the practice of chivalry. Later, Perceval wins the love of Gournemant's beautiful niece Blanchefleur by defending her against a wicked knight. After remaining for an indefinite period with his lady, lost in the joys of love, he finally sets out to find his widowed mother, not knowing she has already died of grief.

One evening he comes to a river, where he sees two men, one of whom is fishing. They offer Perceval the hospitality of the nearby castle, and when he enters the great hall, he sees several hundred men sitting about, and in the center of the hall, lying ill or wounded on a couch in front of a fire, an august and venerable lord whom Perceval recognizes as the fisherman he had seen in the boat. A squire enters bearing a sword which the host presents to Perceval; after this another squire crosses the hall bearing in his hand a bleeding lance; he is followed by two youths each holding a golden ten-branched candlestick, and with these comes a damsel carrying in both hands a *Graal* which shines so radiantly that it dims all the candles in the hall; a second damsel follows carrying a silver plate, and the whole procession passes silently between the sick man's couch and the fire. Perceval wonders at these marvels, but having been instructed by Gournemant not to ask many questions, he refrains from speaking. The next morning he realizes his mistake when he awakes to find the castle deserted, and his horse saddled and waiting at the door. Perplexed, he rides away. Later in the day he comes upon a damsel who tells him that the mysterious fisherman and his host of the previous night are the same person, that he is known as the Fisher King, and that he was wounded through the thighs many years before. Moreover, she informs Perceval that if he had inquired concerning the wonders of the castle, the king would have been healed and the surrounding country freed from divers evils. Because he failed to ask the question, the damsel calls him Perceval the Catiff, and adds to his sorrow by telling him of his mother's death.

Perceval rides on to further adventures, and Arthur's knights, hearing of his skill at arms, determine to seek him out. One day they come upon him buried deep in thought before a wounded bird whose blooddrops on the newly fallen snow remind him of the face of Blanchefleur. The next day a loathly damsel berates him for his sloth, and makes him so ashamed that he resolves never to sleep two nights in the same place until he has discovered the mysteries of the Grail.

The next thousand lines of the story are concerned with the exploits of Gawain, and finally we return to a rather dejected Perceval, who, after

2

five years of futile adventures, has still failed to achieve the quest. Wandering aimlessly through the forest, he meets a group of penitents who remind him that it is Good Friday, and that it is unseemly for a knight to go in armor on so holy a day. They advise him to seek out a nearby hermit, whom the unhappy knight discovers to be his uncle, and to whom he confesses that he has forgotten God through grief over his failure to learn the mysteries of the Grail. The hermit then tells him that he *lacked the grace* to speak at the appointed moment; moreover, he gives his nephew valuable information concerning the Fisher King. He tells Perceval that the maimed King is his (Perceval's) cousin, and that the Fisher King's aged father, Perceval's uncle, has been sustained for twenty years by the Holy Grail. Perceval starts out again in the springtime to continue his quest of the Grail. The story continues with the exploits of Gawain. Perceval is not mentioned again, at least not by Chrétien himself. His continuators let Perceval reach the Grail castle once more.

Apparently Chrétien died in the midst of his work,[25] but soon after his death the romance was taken up by continuators until it reached the enormous proportions of about sixty-five thousand lines.[26]

It will have been noted that in Chrétien's account of the Grail very little is said of its sacred character; it is regarded somewhat as a magical vessel feeding the wounded King, but arousing in Perceval none of those deep religious emotions that later were for Galahad the source of rapturous joy. Moveover, Chrétien in alluding to the mysterious vessel does not call it *the* Grail but *a* Grail. With his successors, however, possibly through the influence of ecclesiastical legend, the Grail, or if that be, the interdeterminate *graal,* became an object of profound reverence; with them it is indeed *the* Grail, and is identified with the cup of the Last Supper. Possibly this difference may have been due to the fact that by the time Gerbert and Manessier wrote, the Galahad-Queste had already become well known, and although Chrétien's continuators preferred to retain Perceval, they could hardly help

---

[25] Cf. Maynadier, H., *Arthur of the English Poets*, p. 112. This assumption, however, is disputed by Wilmotte, *Le Poème du Gral et ses auteurs,* Paris, 1930.

[26] Gautier (or Wauchier) seems to have added more than 20,000 lines to the 10,601 which Chrétien had left. Manessier brought the poem up to 45,000 lines or more, and Gerbert augmented it by another passage of 15,000 verses.

from being profoundly influenced by the prevailing religious enthusiasm that helped to inspire the Galahad Queste.

In noticeable contrast to the conspicuous lack of Christian sentiment surrounding the Grail in Chrétien's *Conte del Graal* is the deeply religious tone of Robert de Borron's *Joseph*. Here the Grail is unmistakably the cup of the Last Supper, sanctified by the Body and Blood of the Saviour; it is, moreover, a " vessel of grace " of which only the pure of heart can partake, and those who, like the unworthy Moyses, violate it are guilty of death. As far as is known, too, Robert de Borron was the first to link Joseph of Arimathea with the Grail story.[27] His description of the Holy Vessel from the time it was used by Christ until it was carried into Britain is here set forth in briefest outline:

Joseph of Arimathea, a soldier under Pilate, loves Jesus secretly, and after our Lord's death receives from Pilate, together with our Lord's body, the cup which the Saviour used at the Last Supper. The Jews, incensed at Joseph's sympathy with Jesus, throw him into prison where Jesus appears to him carrying the holy cup, and telling him that he will be the first of three to have charge of it. He then explains to Joseph the symbolic connection between the sacred vessel and the celebration of the Mass, discoursing at some length upon the Blessed Sacrament, and declaring the bread and wine to be in very truth His Body and Bloody. He then initiates Joseph into the *secrets of the Grail*, which He says are " sweet and precious, gracious and merciful."

Some time after these events, Vespasian, son of the Roman Emperor Titus, is cured of leprosy by the veil of Veronica on which was imprinted the image of our Lord's face; whereupon Vespasian punishes the Jews who put such a holy Man as Jesus to death. He hears of Joseph's imprisonment, and finding him, discovers that he has been sustained by the Grail for forty-two years. Vespasian, after an interview with Joseph, is converted to Christianity.

Joseph with his friends quits Judea, taking the sacred vessel with him, and goes to live in distant lands. After a while his company's prosperity wanes, and Joseph kneeling before the Grail, learns that God is offended at the sins of his companions. The Holy Spirit instructs him to make a square table as a symbol of the one at which Jesus sat, and to place the

---

[27] According to Bruce, Robert took as his starting point various hints in certain uncanonical writings of early Christianity, chiefly the *Vindicta Salvatoris*, the *Narratio Josephi*, and the *Evangelium Nicodemi*, especially the part called the *Gesta Pilati*.—J. D. Bruce, *Evolution of Arthurian Romance*, I, p. 238.

Sacred Vessel opposite the seat which he will occupy. He is also to instruct his sister's husband Brons to catch a fish which is to be placed near the Sacred Vessel. Brons is to sit at Joseph's right hand, but with one empty seat between them, to signify the seat of Judas. The seat is only to be occupied when a son (or grandson) of Brons and his wife Enygeus shall be born to fill it.

Joseph does as he is commanded. Those who sit at the table feel the blessed influence of the Sacred Vessel; but the sinful and unworthy turn away ashamed. One day the hypocrite Moys feigns the proper condition of mind and heart that should permit his sitting at the table, but when he takes the empty seat next to Joseph, the earth opens beneath him and he disappears. Then a voice declares that the son of Brons and Enygeus would himself have a son who would occupy another vacant seat at another table which would be made as a remembrance of this one.

After remaining for some time in this region, Joseph goes to Great Britain to preach the gospel. While he is there, Brons and his wife have twelve sons born to them, all of whom marry save one, Alain le Gros, whom Joseph with joy consecrates to the service of the Lord.

It is revealed to Joseph that Brons is to have charge of the Holy Vessel after him; moreover, that Brons is to be called the Rich Fisher on account of the fish he had caught for the service of the table. As soon as Brons receives the Grail he is to go westward with the Sacred Vessel. Thus will be fulfilled the figure of the Trinity in the three possessors of the Grail. When Joseph delivers to Brons the Sacred Vessel, he will go into eternal joy. The Vessel is delivered, and the Rich Fisher begins his journey to Britain.

The latter parts of the *Joseph* story are fragmentary and incoherent. De Borron does not make it clear whether or not Joseph himself ever went to Britain. The charge of preaching the Gospel is most definitely laid upon Brons and his son Alain.

Borron's plan, while it utilized to a large extent the machinery of Arthurian romance, involved, as V. D. Scudder remarks,[28] " an indifferent pushing aside of the national tragedy, Arthur's betrayal and defeat, as told by Geoffrey and the chroniclers. The new ideal grafted on the old scheme was from the first doomed to failure. There is confusion here, very like the confusion of life itself. To harmonize the two conceptions was left for later phases of the epic. Meanwhile the theme is immeasurably expanded and deepened. Absorbed in the bright trappings and fierce doings of chivalry, we may feel sometimes that the soul had slight showing at the court of Arthur. But no one can ignore it even while blood

[28] *The Morte Darthur of Sir Thomas Malory and Its Sources*, p. 99.

runs swiftest in the veins, when once he realizes that behind the unfolding tale lies this prelude, with its almost sacerdotal elevation of tone, and its initiate suggestion of experience pointing beyond the life of sense to far fulfillment of spiritual desire."

Other stories of the Grail existed about this same time or soon followed: the early thirteenth century *Parzival* of Wolfram von Eschenbach, a Bavarian poet; the *Peredur* of the Welsh *Mabinogion* (although here the Grail is not expressly mentioned) ; a French Prose Perceval known as " Didot *Perceval* "; the *Sone de Nausay,* a French metrical version, unique in that it identifies Joseph of Arimathea with the Fisher King, and places him in charge of a monastery in distant Norway; and still another French *Perlesvaus,* a prose version, of the early thirteenth century. There were also other redactions or translations of the story in German, Old Norse, Italian, Spanish, Portuguese, and Dutch.

Undoubtedly the great popularity of the Grail legends at this time was due chiefly to two causes: revival of keen contemporary interest in the doctrine of Transubstantiation, which the Fourth Lateran Council (1215) formally defined as a dogma of faith, and the great excitement occasioned by the second crusade begun in 1146. The former is probably responsible for converting what originally may have been half-pagan folktales into a thoroughly Christian story; the latter, for giving it chivalric coloring and human interest. Then, too, simultaneous with the second crusade came the establishment of the Knights Templars, a fighting order whose history furnishes many striking parallels to the legends of the Grail. Both questers and Templars had for their goal religious glory; both were seeking a holy object; both turned their faces toward the East. Geoffrey of Bouillon after conquering the heathen Turks was crowned king of Jerusalem; Evelak of the Grail legend after defeating the armies of the heathen Tholomer was made king of Sarras. Galahad's shield bore the Templar's device.[29]

The psychology of the legend's phenomenal growth seems to be that the stories came when the people were ready for them, and a good way to account for their often widely disparate renderings is to appreciate medieval literary tradition and the inventiveness and willing credence of the medieval mind.

[29] See Skeat, *Introduction, Joseph of Arimathie,* E.E.T.S., 44 (1871), p. xv, xli.

It will be observed that in most of these extant earlier versions of the Grail story Perceval and not Galahad is the Grail hero, and there is little doubt concerning Perceval's priority in this rôle.[30]

How, then, we may ask, did Galahad come so easily to supplant him? What was lacking in the first Grail hero that the second Grail hero possessed? All who have attempted to answer this question seem to agree on one point—celibacy. Perceval's character did not accord with the ideal of perfect purity required of the hero of the Grail; he was a worldly knight whose virginity was not insisted upon. And at an age when the idea of celibacy was preached and praised in the Western Church there could be no married state for one whose quest was intimately associated with the priestly service of the Eucharist. Indeed, under the guise of the Grail, the Holy Eucharist became a symbol of and an incentive to the celibate ideal, and Galahad became its stainless champion. To the argument of evangelical chastity, Miss Weston added another of a more subtle and discriminating character. She thought that Galahad's coming was not only a psychological but an artistic necessity. Perceval, she contended, is not *ab initio* a Grail hero, but a knight whose story runs on the most natural and ordinary lines; his is not, like Galahad's, a high romance of complete consecration.

" The genesis of Galahad," said Miss Weston,[31] " is manifest. On the one hand there was the recognition, by those writers who understood the true character of the Grail tradition, that Perceval, his suggestive title notwithstanding, had no real connection with this group of belief and practice, was no initiate, but a hero whose story

[30] At least four, or if we include Chrétien's three continuators, seven writers make Perceval the Grail hero; Galahad holds the position with only three. Miss Weston considered Gawain one of the earliest Grail heroes. Gawain also appears as a Grail quester in several versions. According to F. von Suhtscheck, the Armenian Giut (Wolfram's Kyot), invented the name Parzival, when, around 1150, he translated into French a Persian Manichean compilation of legends which reached Chrétien and Wolfram. (See *Forschungen und Fortschritte*, No. 10, Berlin, April 1, 1931). Parzival means " pure flower or Persian flower," he says. The story itself is supposed to be Old Persian in origin. Oriental descent has often been claimed for it as well as Celtic and Christian.

[31] Weston, J. L., *Legend of Sir Perceval*, p. 398.

ran on the simplest and most human lines. Nay, one who was indeed notably lacking in one of the essential qualifications, that of intelligence. The initiate must be capable of assimilating and profiting by knowledge beyond the capacity of ordinary men; Perceval was a Dummling! His story, a charming story, was popular in and for itself, and so far from gaining lost by insistence on the mystic element inseparable from the fully developed Grail legend. On the other hand, the growing popularity of Lancelot made insistent demands upon the romance writers; it was quite impossible that he, the most renowned of Arthur's knights, should remain without the charmed circle of effort and achievement; equally impossible that the faithful lover of Guenevere should conform to the standard of ascetic purity demanded of the initiate. Galahad, the last word of Grail evolution, is the answer to this double demand; he alone of all the three is the product of direct literary invention, the son of Christian mysticism, and contemporary literary necessity. He came because in the fulness of time he had to come, and his coming closed for seven hundred years the creative activities of the Grail."

CHAPTER II

GALAHAD IN THE VULGATE CYCLE

Our Galahad, then, appears first in that enormous body of prose literature which, because of its popularity in medieval times, is known as the *Vulgate Cycle of Arthurian Romance*. Why these prose romances, which often told the same tales and with even greater prolixity, came to rival the metrical romances in popularity, is difficult to say, but the fact remains that they did, and after the first century they were, particularly in France,[1] the most favored form which the Arthurian stories assumed, spreading thence rapidly to almost every country of western Europe.[2]

The Vulgate Cycle is made up of five great romances: *L'Estoire del Saint Graal* (or *Grand St. Graal*), *L'Estoire de Merlin, Li Livres* (*L'Estoire*) *de Lancelot, La Queste del Saint Graal,* and *La Mort Artu.* Since Galahad appears in these romances, in a more or less conspicuous manner, each romance shall be treated separately in the following pages.

1. *L'Estoire del Saint Graal*

Throughout this *Early History of the Grail,* Galahad is the predestined hero, the knight of promise, the *boine chevalier* who should achieve the adventures of the Holy Grail. The *Estoire,* which Heinzel considers the best starting point for investigation

---

[1] "The matière de Bretagne," says H. Oskar Sommer, "though undoubtedly the fountain-head of many incidents, episodes, and adventures in Arthurian romance, has exercised an infinitesimal, if any *direct*, influence on the several branches of the vulgate cycle. The vulgate cycle, as handed down to our days in manuscripts of the thirteenth and fourteenth centuries, is an entirely French production which originated in the north of France towards the end of the twelfth century and the beginning of the thirteenth. The *trouvères* and compilers, or *assembleurs*, dealt with material that had already become completely acclimatised in France and was in but very few cases modified by recourse to oral tradition."—Introduction to the *Vulgate Cycle of Arthurian Romances*, p. vii.

[2] Cf. Maynadier, H., *Arthur of the English Poets*, p. 77.

16

(in spite of the fact that in point of time it is probably the last composed romance of the cycle), gives an extended account of the holy vessel from the time of its acquisition by Joseph of Arimathea to its arrival in Great Britain, and of all the miracles wrought by it until the founding of the Round Table. A lineal descendant of Robert's *Joseph,* the present romance appears to be modified so as to make it conform to the conceptions brought about by the introduction of the new hero Galahad and the celibate ideal he embodied. But as Bruce points out,[3] Borron's conception of the first Grail keeper did not perfectly fulfill the condition of celibacy required by the medieval church for the ministers of her Sacraments. Accordingly, just as in the *Queste* the Perceval of Chrétien and his successors has to yield the first place to Galahad, so in the *Estoire* Robert's Joseph has to yield the first place to a new creation, Josephe, who fulfills the necessary condition. Moreover, it must be remembered that by the time the *Estoire* was written, Galahad was probably securely established in the rôle of Grail winner; and there remained, as Miss Weston shows,[4] but one step to render his title indefeasible,—he must be shown to be the *predestined* winner, the hero towards whose appearance all the secular evolution of the Grail dynasty had tended.

It would be well nigh impossible in a study of this nature to give, even in abridged form, that tremendously long and complex narrative known as the *Estoire;* let it suffice here merely to indicate the most significant passages in which Galahad occurs and is shown to be this *predestined Grail winner.* Of these passages by far the most important are: (1) the prophecy of the angel regarding the lance; (2) his prophecy relating to the sword; (3) the story of Solomon's ship.

(1) Referring to the marvelous lance, the angel tells Joseph that not a drop of blood will fall from the lance until the Grail adventures shall commence in the land (Great Britain) whither God is to lead Nascien. One man, the angel tells him, will be struck by the lance and will not be cured until the wonders of the Grail shall have been revealed to him (Galahad) who is full

---

[3] Bruce, J. D., *Evolution*, I, 379.
[4] "Perlesvaus and the Cyclic Romances," *Romania*, 51 (1925), p. 361.

of virtues. Galahad, as we shall see in the *Queste,* is full of virtues,
for which he is permitted to enjoy the wonders of the Grail, and for
which reason also he has power to heal the Maimed King with
blood from the sacred spear.

(2) The angel tells Joseph that the sword which has caused so
many afflictions will not cease to afflict the land until the coming
of the Good Knight, Galahad. As related in the *Queste,* Galahad
alone achieves the adventures of the sword, and by this means
removes the cause of these afflictions.

(3) The incident of Solomon's ship seems to be the most con-
vincing of all arguments regarding Galahad's predestined position
as winner of the Grail. Solomon, hearing through revelation that
his race will terminate in a virgin knight, and desiring to bequeath
a treasure to this descendant, constructs, at the advice of his wife,
a wonderful ship in which he places a bed, the spindles of which
are made from the Tree of Life. At the head of the bed he places
a crown, and at the foot, the sword of his father David, to which
his wife attaches hangings of tow, declaring that these shall be replaced by a belt made by the virgin daughter of a king. At the
end of his questing, Galahad finds the ship of Solomon and in it the
sword of David which Perceval's sister, the virgin daughter of a
king, girds upon him, having changed the tow hangings for a belt
made of her own hair.

The author of the *Estoire,* as if to make assurance doubly sure,
concludes his history by relating the genealogy of the *predestined*
Grail winner, a genealogy that removes all doubt as to Galahad's
foreordained position. On the maternal side these ancestors are:
Brons, Alain le Gros, Josue, Aminadap, Catheloys, Manael, Lambar, Pellean, and Pelles (the grandfather of Galahad). On the
paternal side they are: Nasciens, Celidoine, Marpus, Nasciens II,
Alain le Gros, Ysaies or Helyas, Jonas, Lancelot I, Ban, and Lancelot II (Galahad's father).[5]

While the *Early History of the Grail* is " enormously long, full
of marvels and visions and wanderings and allegorizings and
lengthy conversions daunting to any but a medieval mind," [6] it

---

[5] Sommer, *Vulgate Cycle,* VI, 295.

[6] Schlauch, M., *Medieval Narrative,* p. 178.

performed the invaluable service of paving the way for Arthurian connections, and introduced the distinctive and legitimate backgrounds of the new Grail hero Galahad. Perceval, whom the preceding prose cycle romances had already relegated to a secondary although honorable position,[7] was bound by a natural and inevitable process to disappear as Galahad's rival, and Galahad, of whom Miss Weston says, " He had no rival; he never could have one," [8] takes his place in the world of literature as the destined hero of the Grail.[9]

[7] As was seen, the *Estoire* came after the other cycle romances in which Galahad was hero.

[8] " Perlesvaus and the Cyclic Romances," *Romania*, 51, p. 361.

[9] There are several other references made to Galahad in the *Estoire*, but the most important were discussed. Below is a list of the references not given in detail. The page numbers refer to Sommer's version of the *Vulgate Cycle*.

I, 204. Nascien receives a scroll upon which are written the names of his descendants. Galahad's is ninth in order. Nascien hears that his ninth descendant will surpass all other knights of the past and future; he will be like a lion among beasts; he will be like a flood, muddy at the source but clear and beautiful midstream.

I, 242. Mordreins presumes to look at the Holy Grail and is struck blind. He prays that he may live to see Galahad.

I, 261. Mordreins goes to a hermitage attached to an abbey of White Monks, and remains there until the coming of Galahad.

I, 261. The unworthy Moys, for daring to sit in the the Perilous Seat, is condemned to burn in a great fire. He tells Joseph and his companions that the fire will some day be extinguished by Galahad.

I, 268. Symen, condemned to horrible torments for having stabbed his father Peers, tells Josephe (Joseph's son) that he will be delivered by Galahad.

I, 283. King Galaad, youngest brother of Josephe, visits the grave of Symen, and a voice from the grave bids him build there an abbey to alleviate his pains. King Galaad promises to do so, and Symen tells him that the fire will not cease until the coming of Galahad.

I, 285. Josephe when dying gives his shield to Mordrains, making with his own blood a cross on it, and saying that the cross will remain bright red until the advent of the Good Knight. " He will be as marvelous a knight," he says, " as this is a wonderful shield." The Good Knight will come for the shield on the fifth day after receiving the order of knighthood.

I, 290. Lambar and Varlan engage in a deadly combat in which Lambar

2. *L'Estoire de Merlin*

Galahad is not specifically mentioned in the *Vulgate Merlin,* which does not, as its title would indicate, concern itself chiefly with the prophecies and acts of the sage of Caerleon, but following Wace's *Roman le Brut,* wanders off interminably into descriptions of Arthur's wars, the rebellions of his barons, their wars with the Saxons, and redeems its extreme tediousness only by the human touches of Arthur's courtship and marriage with Guenevere, and Merlin's affairs with the wily Vivien.

The first allusion which might be applied to Galahad is in reference to his prophetic birth and his subsequent achievement of the Siege Perilous. After relating to Uther Pendragon the story of Joseph of Arimathea and the table which he made according to the pattern of that at which Christ sat at the Last Supper, Merlin offers to construct a third table, saying to Uther, " I assure you, if you do this, it will greatly advantage your soul and body." Merlin makes the table, and at Pentecost chooses fifty knights to occupy the seats. When the king questions Merlin as to the knight who will occupy the vacant seat, he replies: [10]

> So much I may say, that it shall not be filled in thy time. And he who will fill it will be born from one who ought to engender him. And he hath not yet taken wife, nor knoweth that he must do so. And it will be necessary, first of all, for the man who is to fill it to accomplish this place, before which sitteth the vessel of the Grail, which those who guard it have never seen accomplished."

The second reference of this nature includes a brief description of Elaine the daughter of King Pelles. The author of *Merlin* speaks of her as the most beautiful woman not only in Britain but in the whole world, and tells how in the castle of Corbenic, which King Galafres had built for the Holy Grail in the time of Aleyn,

is mortally wounded by the sword of David which Varlan has removed from Solomon's ship. When he attempts to replace the sword in its sheath, Varlan falls dead. The sword will not be again unsheathed until the coming of a maid (Galahad).

I, 291. Pelleham is succeeded by Pelles, the father of Helayne (Elaine), the mother of Galahad, who shall be the one to achieve the adventures of the Grail when all other knights have failed.

[10] Sommer, *Vulgate Cycle* II, p. 55.

the second Grail-keeper, the lovely Elaine, guarded the " saintisme graal " until the time that Galahad should be engendered on her.[11]

3. *Li Livres de Lancelot*

The Galahad *enfances,* which Malory incorporated in his *Morte* and which are among the most delightfully human touches in the whole Vulgate story, are found in the third book of *Li Livres de Lancelot.* Referred to only in prophecy in the *Estoire* and the *Merlin,* Galahad here makes his first actual appearance on the literary stage.

The introduction of the Galahad and Grail theme into the story of Lancelot was, however, a later addition,[12] since Chrétien's *Lancelot* knew no Grail, and his *Conte del Graal* contained no allusion to *Lancelot.* The inference is, then, that a Cistercian monk (who later composed the *Queste*), wishing to connect the bravest and most beloved of Arthur's knights, Lancelot, with the greatest exploit of the Round Table, the Grail quest, created Galahad and interpolated the romance so as to keep Lancelot the center of interest by making him the father of the Perfect Knight. He studiously avoided giving offense to the religious medieval mind, and at the same time enabled Lancelot not to win but to enjoy vicariously by means of his son's achievement the glories of the Grail. Upon this fact scholars all seem to agree. " As Lancelot was himself disqualified by his sinful association with Guenevere to take Perceval's place," says Dr. Sommer,[13] " he was given a son who had inherited all the great qualities but not the failings of his father." And Dr. Loomis, in a very discriminating analysis of the Lancelot-Galahad evolution remarks: [14] " The two most vigorous forces of the twelfth century forced Arthurian romance into their patterns. The cult of courtly love adopted Lancelot for its hero *par excellence;* and a white-robed monk of the order of Citeaux chose Galahad to represent the perfect seeker after God. . . . With clear

---

[11] *Ibid.,* II, p. 159.

[12] Bruce, J. D., *Evolution,* I, 398.

[13] Introduction to the *Vulgate Version,* p. viii.

[14] Loomis, R. S., *Introduction to Lancelot et Galahad* par Myrrha Lot-Borodine et Gertrude Schoepperle, pp. viii, x (1926).

purpose the author (of the *Queste*) performs a complete trans-valuation of the values of the chivalric Lancelot story."

The dependence of the *Queste* on the *Lancelot* is clear, since the latter contains the Galahad *enfances* and all the important links in the chain of the Grail hero's life up to the time of his appearance at Camelot.

Before the story of Galahad's birth we find two important prophecies concerning him; the first is that of the clerk Helyes who explains to Galehot, Lancelot's friend, the meaning of Merlin's speech regarding the lion and the leopard. Lancelot, Helyes tells Galehot, is the leopard who will be debarred from achieving the adventures of the Holy Grail, while Galahad is the lion who will surpass all other knights, and bring these adventures to an end. Galehot asks why the bravest of all knights will thus be limited, and the clerk replies: " Prowess and chivalry are not sufficient; the achiever of the Grail must be chaste all his life, and your knight (Lancelot) is not." Loyal to his friend, Galehot presses the question farther asking if the Grail Knight will be as brave as the leopard. " Certainly," replies Helyes, " Merlin has told us that from the chamber of the Maimed King will issue a wonderful beast, different from all other beasts; when that beast comes, the enchantments and adventures of Great Britain will end. He who will achieve the Grail will be chaste, and no knight will surpass him in chivalry." [15]

The second prophecy occurs on the occasion of Lancelot's visit to a cemetery in which he finds the grave of King Galahad of Hocelice (Wales). In a church near this cemetery Lancelot finds a cave from which flames constantly issue, and he hears that whoever opens this cave will achieve the adventures of the Grail. Lancelot tries with all his might, but is unable to open it. This adventure he learns is not for him but for the Good Knight Galahad.

In the third part of the *Lancelot* proper occurs the story of Galahad's conception and birth which it will not be necessary to rehearse here since it is taken over practically in its entirety by Malory, and will be found in detail in a later chapter.[16]

[15] *Vulgate Version*, IV, p. 26.   [16] Chapter V.

After Galahad's birth we hear almost nothing of him until his arrival at Camelot to claim the Siege Perilous. Like the Divine Knight whom he emulates, the child Galahad grows in wisdom and age under the careful eyes of his devoted mother and the nuns to whose keeping he is entrusted at the age of six. Twice we catch glimpses of the infant Galahad: on the occasion of Bohort's visit to the Grail castle, and again when Elaine visits Arthur's court bringing the little Galahad with her. In the former instance Bohort is delighted to see the lovely two-year-old child, whose entrance into the room is accompanied by the mysterious dove bearing a censer, and a damsel bearing the Grail. That night he is visited by a strange old man playing upon a harp, who tells him that no one but Galahad will be able to achieve the adventures of the Grail castle, and that Lancelot might have achieved them had it not been *par le foiblece de ses sains.*

Shortly after Easter in the year in which Galahad is eighteen, a holy hermit tells the youth that he will be knighted at Whitsuntide, and admonishes him to enter the order of chivalry pure and chaste. Galahad promises to do so, and quietly awaits the accomplishment of God's will. A day later Arthur, hunting in the forest, hears Mass at the hermitage, and learns from the hermit that the knight who will sit in the Perilous Seat and achieve the adventures of the Holy Grail is coming to court at Whitsuntide. With great joy Arthur summons all his knights and vassals to meet at Camelot where he will hold a great court at the approaching feast.

4. *La Queste del Saint Graal*

It is upon this romance, more than any other, that literature has drawn for its conception of Galahad. The *Queste* is dated about 1220, and although for many years it was believed to be the work of one Walter Map,[17] Pauphilet has shown in his excellent critical

---

[17] " I have studied the Galahad *Queste* closely," says Miss Weston, " and have compared versions gathered from widely different sources, French originals, and translations, and I am distinctly of the opinion that we possess the romance practically in its original form. It is a homogeneous composition; it is not a compilation from different sources and by different hands. There is no trace of an earlier and later redaction, save only in the direct edifying passages, which in some cases appear to have undergone

study of this work [18] that it was really the work of a Cistercian monk whose name is not known. Pauphilet's analysis of the present romance is profound and scholarly, and constitutes, as Mr. Comfort says, " a valuable interpretation of this document as a chapter in the history of medieval religious thought." [19]

The romance begins where the *Lancelot* leaves off, and there is true dramatic skill shown in its opening passages.

On Whitsunday eve a damsel rides into the great hall at Camelot, and in the name of King Pelles summons Lancelot to follow her. She leads him to an abbey of nuns in a forest where Galahad has been brought up. Here, at the request of the nuns, Lancelot dubs Galahad, and returns to the court. That day the king and his knights suddenly discover from an inscription on the Siege Perilous that this seat is to be occupied the very next day (Whitsunday 454 A. D.) by him for whom it is destined.

Before Arthur and his knights sit down to dinner on the great feast of Whitsunday, Kay reminds them that custom calls for some adventure. They are not long seeking this, as news is brought of a marvelous sword stuck in a stone floating in the river. The knights hasten to try their skill at removing the sword which bears an inscription declaring that only the best knight in the world will be able to remove it. Failing in the trial, the knights return to the great hall, and scarcely are they seated when, all at once, the doors and windows suddenly shut as of themselves, and an old man robed in white enters leading by the hand a young man clad in red armour, without sword or shield, and leads him to the Siege Perilous upon which appears in golden letters the name of Galahad. Before the feast begins, Galahad succeeds in drawing the marvelous sword from the stone in the river.

The next day, in order to test Galahad's prowess, the king holds a great tournament in which Galahad, though shieldless, shows himself superior to all the other knights except Lancelot and Perceval. That evening as the knights of the Round Table are assembled in the hall, there is heard a loud clap of thunder, and suddenly a great light floods the place while the

---

amplification. The difference between the versions is not that of incident or sequence, scarcely even of detail, but rather of clearness and coherence with which the incidents are related in some of the versions as compared with others. I am strongly inclined to think that there is no peculiarity in any of the *Queste* MSS. which cannot quite well be ascribed to the greater or less accuracy of the copyist, or his greater or less taste for discourses of edification."—*Legend of Sir Lancelot du Lac*, pp. 132-3.

[18] *Études sur la Queste del Saint Graal Attribuées à Gautier Map*, p. 135 ff. See also Chapter III, below.

[19] Comfort, W. W., *The Quest of the Holy Grail*, Introduction, p. v.

Holy Grail covered with white samite is borne into the hall by invisible hands. The palace is filled with delicious odors, and each knight is satisfied with the kind of food he most desires. When the Grail vanishes, Gawain vows to go in quest of it, and the other knights vow to do the same. The hermit Nascien forbids the ladies to accompany their knights on this quest, and admonishes the knights to confess their sins before setting out.

Arthur fears that he will lose the greater part of his knights, but since they are forsworn, he cannot prevent them. Beginning with Galahad, the one hundred and fifty knights all swear not to return to court until they have found the Grail. On the fifth day after setting out, Galahad comes to an abbey of white monks where his ancestor Nascien is buried, and here he meets Baudemagus and Yvain. Behind an altar in this abbey, hangs a marvelous white shield with a red cross on it, the shield by which Mordrain gained victory over the pagan Tholomer. Baudemagus attempts to carry off the shield, but a mysterious White Knight rides after him, unhorses him, and commands Baudemagus' squire to carry the shield back to Galahad to whom, he says, it rightfully belongs.

Galahad then achieves the adventure of removing the corpse of a knight from a devil-haunted tomb, and, accompanied by Melian his squire (son of the king of Denmark), leaves the abbey. Parting for a while with Galahad, Melian picks up a gold crown which he finds on a chair in the forest, and is severely wounded for this by a knight who later is himself wounded and put to flight by Galahad. Leaving the disabled Melian at the abbey, Galahad next conquers the seven terrible giants outside the Castle of Maidens, and delivers the captive women. He meets Lancelot and Perceval, engages in combat with them, and unhorses both knights. Perceval's aunt, a recluse who lives in the forest, tells Perceval that the unknown knight who unhorsed him and Lancelot is Galahad, the best knight in the world.

The story then relates the adventures of Lancelot and Perceval in the quest of the Holy Grail. On one occasion Perceval, attacked by twenty armed men, is rescued by Galahad. The adventures of Bors, Gawain, and Hector, are also related.

Galahad one night seeks shelter in a hermitage near Corbenic. During the night a damsel comes in search of him, bidding him rise quickly and accompany her to a ship where Bors and Perceval await him. The three knights recount their several adventures while the vessel swiftly bears them to a desert, fourteen days' journey from Logres. There, at the advice of the damsel, they transfer themselves to another and more magnificent vessel (Solomon's ship), and then the damsel reveals herself as Perceval's sister. In Solomon's ship there is a beautiful bed on which is laid King David's sword half-drawn from its scabbard. Perceval's sister relates the story of the dolorous stroke made with this sword, and explains the inscriptions thereon. Galahad is the only man in the world, she says, who will be able to draw the sword from its scabbard. She also explains the origin of the three spindles of different colors which make part of the bed. The three companions find a scroll confirming all that Perceval's sister has told them. The maiden replaces the tow and hemp hangings of David's sword with rich hangings made of her own hair braided with jewels. She calls the sword with its new ornament "L'Espee as Estraingnes Renges," (the Sword with the Strange Hangings), and the sheath "Memoire de Sanc" (Memory of Blood). She girds the sword on Galahad and he vows to be her knight, since she has dedicated herself to a life of perpetual chastity.

The ship moves out to sea, some time later landing near the castle of Cartelois. Here Galahad, Bohort, and Perceval, slay the wicked sons of the aged Count Ernol, and Galahad receives a command from God to go to the Grail Castle and heal the Maimed King. On the way, he and his companions meet with a stag and four lions; the significance of this is expounded to them by a hermit. They also encounter a group of knights whose custom is to procure the blood of a virgin princess in order to cure the leprous lady of their castle. Perceval's sister being told of their motive, voluntarily yields her blood to save the sick lady, but sacrifices her own life in so doing. In accordance with her desire, her body is laid in a ship and put out to sea, while in her hand is placed a scroll telling of her life and the manner of her death.

By God's grace, Lancelot is directed to the ship which bears the body of Perceval's dead sister, and there he learns from the scroll who the girl was, and what was her history. He remains with her in the vessel, and is later joined by Galahad. Thus, for six months father and son live together, until God commands Galahad to finish the adventures of the Grail.

Galahad visits the abbey in which the blind Mordrain is dying, and the latter, healed by Galahad's visit, expires contented. Galahad then achieves the adventures of the boiling fountain and the burning tomb. He meets Perceval, and for five years (during which time they bring to an end all the adventures of Logres), the two knights wander together until they reach the Grail castle. Bohort joins them, and the three knights arrive at Corbenic, to the great joy of King Pelles. Here Galahad achieves the adventure of piecing the broken sword with which Joseph of Arimathea had been wounded. A voice then warns all who have no right to sit at Christ's table to withdraw. As soon as all have left the hall except King Pelles, his son Eliezer, his niece, and the three questers, four damsels enter bearing on a bed the Maimed King who expresses his confidence that with Galahad's coming his sorrow will be relieved and that he soon will die. A voice now commands all save the three questers to depart. Then a bishop, accompanied by four angels, comes down from heaven, and by the letters on his forehead the knights know that the bishop is Josephe. The angels make preparations for the Mass, which is said by Josephe, the Holy Grail being in the centre of the table. Josephe kisses Galahad, and then bids him kiss the other questers. Finally, having assured them that they will be fed and rewarded by the Saviour, he vanishes. Christ, with bleeding hands and feet, now rises out of the Grail, feeds them from the Grail, and declares that this vessel is the dish of the Last Supper. They will see it more clearly, He says, in the Spiritual Palace at Sarras. Obeying Christ's command, Galahad heals the Maimed King with blood from the lance.

That same night a voice bids the knights depart from the Grail castle. They go to the sea where they find Solomon's ship waiting for them, and on it the Holy Grail. Galahad, remembering the happiness he has just experienced in tasting the sweetness of the Grail, longs for death, and God promises him that his desire shall be fulfilled. The ship arrives at Sarras, and the knights carry the Holy Grail to the Spiritual Palace, where Our Lord had consecrated Josephe the first bishop. The ship which bears the body of Perceval's sister arrives at Sarras at the same time as Solomon's ship, and the knights bury the maiden in the Spiritual Palace.

Many miracles are performed by the Holy Grail as the knights carry it through the streets of Sarras. The pagan king Escorant, fearing their power in his kingdom, casts the three knights into prison, where the Holy Grail nourishes and comforts them. After a year Escorant dies, but not before he has asked the Grail knights' pardon for his cruel treatment of them. Against his will, Galahad is unanimously acclaimed king of Sarras, and one year from the day on which he is crowned, while assisting at Mass, he receives a summons to approach the holy vessel and see what he long has wished to see. Overcome with joy, he prays for death, and having received the last sacrament from the hands of Josephe, he bids farewell to his companions and expires. At the same moment, Bohort and Perceval see a hand reach down from heaven and bear away the Grail and the lance, and from that day to this no mortal eye has ever beheld them. Galahad is buried at Sarras, and some fourteen months later Perceval expires, and is interred by his sister's side. Bohort returns to Arthur's court, and relates to the king and his remaining knights the adventures of the Grail. Arthur has the adventures recorded, and put in the abbey at Salisbury.

From an artistic point of view, the *Queste* does not excel or even equal many of the other prose romances, in fact its "forest of allegories" [20] is rather baffling to the most sanguine of literary travelers. But it has one important claim to distinction—it was the first to break the established tradition by throwing upon legends of purely human love, the *amor courtois,* the light of an ascetic ideal. "Perspective and causality, absent in the lighter phases of romance, enter with Galahad and the Grail. Dignity is added to

[20] Pauphilet, A., *Romania,* XXXVI, 605.

knightly life: Arthur and the Table Round are summoned to a destiny higher than they had known. Fulfillment is the watchword of the hour, and Galahad is the Fulfiller." [20a] This break, as W. W. Comfort points out,[21] is precisely what constitutes the originality of the *Queste.* " Literary tradition," he says, " had had its way with Gawain, Lancelot, Arthur, Guenevere, Bors, Hector des Mares, Perceval, and the rest of the great personages at the court. This tradition had portrayed in these personages divers qualities dear to twelfth-century French chivalry, but it had not undertaken to represent any of this society as impeccably chaste, as pure, as ' virgin.' Perceval was the purest of them all, but even his literary title was not clear enough in the eyes of our author to entitle him to serve as protagonist in this new spiritual Quest. As for the rest of the courtiers, they were all far from perfect: they were guilty of pride, cruelty, and incontinence. Their past record, known of all, debarred them from any hope of success in this exacting competition. Yet they were favorites with the social class whom the Cistercian apologist wished to reach with his revival call. He wished to call this proud and luxurious public to a militant career of virtue and self-abnegation. How should he catch their attention and turn it to his own purpose? By taking the old favorites, by showing their delinquencies and their unworthy traits, and by creating beside them a new character to embody those virtues which alone could win in the Quest. So he created Galahad, son of Lancelot, who thus belongs in the old corrupt society, but who distinguished himself from all his relatives and associates by his possession of those qualities which the ascetic author had determined to extol." This is practically the substance of M. Pauphilet's idea in his critical analysis of the *Queste,* of which more shall be said in the following chapter.

5. *The Mort Artu*

Galahad, having achieved his quest and tasted the fruits of his victory, disappears completely from the remainder of the story. The *Mort Artu,* the last and perhaps most widely read of the

[20a] Scudder, V. D., *op. cit.*, p. 275.
[21] *Introduction to the Quest of the Holy Grail*, p. vi.

Vulgate romances, upon which Malory, Tennyson, and, in our own day, Robinson, have drawn with such satisfactory results, contains no allusion to Galahad except in the opening lines when Bohort, the last of the Grail questers, tells the knights of Arthur's court of Galahad's and Perceval's death and the adventures of the Grail. Bohort's story acts as a connecting link between the *Mort Artu* and the preceding romance, and the subsequent story has nothing to do with Galahad and the Grail. It is, as the title shows, the denouement of the Arthurian epic, and deals chiefly with Arthur's last wars, the discovery of Lancelot's and Guenevere's fatal love, and the final breaking up of the Round Table. In order to show that this catastrophe was the inevitable result of the sin of Arthur's queen and Arthur's bravest knight, the writer spares no pains in point of plot or incident to make all tend to this last sad end. The *Mort Artu* furnished a fitting close to the *Vulgate Cycle,* and terminated for an indefinitely long period the creative activities of the Arthurian legend.

Perlesvaus

Before concluding this chapter it will be necessary to say a word of still another Grail romance which appeared early in the thirteenth century and which has Perceval (or *Perlesvaus* as the author calls him) as the hero.[22] In this rather confused tale in which Lancelot is a prominent figure, the necessity of personal chastity is made paramount, and Lancelot, because of his sinful love for Guenevere, is debarred from the adventures of the Grail. Permeated with the same religious sentiment which distinguishes the Galahad romance, the *Perlesvaus* appears to have been compiled with the express purpose of reinstating Perceval in the rôle of Grail winner, from which position he had been deposed in favor of Galahad. " Now the Grail being what it was," says Miss Weston,[23] " this was simply impossible. To depose Galahad, the creation of an imperative demand, at once psychological and literary, in favor of Perceval who had been deliberately set aside as failing to fulfill the essential conditions of the rôle, and that at a

---

[22] Translated from an anonymous French MS of about 1220, by Sebastian Evans, and known as *The High History of the Holy Grail.*

[23] Weston, J. L., *Legend of Sir Perceval*, p. 340.

date when the Lancelot-Galahad romantic development had, like Aaron's rod, swallowed up all its rivals, is unthinkable. To state such a problem fairly is to refute it. With Galahad it was emphatically a case of ' *J'y suis, j'y reste* ' and, Wagner notwithstanding, he holds his position today! "

These, in fine, are the distant places whence our hero comes to us. Although he occupies a prominent place in English literature, his roots are fixed in the legends of another people. A comparatively late edition to Arthurian romance, Galahad is a logical and artistic necessity to the completion of the great cycle. " He came because in the fullness of time he had to come," [24] and his coming was joyously received because of man's instinctive love of the good. And now there remains but to show how this Galahad of the Middle Ages came to occupy his present position in the world of English literature.

Before tracing Galahad's course through centuries of English thought, however, I shall in the following chapter indulge in a brief speculation as to the possible genesis of the Galahad character and the reason for his coming into being.

[24] Weston, J. L., *Legend of Sir Perceval*, p. 398.

CHAPTER III

The Possible Genesis of Galahad and the Old French "Queste"

As we have already seen,[1] the first literary work with which Galahad[2] is definitely identified is the twelfth century romance known as *La Queste del St. Graal.* Before attempting to discuss the purpose of this romance, it would seem to be a profitable procedure to outline first the generally accepted explanations of the origins of this romance, or rather, those which find general agreement.

(1) The most prominent of these is the theory that *La Queste del St. Graal* was written by the monks of Citeaux to induce its readers to lead more Christian lives. Pauphilet,[3] in an exhaustive study of this early romance, piles up evidence in support of this thesis. "It it not the author's motive," he says, "simply to add an episode to the Round Table legends."[4] He goes on to point out how the author of the *Queste* in numerous passages manifests his intention of opposing his work to the literature of his time. "He (the Cistercian monk) despises the valor, the purely chivalrous exploits; he reproves the *amour courtois,* which he sees confounded with the 'vile sin of luxury.' He borrows from the romances of the Round Table and especially from *Lancelot* certain of the most brilliant heroes, Gawaine, Yvain, Lancelot, Hector. . . . He gives the impression that around the Grail the world takes a new aspect where the traditional valor of men and of things is reversed."[5] The monk, as Pauphilet shows, has attempted to depict the moral life of man, representing it as a universal conflict of the good against the bad, of God against Satan. In this struggle, man com-

---

[1] Chapter I, p. 3; Chap. II, p. 23.

[2] By "Galahad" we mean here not the Grail seeker *as such*, but the particular type—the ascetic Christian Quester—as he appears for the first time in the Old French *Queste.*

[3] *Études sur la Queste del St. Graal,* Paris, 1923.

[4] *Ibid.,* p. 14.

[5] Pauphilet, A., Introduction, *La Queste del St. Graal,* p. viii.

31

bats by means of faith, piety, austerity, his weaknesses, the most redoubtable of which are luxury and pride. Moreover, the author of the *Queste,* who shows himself to be well-versed in theology, liturgy, and ecclesiastical polity, is bent on proving the doctrine of Transubstantiation against prevalent heresies, on showing the intercessory power of the saints, on demonstrating the rewards which will come to the chaste, the humble, and the merciful. But over and above all, he wishes to show that the *quest motif,* the central idea of this romance, is bound up in the search of the individual for God—without family ties, without worldly connections of any sort. The influence of the Church is represented entirely by the monks whom the knights encounter in the forest. Secular priests, bishops, the Pope himself, are not alluded to. Considering the *Queste del St. Graal* from a dogmatic or didactic point of view, it is quite obvious, according to Pauphilet, that the author was preaching.

(2) A second theory adduced for the origin of the *Queste* is on the more remote grounds of literary or artistic utility, but concerning this point of view, there has been more or less controversy. Miss Jessie Weston [6] insists that the romance was a psychological necessity; that some new development was demanded by the story-tellers in order to bind together the many loose ends of the story, and to remove the manifold disasters which hung so heavily over it. A hero was due who should possess certain qualifications necessary to the satisfactory completion of the story, and therefore a hero was created who, because he *did* possess these qualities, simply had to make his triumphal procession through the adventures which had proved stumbling-blocks to his predecessors.[7]

Miss Dorothy Kempe,[8] on the other hand, believes that the *Queste del St. Graal* was an artistic mistake. She maintains that the combination of the old Arthurian tales and the Christian leg-

---

[6] Weston, J. L., *Legend of Sir Perceval,* p. 398.

[7] True, there had been earlier quests with Perceval, Gawain, and Lancelot as their respective heroes. In some instances these had proved successful. But in the course of time their lives had been shadowed by some sin or slight defection which debarred them from the rôle required for the newly created hero.

[8] *Introduction to Lovelich's Holy Grail,* p. vi, E. E. T. S., Ex. Ser. (1874)

endary elements from an artistic point of view spelled disaster. The introduction of the new hero is, according to her, a pious anti-climax to the most virile cycle in English literature. Here we find a man (Galahad), whose powers are chiefly spiritual, completing an epic which had been calling for a man of physical prowess, a Christian saint intruding into a pagan arena, armed with weapons incongruous enough to be ridiculous. The transition is abrupt, and the sympathies of the author seem foreign to the materials with which he worked. The very ease with which a superhuman hero swept in and accomplished the adventure (the quest) which many knights drawn from hard life failed to accomplish, detracts from the completeness of the story. Indeed, many scholars are of the opinion that whatever beauties are found in this work come from a simplicity of style, a rather good craftsmanship—from anything, in fact, except a deep and comprehending artistry which fully grasped the real meaning of the existing legends and knew just what was required to make them whole.

There are, however, a sufficient number of scholars [9] who insist that the *Queste del St. Graal* is an artistically beautiful thing, capping the entire edifice which legions of Arthurian architects piled up during the course of ages (and numerous translations testify to this conception), that we may seek a reconciliation. It might, therefore, satisfy diverse schools to say that the Galahad *Queste* was accidentally artistic, drawing beauty from intrinsic idealism, but that, as a part of the legends into which it was fitted, it was essentially valueless.

(3) Yet, there is a possibility (which seems to be something more than a possibility), that the elements of the story are not as basically diverse as at first they might appear to be; that the Cistercian author's genius, for example, lay not so much in his ability to unite factors which were well-nigh irreconcilable, as simply, by intuition and divining, as Richard Wagner did in the Parsifal, to re-unite parts of a whole which originally were essentially one; that this double-trunked tree, the branches of which appear intertwined in accidental unity, actually took root from a single seed, and that the diggers and delvers must go even deeper

[9] Evans, Gietmann, Pauphilet.

than they have thus far gone in order to convince themselves of this possibility.

Scholarship has brought out the well known fact that there are striking similarities in the folklore of peoples who are flung far apart both from a racial and geographical point of view. F. R. Schröder [10] has tried to show, for example, in his work *Die Parzivalfrage* how the Parzival story was the heritage of oriental (Persian) peoples long before its advent into western literature; how the idea of *Perfect Man, the Electus, Perfectus, " der Erlöser,"* the *Logos, teleios anthropos,* of Hippolyt († 235 A. D.), *der Urmensch, der Vollkommene Mensch* " gemahnt an die Gestalt Parzivals," and how the Perfect Man and the quest for perfection existed as part of the religious belief of many oriental sects. He goes to great lengths to prove that the whole machinery of the Parzival story is the ritualistic expression of Manichaeism with its composite tenets of Gnosticism, Islamism, Judaism, and Christianity.

The task of identifying Christian beliefs and traditions, as often expressed in the Grail legend, with pagan folklore and religion of great antiquity has, of course, often and sagaciously been attempted and at some length. Of late, Roger Sherman Loomis, in his scholarly work *Celtic Myth and Arthurian Romance,*[11] has taken great pains to indicate the Celtic pagan derivations of the Grail elements. The Grail castle, according to Dr. Loomis, is a parallel of the Other World fortress of Curoi, but it is " also identifiable with the abode of other Welsh gods, Manawyddan, Bran, and Beli. . . ." [12] Further, he quotes Dr. Nitze to the effect that, " Manannan and the Fisher King are to all intents and purposes the same person." [13]

[10] Schröder, Franz Rolf, *Die Parzivalfrage* (1928), p. 5. See also H. Güntert, *Kundry,* Heidelberg 1928, p. 41. Comp. Franz Kampers, *Das Lichtland der Seelen,* Köln, 1916; Max Unger, *Neue Parzivalforschung* (*Kölnische Zeitung,* Nov. 29, 1931.) The name of Parzival's father, Gahmuret, is alleged to be Avestian Gaya Maretan, " mortal life " or " Urmensch " or Iranian " Urkönig." " Parzival " means " the chaste flower," in the opinion of the Orientalist, von Suhtschek. (See footnote p. 14.)

[11] Chapters XV, XVI, XVII, XXIII, XXVII.

[12] *Celtic Myth and Arthurian Romance,* p. 176.

[13] *Ibid.,* p. 181. On " Fisher King," also Schwietering, *Zeitsch. f. d. Altertum,* 60 (1923), 259 f. F. R. Schröder, *Parzivalfrage,* p. 27. " Fisher

Now Manannan was the son of Lir, King of the Land of Promise.
Manawyd, the Welsh counterpart of Manannan, is, according to
Dr. Loomis and Dr. Nitze, another type of the Fisher King, as is
Bran the sea-god.   Due to his infirmity he is usually presented
in the sedentary occupation of fishing, if we accept the explanation
of some conteurs.   The Siege Perilous, Dr. Loomis adds, is hinted
in the seat of watch in Curoi's castle of the king's seat at Nuada's
court.[14] And so on.

The excellence of such studies as these is manifest, and far from
detracting from the thesis of the present chapter, only make the
ultimate reconciliation all the easier.

There are, on the other hand, those who, due to their ardent
sympathy with the mind of the Cistercian of the Middle Ages,
sometimes fall into the snare of overemphasizing the elements of
Christian mysticism in the whole Grail idea.   They seem convinced
that an allegory is designed primarily to obscure the truth, and
feel certain that their task is *a priori* a difficult one.   The conse-
quence of such a premise is a still more mysterious and unintelli-
gible explanation than was the object to be explained—a sort of
progressive obscurantism.   They would be cautious and exact, but
in drawing out the single strands, they not only destroy the fabric,
but become entangled in the web made thereby.

In order to effect a reconciliation between these two views, scholars have sought for some common denominator between Christianity and paganism in the Grail story; they have asked themselves
whether there is not, in the inherited traditions of mankind, something simple enough, and fundamental enough, and universal
enough to permeate the entire mass of folklore, and serve as an
ultimate explanation of these interminable parallels.

But is such a common denominator to be found?   Is there a
reconciliation existing between pagan folklore and Christian tradition?   The present writer believes there is, and, if there is, *it is
to be built upon the Church's doctrine of Original Sin and man's
rehabilitation through Grace.*

The story of the first man's creation in a state of innocence, of

King," according to the latter, is cult language for " priest " or " Mysta-
goge "; in Greek: *halieus.*
[14] *Ibid.,* p. 216.

his fall, and the consequent proneness to sin in his children, of the loss of his former happiness in the Garden of Paradise bringing with it a subjection to ignorance, concupiscence, sickness and death—all this is too well known to require elaboration. According to the third chapter of Genesis, Adam, at the instigation of Eve, disobeyed God and was driven in shame from Paradise, with the promise, however, that one day a Redeemer would come to save him and his posterity. The exegesis of that part of the Bible need not detain us, as it is more to our point to seek the implications which became a part of Catholic dogma as officially proclaimed by the Popes and Councils of the Church.

Original sin, the most important corollary, takes its Scriptural substantiation from Saint Paul (*Romans* v, 12, ff.) :

> Wherefore as by one man sin entered the world, and by sin death; and so death passed upon all men, in whom all have sinned. For until the law sin was in the world; but sin was not imputed, when the law was not. But death reigned from Adam unto Moses even over them also who have not sinned after the similitude of the transgression of Adam, who is a figure of him who was to come.

From these and other Scriptural passages, from tradition and the teaching of the Fathers, the Church has pronounced certain definitions which are essential to the integrity of Catholic belief. The Second Council of Orange, in 529, the decrees of which were confirmed by Pope Boniface II, declared that Adam through original sin lost sanctity and justice and was entirely transformed to a lower state both as regards body and soul.[15]

The cumulative doctrine of the Church throughout the early centuries had definitely expressed the further ideas that this sin

---

[15] *Conc. Arausicanum II.* Can. 1. Si quis per offensam praevaricationis Adae non totum, id est secundum corpus et animam, in deterius dicit hominem commutatem, sed animae libertate illaesa durante, corpus tantummodo corruptioni credit obnoxium, Pelagii errore deceptus adversatur Scripturae dicenti: " *Anima quae peccaverit, ipsa morietur* " (Ez. 18, 20) ; *et:* " *Nescitis, quoniam, cui exhibetis vos servos ad obediendum, servi estis ejus, cui oboedistis?* " (Rom. 6, 16) ; *et:* " *A quo quis superatur, ejus et servus addicitur* " (2 Pet. 2, 19).

The foregoing was substantiated by the Council of Trent, Session V, June 1546, Can. 1.

of Adam had injured not only himself but all mankind,[16] that
their manner of sharing in this sin was not by imitation but propa-
gation since it was a true sin,[17] that it differed from actual sin not
only by reason of the consent but also by reason of the penalty,
which in the case of original sin was only the privation of the
Beatific Vision,[18] and that it was remitted only by the sacrament
of Baptism.[19]

[16] The complete *ex professo* doctrine must be sought in the canons and
chapters of the Councils of the Church, and for our purpose in those
which were held before the twelfth century.

Cf. The Second Council of Milevitanum and the Plenary Council of
Carthage, which were confirmed in 418 by Pope Zosimus, Canons 1, 2,
and 3; the letter of Pope Celestine I (21) to the Bishops of Gaul on
Semipelagianism, Chapter 4; the Canons of the Second Council of Orange
(Arausicanum) against Semipelagianism (529) confirmed by Pope Boniface II, Canons 1 and 2; the Council of Rome (861-863) Canon 8; *Symbolum Fidei* of Pope St. Leo IX. (Citations found in Denzinger's *En-
chiridion Symbolorum et Definitionum.*)

The Council of Carthage in 418, the decrees of which were approved by
Pope Zosimus, anathematized all who said that the words, " in remission
of sin," when used in infant baptism, were not to be taken in their true
sense. Can. 2.

Item placuit, ut quicunque parvulos recentes ab uteris matrum bap-
tizandos negat, aut dicit in remissionem quidem peccatorum eos baptizari,
sed nihil ex Adam trahere originalis peccati, quod lavacro regenerationis
expietur, unde sit consequens, ut in eis forma baptismatis " in remissionem
peccatorum " non vera sed falsa intelligatur, Anathema Sit.

The Second Council of Orange speaks of the injury wrought to Adam's
posterity by his sin, in the Second Canon:

Si quis soli Adae praevaricationem suam, non et ejus propagini asserit
nocuisse, aut certe morte tantum corporis, quae poena peccati est, non
autem et peccatum, quod mors et animae, per unum hominem in omne
genus humanum transiisse testatur, injustitiam Deo dabit, contradicens
Apostolo dicenti: *Per unum hominem peccatum intravit in mundo, et per
peccatum mors, et ita in omnes homines mors pertransiit, in quo omnes
peccaverunt.* (Rom. 5, 12.)

[17] Carthage, up supra, Can. 1: " Placuit . . . ut quicunque dixerit,
Adam primum hominem mortalem factum. Ita ut, sive peccaret, sive non
peccaret, moreretur in corpore, hoc est de corpore exiret non peccati
merito, sed necessitate naturae."

[18] Letter of Pope Innocent III, " Majores Ecclesiae Causas ", to Ymber-
tum, Archbishop of Arles, in which is found: " Poena originalis peccati
est carentia visionis Dei, actualis vero poena peccati est gehennae per-
petuae cruciatus."

[19] See the Decrees of the Council of Carthage (418) on Original Sin

Incomplete as this outline must necessarily be, it clearly shows us that, in the traditions and teachings of the Church, the effects of original sin were not confined to Adam; all posterity shared in the punishment expressed in the words of Genesis: " Cursed is the earth in thy work." (Chapter III, 17.)   The only hope of restoration was offered in the promise of a Redeemer who would some day come and make satisfaction.   As Dr. Karl Adam expresses it: [20]

When Adam fell away from God, all humanity in him and through him fell away likewise.   That is a basic conviction of Christianity, which was adumbrated in certain post-canonical Jewish writings, and received formulation as a Christian doctrine especially at the hands of St. Paul. *At the basis of this Christian dogma of an original and inherited sin, and of our redemption through the new man Christ, lies the great and striking thought that mankind must not be regarded as a mass of homogeneous beings successively emerging and passing away, nor merely as a sum of men bound together by unity of generation, as being descendants of one original parent, but as one single man.   So closely are men assimilated to one another in their natural being, in body and mind, so profoundly are they interlocked in thinking, willing, feeling, and acting, so solidary is their life, their virtue and their sin, that they are considered in the divine plan of redemption only as a whole, only as a unity, only as one man.*   This one man is not the individual man, but the whole man, the totality of the innumerable expressions of that *humanity* which is reproduced in countless individuals.   This one man includes all men who were thousands of years ago and all who shall be thousands of years hence. Such is the one man, the whole man.   And the guilt and destiny of every single man are not merely his own guilt and his own destiny; they concern the whole of humanity in proportion to the importance which Providence has assigned him in the organism of humanity.

Now, among the many parallels in pagan myth and folklore which went into the Arthurian romances some stand out more

and Grace; Council of Rome (861-863), confirmed by Pope Nicholas I in Canon 8, decrees as follows:

Omnibus enim, qui dicunt, quod hi, qui sacrosancti fonte baptismatis credentes in Patrem et Filium Sanctumque Spiritum renascuntur, non aequaliter originali abluantur delicto, anathema sit.

Finally, in the *Symbolum Fidei* of Pope Saint Leo IX of 1053, we find: "Animam non esse partem Deo, sed ex nihilo creatam, et absque baptismate originali peccato obnoxiam, credo et praedico."

[20] *The Spirit of Catholicism*, p. 33.

prominently than others, and although it would be purely gratuit-
ous to pick out one or another as fundamental, since the mass is
presented to us a vast tapestry, still it is but natural that we lay
more stress on those which seem to have caught deepest root in
most widely different localities, and which have passed through the
greatest number of forms. *Among these is the legend of the
Maimed or Fisher King, the idea of lands dwelling under a curse
of barrenness or of enchantment, and of certain deeds of prowess
and valor which could not be accomplished until a certain expected
knight should arrive.*

The idea of the Maimed King and the Promised Knight is not
confined to the medieval Grail story. The crippled, bleeding, sick
or wounded man helplessly waiting for a savior is almost a commonplace in ancient and medieval literature. To point out particular examples in literature of the longing of mankind for some-
one who would come and lift the spell, or spells, would be merely
repeating known tales. It is enough, however, to suggest that the
Cistercian author of the Galahad *Queste* observed a parallel between
the *fall* of Adam and the wounding of the Grail King (the
"Fisher" King), between the hope of a Redeemer (Christ), and
the coming of a Perfect Knight (Galahad). Pehaps not as a
different aspect of the same thing did he see it, but certainly as
a story which possessed certain similarities. A mained king,
according to ancient traditions,[21] usually found disfavor with the

[21] Dr. Loomis, in his scholarly work, *Celtic Myth and Arthurian Romance*, quotes at length from Macalister's study of Tara (PRIA, XXXIV,
C, 324): "The king of Temair was a god incarnate. This is the all-
important fact which results from a study of the traditions of the early
kingship that have come down to us. . . . When a good king was on the
throne the gods condescended to take up their abode with him; when
the king was illegitimate they withdrew themselves. . . . Contrast these
characterizations from the *Lebor Gabala* 'Good was that king Eocho mac
Eirc; there was no rain in his time, but only dew; there was no year
without its harvest; falsehood was expelled from Ireland in his time.'
'In evil case was Ireland in the time of Coipre, for the earth did not yield
her fruit, because there was but one grain in the ear, one acorn on the
oak, one nut in the hazel; the creeks were unproductive, the cattle were
dry, so that there was an intolerable famine throughout Ireland for five
years in which Coipre was king.' We have seen in the last section that
Eochu mac Eirc was the impersonation of the Divine Wisdom at the head

gods who had marred him thus, and so it was quite natural in the
mind of the monk for such a ruler to find a parallel in Adam.
Amfortas, the Grail King of Wolfram, was wounded because of his
illegitimate love for Orgeluse.　The latter name could suggest
to a medieval author the sin of pride, and again remind him of
Adam and mankind.　The Fisher King in question was, moreover,
wounded through the thigh, as if to imply that all his posterity
would inherit something of his imperfection; Adam also received
a wound, and theologians describe him after the fall as *Spoliatus
gratuitis et vulneratus in naturalibus.*[22]　" By one man sin entered
into the world," says Holy Scripture, *" and by sin, death."*
(*Romans* v, 12).

Now, it was not necessary that the Cistercian author of the
Queste should understand that Adam and the " Fisher King " had
a common origin in the dim past; it was enough that he divined
some sort of parallel and the occasion of an allegory.　And how
strikingly apparent the parallel was! Here he found both in pagan
folklore and Christian tradition an imperfection existing in the
whole mass of the people (members) because of the injury suffered
in their head; in both pagan folklore and Christian tradition he
found that the only hope of restoration was in the promise of a

of the 'epic' pantheon: and though the historians have made him a
king, he retains sufficient godhead to secure the blessings named for his
people. . . . As Dr. Baudis points out, this idea is also at the basis of
the prohibition of the rule of a blemished king." The euhemerized
god Nuada, after losing his arm at the first battle of Moytura, was forced
to retire from the kingship.　His successor Bres was satirized for his
churlishness so that great red blotches broke out over his face disqualifying
him in turn.　(*Folklore*, XVII, 29.)　By this time Nuada had acquired
his famous silver arm and was able to resume his throne.　*There can be
no doubt therefore that the Irish believed that the health or sickness of
the god in his earthly representative, the king, reflected themselves in the
abundance of the crops and the yield of the cattle.*　Nevertheless it is
significant that only the Welsh Bran affords a clear prototype of the
Maimed King and the names of most of the Maimed Kings of Romance
are of Welsh derivation.

[22] The *gratuitis* were both supernatural and praeternatural gifts (im-
munity from sickness and death and all the ills that afflict mankind);
the *naturalibus* were man's natural appetites which had been vitiated. *Vide*
Toner, *De Peccato Originali*, p. 126.

Redeemer who would some day come and make satisfaction. From Christian tradition he knew the results of the fall: that mankind was to be barred from Heaven until One should come to make amends; that the spell of satan lay over all; and that the world was barren of good works because the grace or favor of God was not with men.

Indeed, this is the very substance of the sermon which Trevrizent gives Parzival, the hero of Wolfram's story, when Trevrizent is about to explain to him the history of the Grail King. In the heavenly chorus of angels, Lucifer's seat became vacant. " Lucifer's sin was pride," say he to Parzival, and continues: " Adam took the place of Lucifer who sinned while he was ' âne gallen ', pure, without stain. Adam [and Eve] brought misfortune into the world."

> " diu erde Adâmes muoter was:
> " von erden fruht Adâm genas.
> " dannoch was diu erde ein maget;
> " Noch hân ich iu niht gesaget
> " wer ir den magetuom benam.
> " Kâins vater was Adâm:
> " der sluoc Abêln umb' krankez guot.
> " dô ûf die reinen erden'z bluot
> " viel, ir magetuom was vervarn:
> " den nam ir Adâmes barn,
> " dô huop sich êrst der menschen nît:
> " alsô wert er iemer sît."

But of a pure virgin Christ was born to redeem " Adâmes künne." Purity, Adam, Christ, Parzival, Amfortas—all are here combined. Adam's children, ate of forbidden herbs; and since then mankind is crippled. Adam robbed earth of its virginity, according to medieval conception, because Cain's blood entered mother earth, and a curse since rests on mankind. The legends all showed a similar picture: men barred from attaining mysterious quests (the Grail); evil spells cast over lands and peoples; barrenness and sterility, and a thousand other ills afflicting manking until some Great Deliverer should come.

It was but natural, then, that the story of the Perilous Seat in

[22a] See Wolfr. Parzival, 464, 11 ff (Book IX). See also Parzival 518-520.

4

which no sinful man could sit, the castles which lay under spells until the Perfect Knight should come, the lands which would be barren until that time—all were similies, in the mind of the monk, which well expressed the long waiting of the world of the Old Dispensation. It must be stressed that there is nothing to indicate a realization on the part of this Cistercian moralist that he may perhaps have found the key to the ultimate solution of the Grail mystery; for him it was sufficient to find in a story which had caught the popular fancy strikingly analogues with which to clothe his dogmas.

If all this be true, it is easy to see why Galahad came—why he had to come. Perceval's story prepared the way for him. The story as far as the pagans were concerned was never finished. They were still waiting. Folklore loses its value and descends to mere fiction unless it preserves the beliefs and traditions of a people. And there was nothing in the religion of the pagans, who had forgotten their origins and disintegrated into mere cults, which could complete the story. Judaism itself still waits. The only people who could finish the story were those who saw in Jesus Christ the Redeemer Who had been promised in the Garden of Paradise. *For them the Fisher King was the figure of Adam who by the coming of a Perfect Man was healed along with his posterity of the curses that lay upon him.* To quote Dr. Adam: [23]

With this new mental attitude we are able to appreciate the fundamental Christian conceptions of the first man and the new man, of Adam and Christ, in their profound significance. Adam, the first man, called to share by grace in the divine life, represented in God's eyes the whole of mankind. *Adam's fall was the fall of mankind.* Detached from its original supernatural goal, mankind then, like some planet detached from its sun, revolved only in crazy gyration round itself. Its own self became the centre of its striving and yearning. Man came to feel God, the very source of his spiritual life, as a burden. The first "autonomous" man in the ethico-religious sense was Adam, when he took the fruit of the tree of life. And so man no longer had any source whence he might renew his strength, except his own small self. *He had abandoned the eternal source of living water, and dug himself a poor cistern in his own self. And the waters of this cistern were soon exhausted. Man fell sick and died. His self was his sickness and his self was his death. And*

---

[23] *The Spirit of Catholicism,* p. 34.

all mankind died with him. Then, according to the eternal decision of God's love, the New Man came, the man of the new, permanent and indissoluble union with God, Christ the Lord. In Him erring mankind, man radically cut off from the divine source of his life, was finally reunited to God, to the Life of all lives, to the Fount of all power, truth and love. Mankind—not merely this man and that, not you and I only, but the whole of mankind, the unity of all men—was brought home again from its terrible diaspora, from its dispersion, back to the living God. The whole man came once more into being, permanently united with God, and so effectively united that he could never more, as the unity of mankind, be for any fault cut off from the divine source of life. Therefore Christ, as the God-man, is the new humanity, the new beginning, the whole man in the full meaning of the phrase.

To return now to our present problem. It would seem logical at first to follow Pauphilet and to identify Galahad with Christ. But to do that would be to lose sight of the ulterior motive of the monk and to leave the Quest of the Grail in its former state of confusion. To develop this aspect of the theory it will be necessary to digress for a moment and consider briefly the problem in the hands of the moralists who made the interpolations, and their mental attitude towards that problem.

As has been suggested, the author of the *Queste* caught something of a parellel between certain legends and his own religious beliefs. If his chief aim were merely to finish the legends by adding new material from their original sources, garbed in the changing raiment of the legends in their present state, he would have introduced Christ as Galahad. (All this, of course, implies the baseless premise that he knew both shoots came from a single source.) But the point is this: he had no such intention. He intended to edify—and how he has suffered at the hands of scholars and critics for what seemed to him a lofty aim! There would have been no purpose in borrowing an elaborate and involved allegory to explain what to him and his followers was a dogmatic fact. The story of Christ was to him, as was the story of Adam, an historical fact. It was to be preserved and taught with scrupulous simplicity, just as the Old Testament writings were sacred among the Jews. In fine, he had the key to the vast and varied but unfinished cycles of romances and forebore using it, simply because the Fall and Redemption of mankind taken corporately—

the matter of original sin and the rehabilitation of mankind in grace—were dogmas about which he and his followers could do nothing.

A very different thing, however, was the question of actual sin and the grace which makes each individual faithful to God. This was not a *fact* in the same sense as was the other. It was rather a *state,* and was eminently the subject of exhortation. Now, to exhort men to change their ways of living requires very much more than recitals of fact. There is, for the vast majority of mankind, need to strike the heart with fear of consequences of wrong, need to build up ideals of right, need to show how divine help will be given to overcome what seem to be insuperable obstacles; in a word, there is every room for the monitory allegory. So with the most gripping tales in the world on the one hand, and a definite purpose of edification on the other, it is only to be expected that *the Cistercian author of " La Queste del St. Graal," in creating Galahad, had in mind, not Christ, but a mortal man who walked undaunted to his goal because he kept the commandments of God and was clothed in grace.*

Nor is the argument entirely *a priori.* Our suspicions are confirmed by facts. In the first place, as a result of the spread of Christianity and of the influence of the Crusades, the old legends were becoming Christianized. Those who knew of Arthur as a king, and Lancelot as the bravest knight in all the world, also knew that Christ had lived and died in Palestine. It would have been a sheer anachronism to bring Christ to Camelot and to take Him out of His traditional setting. Furthermore, the reverence of the monk was too great to identify Him Who was born of the Virgin Mary with a man, however ideal he might have been, who was born of Elaine's deception on Lancelot. And not the least of the reasons opposed to Pauphilet's theory is the fact that the Cistercian's belief in the divinity of Christ (which meant absolute omnipotence) was so firm that it could not conjure up the picture of a God spending years upon a knightly quest and undergoing the trials, temptations, and disappointments common to knighthood.

The case of ordinary mortals was different. Their entire life was a sort of quest. Wherever they journeyed, they were likely to encounter one of the three arch enemies, the world, the flesh, and the devil, and these encounters could be described with all the glamor and pageantry of the ages of chivalry if they were expressed in terms of romances of the day. There were necessary modifications, however. The victors were those who first sought God in all they did, and not those who sought the favor of kings or even of nations. Personal sanctity was required as a necessary condition before the supernatural strength would be given to enable them to issue in triumph. The reward for prowess could not be the love of women and the amassing of property; it must be in one form or another the possessing of God—the Beatific Vision.

So the knights of Camelot, in the mind of the Cistercian monk, rode away from the worldly distractions of the court, and wandered wherever circumstances led them, knowing that their trials would come and that if they passed them safely, the goal would be theirs. And the goal was the possession of the Grail!

But what was the Grail to Galahad and to the knights in the " Queste " ? Scholars for many years have labored untiringly to find answer to that question.[24] It must have been something of tremendous importance to have inflamed half of Arthur's knights to such a pitch that they turned their backs on wives and ladies of their choice, on tried and true companions, on all the glory which might have been theirs had they remained at home, and set out whither they knew not. To have been the object of such sacrifices a mere cup, even though a " magical " cup, and nothing more, would be absurd! Of course an allegory can wander away from from probability if it must, but if it is to make an impression on the simple it must not be too difficult of interpretation.

In the light of the Church's doctrine of Grace, the idea of a

[24] Dr. Loomis thus sums up the prevailing theories: " There is no questioning the fact," he says, " that the scholars who have offered the three chief solutions for the problem of the Grail have been able to make out an excellent case. The Grail as Celtic talisman, as fertility symbol, as Christian relic,—each conception is supported by masses of detailed evidence. The judicious scholar is driven to admit that the Grail has signified many things to many men at many times. Each interpretation is partially true for us just as it was true for the redactor who placed that particular interpretation on it."—*Celtic Myth and Arthurian Romance*, p. 139.

" cup ", however, seems very fitting. The Christian soul is seeking God,—God incarnated in a Man. Man's spiritual encounters are brought down to terms of physical combats; it is eminently appropriate, therefore, that his reward be expressed by a material, tangible object; for God—the ultimate object of man's search—as a spiritual and simple substance could never fall under the senses. What figure or symbol was more likely to thrust itself on the minds of medieval men (whose theologians at that time were everywhere discussing the doctrine of Transubstantiation) than the chalice of the Last Supper as the fountain of grace in which Christ the God-Man declared Himself to be truly present? [25]

This, indeed, is the theory of the learned theologian Etienne Gilson, set forth in an enlightening article, *La Mystique de la Grace dans la Queste del St. Graal.*[26] The Holy Grail, according to Gilson, is nothing else but the grace of the Holy Spirit, and the cup is merely the symbol of the love with which the Christian soul is nourished. That this idea was unmistakably in the mind of the author of the *Queste* is shown in the words he puts upon the lips of King Arthur after the first appearance of the Grail: [27] " Surely, my lords, we ought to be glad and rejoice greatly that our Lord has given such evidence of His love, that He has consented to feed us with His grace upon such a high festival as Pentecost." According to Gilson, the author of the *Queste* could not have given a clearer definition of the Grail than this: *The Grail is the Grace of the Holy Spirit, unquenchable and delicious source from which the Christian soul drinks.* This definition, which is of so great importance in the proper understanding of the *Queste,* is further developed by the hermit in his advice to Hector, when, speaking of the Holy Grail, he says: " A spring indeed it is, which can never be exhausted however much one may draw from it; *for it is the Holy Grail, that is, the grace of the Holy Spirit.*" [28] Pauphilet [29] is of the same opinion as Gilson in maintaining that the grace of

[25] The dogma of Transubstantiation was declared at the Fourth Council of Lateran in 1215.

[26] *Romania*, 51 (1925), p. 322 ff.

[27] Comfort, W. W., *The Quest of the Holy Grail*, p. 13.

[28] *Ibid.*, p. 128.

[29] *Études sur la Queste del St. Graal*, p. 24, 25.

God and the Grail are identical, but Pauphilet goes a step farther
and calls the Grail " the romantic manifestation of God." *" Plus
exactement, le Graal, c'est la manifestation romanesque de Dieu."*
On this point Gilson has some very definite distinctions to make.
He tells us that while it is true that the attributes of the Grail
are the same as those of God Himself, still, it is not exact to conclude from this that the Grail *is* God.   In order to understand the
thought in the mind of the Cistercian author of the *Queste,* it is
wise, according to Gilson, to begin with the Augustinian conception
of grace with which St. Bernard and the Cistercians were inspired.
First, the definition of God Himself is that *He is Love, Deus
Charitas est.*[30]   *Grace is what God has gratuitously conferred on
us of His love in order to call us back to Him.*   Charity is *from*
God, *Charitas ex Deo est.* (*I Epis. St. John,* 4, 7.) God and grace,
then, observes Gilson, can bear the same name, *Charitas,* although
an infinite difference separates them, since grace is a created gift,
whereas God is the creator of it.[31]   From this it follows that it is
impossible to attribute to God the name *Charitas* in the same sense
as that in which we attribute it to grace.   Indeed, according to
Gilson, it would be altering the significance of the entire work to
interpret a symbol of grace as if it were a very symbol of God.[32]

Now, how does all of this help to explain the genesis of Galahad?
The answer is simple.   The Cistercian author of the *Queste del
St. Graal,* having set himself the task of fashioning from the widely
popular Arthurian legends a romance whose central theme should
be grace and man's rehabilitation through grace, found it necessary
to create a character in which the fullness of this grace (or God's
love) should appear.   He wished to show how the life of grace func-
tions in a Christian soul, to demonstrate the varying degrees in the
romance of divine love, and so he created Galahad, who, from his

[30] *I Epis. St. John,* 4, 16.

[31] This doctrine, as Gilson shows, is formulated by St. Bernard in terms
of perfect precision: *Dicitur ergo recte charitas, et Deus, et Dei donum.
Itaque Charitas dat charitatem, substantiva accidentalem.   Ubi dantem
significat, nomen substantiae est; ubi donum, qualitatis.—De diligendo
Deo,* cap. XII, art. 35.

[32] *" La Mystique de la Grace dans la Queste del St. Graal,"* Romania,
51 (1925), p. 325.

initial call to his final ecstasy exemplifies all this perfectly. Galahad is the flower of Cistercian mysticism, a hero in whom the grace of God shows forth so translucently that even his exterior borrows some of the shining beauty of the soul within.[33] The author of the Queste insists upon purity because purity is an absolute necessity for the perfect contemplation of God. "Blessed are the pure of heart for they shall see God." (*St. Matthew* v. 8.) This reward of purity, namely, *seeing* God, does not refer solely to the Beatific Vision and the delights which will come to the just soul after death; it refers more specifically to the souls of men still in the trammels of the flesh, who keep their members free from the corruption of sin [34] and are therefore able to look steadfastly with the eyes of faith on the Divine Guest of their soul and to hold constant communion with Him. These men, like Galahad, indeed *see* God; they are true mystics, possessed of an abiding consciousness of the indwelling of the Holy Spirit, of that Spirit Which is the essence of all Love, the love that unites the Father to the Son, the Love that unites man to man and men to God, the Love in which all creation lives and moves and has its being. And it is this Spirit which "giveth testimony to our spirit that we are the sons of God." (*Romans* viii, 16.)

Finally, Galahad the pure, who by reason of his fidelity to grace overcomes all obstacles, sees the Holy Grail, and is made king of Sarras. This kingship is a purely symbolical idea of the spiritual kingship which every just soul enjoys in union with the kingship of Christ. By his conquest over sin, man becomes a son of God, and if a son, an heir also. "Heirs indeed of God and joint-heirs with Christ." (*Romans* viii, 17.) And since kingship is so universally considered to be a supreme reward, Galahad becomes king of the city of his own soul, and rules in the realm of the Grail.

Thus we have the main outlines of a theory which may help to explain the origin of the type of Grail-seeker known as Galahad. It is not entirely new, in that other commentators, notably Pau-

---

[33] Gilson suggests that the author of the *Queste* in drawing the picture of Galahad may have had in mind the physical beauty of St. Bernard. " It would not be impossible," he says, " that Galahad preserved some of the traits of the illustrious abbot of Clairvaux."—*Ibid.*, p. 333.

[34] *Romans* vi, 19-23.

philet and Gilson, have cleared the way for it. After all, a theory is a working model to explain known facts. It is " true " until it fails to keep pace with scientific knowledge. It can be altered *ad infinitum* as data are heaped up in its rejection or support. But at the outset it is sketched on high points, and the present theory attempts to reconcile a few high points in seemingly parallel traditions, on the notion that truth, is, after all, one.

This *Original Sin and Grace Theory* is in one sense a reversal of many preceding ones, because it acknowledges the didactic character of the elaboration, while it stresses the psychological necessity of Galahad's coming, or the coming of a Perfect Man. It denies, however, the proposition that this elaboration was essentially fatal in that it was an incongruous grafting, having a few accidental beauties, and rather holds it up as the only logical conclusion, an artistic necessity having many accidental defects. The fact that the transition appears to many so violent and abrupt may be, nay undoubtedly is, one of these defects, and is due, no doubt, to the fact that the elaborator had no idea that he was anything more than an elaborator. His failure merely to complete the legends by introducing a figure corresponding to Christ, and his developing a Galahad solely for edification, is further indication of this. But however manifold these crudities may be, the theory would suggest that he did fulfill the long unfulfilled prophecies from the only source possible, for the traditions of paganism had become lost in their own ramifications.

These suggestions may never be proved, but for the same reason (namely, their very generality), they may likewise never be disproved. It will be all the author desires if they merely indicate some possibility of an ultimate reconciliation between pagan lore and Christian tradition, or if they help to throw the feeblest ray of light upon the possible genesis of Galahad.

CHAPTER IV

GALAHAD FROM THE *Queste* TO MALORY

At the end of the twelfth century the Arthurian legends in literary form had spread with amazing rapidity over the continent of Europe so that not only Germany, Spain, Italy, and Holland, but even distant Norway, had thrilled to the stories of Arthur and the Grail. It was not, however, until the third quarter of the fourteenth century that the stream of Arthurian romance began to flow at all abundantly in English.[1]

To Layamon, a priest of Ernley, belongs the distinction of being the first to celebrate Arthur in the English tongue. His *Brut* (c. 1200) being within a century removed from Geoffrey's *Historia* was still close enough to claim a share, and the last share, in the great Geoffreyan tradition. Of all the pseudo-historians who came after Geoffrey, and before the Elizabethan Holinshed, only two can be said to have contributed materially to the development of the Arthurian story, the French poet Wace and the Saxon poet Layamon.[2]

Layamon, not satisfied with following Wace's amplifications of Geoffrey's chronicle, doubled the French poet's lines; and though Layamon lacks the compelling grace of Wace's style, still his frankly patriotic *Brut* possesses some of the wild, impassioned notes of early Anglo-Saxon verse, which along with its sombre ancestral enthusiasm for war brings it very much nearer to the Old English mood than the narrative of the courtly French versifier. Blunt, and even plebeian at times, Layamon writes with a vigor becoming his martial themes, and, as Legouis says,[3] exhibits somewhat of the "massive ironies of the Anglo-Saxon epic."[4] Like its French source, the English *Brut* is a colorful pageant of medieval society—knights and ladies, minstrelsy and tournaments,

[1] Cf. MacCallum, W. M., *Tennyson's Idylls and the Arthurian Story*, p. 62.
[2] Cf. Maynadier, H., *Arthur of the English Poets*, p. 50.
[3] *History of English Literature*, p. 54.
[4] *The Brut*, Chap. LXXVII.

50

perilous adventures and gorgeous cavalcades—all centered about the three great ideals of the Middle Ages: love, chivalry, and religion.

Galahad, as is to be expected, finds no place in the *Brut,* since the latter is drawn largely from Geoffrey, and Geoffrey's *Historia* antedates the literary story of the Grail. We do, nevertheless, find in Layamon's epic many of the knightly virtues that were to characterize Galahad; for the zealous priest was a devoted champion of the Faith, and his heroes were Christian knights of the highest order. That his conception of the Round Table was that of an ideal society drawn from the flower of knighthood is attested by the following description: [4]

. . . And all the knyghtes weren so gode that no man knew the werst; and therefore kyng Arthure made the rounde table, that when thai shulde sitte to the mete, all shulde bene aliche hye, and evenlich seruede at the table, that none myght maken auant that none were hyer than othere.

The literary interest of the period following Layamon lies chiefly in the prevalence which the vernacular idiom obtained over the French, and the general impetus given to learning. Of the England of this time it may be said that it prepared rather than accomplished great literary achievements. The court was yet essentially French; in the schools Latin was studied through the French, and the majority of literary men still wrote in Latin. Soon, however, this condition was changed. Edward III, in 1362, ordered that the pleadings in all lawsuits should thenceforth be carried on in English, and Henry IV extended the same rule to parliamentary proceedings. English now replaced the French in the "grammere scoles of Engelond." In the rush of a great national movement expressed finally in the Hundred Years' War, which freed England from the political ties of France, the French language lost its official prestige, and English became the speech not only of the common people but of courts and Parliament as well. The popularity of the English version of Mandeville's *Travels,* was a proof of the growing importance of the native language.

On the Continent, the names of Dante, Petrarch, and Boccaccio, now loomed large and bright on the literary horizon. In England

[4] Brut, Chap. LXXVII.

Chaucer portrayed in his inimitable fashion the manners and
customs of business man and courtier; Langland and Wyclif wrote
against ecclesiastical abuses and preached the equality of men;
Gower and Lydgate strained their powers to perpetuate the traditions of literary England.   On the whole, it was a period when,
as Legouis says, " The English language . . . now had faith in its
destiny." [5]

English Arthurian literature, silent since Layaman's *Brut,* once
more found its voice, and when, in the fourteenth century the
English rediscovered the Arthurian stories, the tendency was to
develop the cycle along national lines, and to concentrate on the first
and the last acts of the drama of Arthur—the Merlin and the Mort
Artu.   The majority of fourteenth century writers passed over the
religious elements inextricably woven into the fabric of Authur-
ian romance, and preferred to weave their story around the figure
of the great king.

The Grail motif was not entirely neglected, however, and
although those works in which it appears have no great title to distinction, still they at least reveal the fact that England was aware
of the religious background of its national cycle, and that it was
eager to preserve the tradition of Galahad and the Grail.   It must
be remembered, too, that the fourteenth century was a period of
prevailingly religious poetry as seen in the *Ormulum,* a poetic para-
phrase of the gospel lessons of the year, somewhat after the manner
of the Cædmon Paraphrases; in Richard Rolle of Hampole's *Pricke
of Conscience,* a series of poetic meditations on death, judgment,
heaven, and hell; in the deeply religious *Pearl, Patience,* and
Cleanness, poems found with the manuscript of *Sir Gawain and
the Green Knight;* and in the works of the unknown author of the
Cursor Mundi.   The audiences for whom such poetry was written
would naturally lend a sympathetic ear to the religious note in
Arthurian literature, and those versed in the school of Richard
Rolle's mysticism, would be quick to see and appreciate the allegory
of the Grail.

None of the works in which Galahad appears during this period,
except perhaps the *Alliterative Joseph of Arimathie,* can boast of
great literary merit, nor can any of them claim with Malory the

[5] Legouis and Cazamian, *A History of the English Literature,* Vol. I,
p. 61.

distinction of having established Galahad permanently as the Grail hero of English Arthurian romance. The five works continuing the Galahad tradition are: *The Alliterative Joseph of Arimathie, Hardyng's Chronicle,* the *Prose Merlin,* Lovelich's *Holy Grail,* and Lovelich's *Merlin.*

The Alliterative Joseph of Arimathie, of unknown authorship, is, according to Skeat, not only one of the finest but one of the oldest pieces of alliterative poetry since the Conquest.[6] The poem, sometimes called the *Seint Graal* or *Holy Grail,* is a fragment of 709 alliterative verses written continuously like prose, of which apparently little is lost, the lost portions being, Skeat maintains, in the introductory lines. The story deals with the events which preceded the bringing of the Grail to England, and the adventures of Joseph of Arimathea, Galahad's famous ancestor, at the court of King Evelak of Sarras, but particularly with the episodes of King Evelak's shield, to which so much importance was attached in the Galahad *Queste.* The object of the poet was clearly to translate as much of the *Estoire* as pleased his fancy, a task of which he fairly acquitted himself. In the brief outline the story is:

After our Lord's entombment, Joseph of Arimathea is seized by the Jews and imprisoned in a dungeon, where he remains for forty-two years, until released by Vespasian. After his release, he tells Vespasian that the time of his imprisonment has seemed but three days. Being first baptized himself, he proceeds to baptize Vespasian and fifty others; Vespasian wreaks vengeance on the Jews for having imprisoned Joseph. In obedience to a divine voice, Joseph, with his wife, his son Josephes (or Josaphe), and a company of fifty people, leaves Jerusalem, and arrives at Sarras, taking with him the Holy Grail, or Sacred Dish containing Christ's blood, which is carried inside an ark. Joseph tries to convert Evelak, the king of Sarras, at the same time declaring the doctrine of the Holy Trinity. The king provides for the wants of Joseph's company, but has his doubts about the truth of the doctrine. The following night he is converted by two visions. In the first he sees three stems growing from one trunk, and appearing to coalesce into one—an emblem of the Trinity in Unity. In the second he sees a child pass through a solid wall without injury to the wall, an emblem of Christ's spotless incarnation.

---

[6] "We may safely date it not later than A. D. 1360, but I prefer rather to date it about 1350, for its meter is of a more rugged and earlier character than even that of 'William of Palerne'."—W. W. Skeat, Introduction, *Joseph of Arimathie,* E. E. T. S., No. 44, p. x.

Josaphe, the son of Joseph, also has a vision: on peering into the Grail-Ark, he beholds Christ upon the cross and five angels with instruments of the passion; afterwards eleven more angels appear, while Christ seems to descend from the cross and to stand beside an altar,upon which are the Lance, the Three Nails, and the *Dish with the Blood* (*the Holy Grail*). Christ then ordains Josaphe bishop, and bids him and Joseph go to Evelak's palace. A clerk is appointed by King Evelak to dispute with Joseph, but is miraculously struck dumb, whilst at the same time his eyes fly out of his head. Evelak repairs to a temple of idols, hoping to secure the clerk's recovery, but the idols are powerless. Soon after a messenger arrives to tell Evelak that his land has been invaded by Tholomer, king of Babylon, whereupon Evelak prepares for war. Before he sets out, Joseph and Josaphe have a private interview with Evelak, wherein Joseph tells the king that he is acquainted with all his previous history, and Josaphe gives Evelak a shield with a red cross upon it, telling him to pray to Christ in the hour of peril. In the first encounter, Tholomer's men are successful, but lose their tents. Evelak then collects more men, and is joined by his wife's brother, Seraphe, with five hundred men. In the next battle, King Evelak and Duke Seraphe perform, but at last Seraphe is sorely wounded and Evelak is made prisoner. As Evelak is being led to death he remembers Joseph's advice; he uncovers the shield with the red cross, and prays to Christ. An angel, in the outward form of a White Knight, comes to the rescue, slays Tholomer, heals Seraphe, mounts Evelak upon Tholomer's horse, and helps him to achieve a complete victory, after which he vanishes.

> Þenne was Eulac taken . and woundet ful sore;
> And the kyng tholomer . takes him to kepe,
> Ferde in-to a forest . fast bi-syde,
> forte fallen him feye . er thei a-ȝeyn ferden.
> Þenne he vn-keuered his scheld . & on the cros bi-holdes;
> He seiȝ a child strauȝt ther-on . stremynge on blode,
> And he bi-souȝte him of grace . as he was godes foorme.
> Þenne he seiȝ a whit kniht . comynge him a-ȝeines,
> bothe Armure and hors . al as the lilye,
> A red cros on his scheld . seemed him feire;
> Rydes to tholomer . rad wiþ þat ilke,
> Baar him doun of his hors . and harmed him more,
> strok him stark ded . that he sturede neuere.
>
> *Joseph of Arimathie*, ll. 555-567

Meanwhile Joseph has an interview with Evelak's queen, who is at heart a Christian, and whose early history is related. Evelak returns home and is baptized, being named Mordreins; Seraphe is also baptized, receiving the name Naciens. Joseph baptizes five thousand of Evelak's subjects, and abides at Sarras, while Josaphe and Nasciens set out upon a missionary journey, the Holy Grail being left at Sarras, in the charge of two

of Joseph's company. The poem here closes with a brief reference to the
subsequent imprisonment of Josaphe by the king of North Wales, and his
release by Mordreins (Evelak).

This rather abrupt ending of the poem leads one to infer that,
over and above the hundred lines Skeat thinks are missing in the
introduction,[7] there is also a missing portion belonging to the last
part, having to do with Joseph's death after leaving Sarras, and his
deathbed prophecy concerning Galahad and the shield. As related
in the *Estoire* and the *Queste,* Joseph when dying ordered that the
shield which had won for Evelak victory over the Babylonians and
his conversion to Christianity, should be brought to him, and before
bequeathing it to Evelak, made the sign of the cross upon it with
his blood, and charged Evelak to treasure it always as a remembrance of him. He then revealed to Evelak that no one would hang
this shield about his neck until Galahad should come, *juskes a tant
!que galaad le boins chevalier, li derrains del linaige nacien, l'e
pendera au sien col.* Moreover, he directed Evelak to place the
shield over the tomb of Nacien until Galahad should come to claim
it on the fifth day after receiving the order of knighthood.

That the inference of the lost ending is plausible appears from
the fact that all the other episodes related in the poem are identical
with those related in the *Estoire* and the *Queste.* Moreover, it is
hardly probable that a poet so well versed in the technique of the
art would purposely have marred his poem by failing to give it
climactic coloring, or would have concluded a rather stirring
narrative with an event so commonplace as Joseph's sudden departure from the city of Sarras. The English *Joseph of Arimathie* is,
of course, a condensation by the poet of the usual Joseph of Arimathea material as represented in the *Estoire* and Robert de Borron.
In all these stories Galahad is prophesied, either implicitly or
explicitly, as the one who is to restore *la terre foraine* and to lift
the manifold enchantments under which the land is laboring.

Although Galahad is not mentioned in the poem, it is worthy of
conjecture as to whether the English poet rejected the Galahad
material as not relevant to his unity of design of telling only the
story of Joseph, or as to whether he failed to see the climactic

[7] Skeat, W. W., Introduction to *Joseph of Arimathie,* p. viii.

value of introducing Galahad, as did the author of the *Estoire*. Whatever may have been his motive, " The Joseph of Arimathea legend," as V. D. Scudder observes, " was now connected with the Galahad motif, and as the Perceval legends represented the earlier type of Grail story, so the Middle English *Joseph Arimathie* reflects the latest type (the Galahad-Grail) stamped with religious fervor, permeated by ecclesiastical influence, remote from folk-lore and indifferent to the militant ideals of chivalry." [8]

Similar to that of the *Joseph of Arimathie* is the account given of the adventures of Joseph and the shield in *Hardyng's Chronicle*.[9] Hardyng professes to follow Mewyn, the " Britayne Chronicler," who is probably, says Skeat, no other than Melkin, and Melkin Skeat identifies with Nennius.[10]

Hardyng relates how Joseph of Arimathie came into Britain with Vespasian, and of how he converted the King Aruiragus, and gave him a shield of

> ye armes that wee call sainct George his
> armes, whiche armes he bare euer after;
> and thus became that armes to bee ye
> kynges armes of this lande, long afore
> sainct George was gotten or borne.   (Chap. XLVII).

and how Joseph by his preaching won the king to a law divine. The chronicle, which is a narrative of English kings from Brutus to Edward IV, during whose reign it was written, relates that Uther Pendragon founded the Round Table at Winchester chiefly for the recovery of the Sangreal, and also in commemoration of the King's marriage with Igerne. Hardyng says that the Seige Perilous will be achieved only by the most religious of all knights, and calls Galahad the chief knight of the Round Table.

> And at the day he weddid her and cround,
> And she far forth with child was then begonne,

---

[8] *Morte Darthur of Sir Thomas Malory*, p. 158.

[9] *Hardyng's Chronicle*, edited by Sir Henry Ellis, 1812.

[10] " Melkin," says Skeat, " is possibly the same as ' Mewynus, the Bryton chronicler," mentioned in *Hardyng's Chronicle*, ch. i, and in ch. xliii, where MSS have the various readings: *Newinus, Nenius,* and *Neninus*, which look very much like Nennius.—Skeat, *Joseph of Arimathie*, E. E. T. S., Vol. 44 (1849), p. xxi.

To comfort her he set the Table Rounde
At Winchester, of worthiest knights alone
Approved best in knighthood of their sone.
Which Table Round, Joseph of Arimathie
For brother made of the Saint Gral only.
In which he made the Siege Perilous,
Where none should sit, without grete mischief,
But one that should be most religious
Of knights all, and of the Round Table chief,
The Saint Gral that should recover and acheve.

The account of Galahad's achievement of the Siege is attributed by Hardyng to Mewyn, but in this case Skeat's supposition that Mewyn may be Nennius could hardly be correct. More than likely Hardyng, who like the other pseudo-chroniclers was at little pains to reconcile fact with fable, means the book of Merlin, which purported to be, after a fashion, a chronicle of Britain, although Merlin was not the " Britayn chronicler." The passage which expressly refers to Galahad as the promised knight is as follows:

In Mewyn's books, the Britayn chronicler,
As writen is the Britons iestes emong,
That Galaad the knight, and virgyne clere
Should it acheue and auentures all in fere
Of the seynt Graale, and of the great Briteyn,
And afterwards a vurgyne dye certeyne.

The Chronicle relates how Galahad came to Auelon, and found there a spear and a white shield bearing a red cross, the shield having been left there by Joseph and the spear by Nascien. Four hundred years after Joseph's time Galahad finds the Saint Grail in Wales, after which he goes to Sarras and is made king of that city. Here Galahad founds the Order of the Holy Grail, choosing for his society twelve knights in memory of the twelve Apostles.

Where thenne he made xij. knightes of the order
Of saynt Graall, in full signifycasyon
Of the table (of) whiche Joseph was the founder,
At Aualon, as Mewyn made relacyon;
In token of the table and refyguracyon
Of the brotherhede of Christes souper and maundie
Afore his death, of hyghest dignytes.

Galahad dies at Sarras, but sends Perceval with his heart to

5

Arthur, praying the king to bury the heart beside king Evelak and duke Seraphe and Joseph in Our Lady's chapel at Glastonbury. This was done, and the famous shield was hung over the tomb in which Galahad's heart was buried.

Like *Hardyng's Chronicle,* the *Prose Merlin,*[11] as well as the poems of Henry Lovelich, are typical of the period from which they sprang. The century and a half following Chaucer (1400-1550) was the most volcanic period of English history. The land was swept by vast changes, inseparable from the rapid accumulation of national power. The bloody War of the Roses sapped the energy of England, and a king who was but a puppet in the hands of his powerful nobles helped to hasten his country's destruction. Such a situation prevented any literary development and gave little encouragement to men of letters. Even the best writers of the period, Lydgate, Occleve, and the less important Hawes, confined themselves largely to translations and to subjects little adapted to artistic creation. On the whole, it was a period of imitators and reiterators and outworn themes. Not until the first Tudor king Henry VII ascended the throne did this period of literary inactivity come to an end.

As Langland and Chaucer had their host of imitators, so the medieval French romancers were not without their school of redactors, interpolators, and translators, to which latter group the writer of the *Prose Merlin* belongs. An author of undoubted ability, he nevertheless reflects in his work all the faults and shortcomings of his age: he is tedious to a fault, and he has a total disregard for the elements of climax and suspense. His *Merlin,* not always an accurate retelling of the Old French tale of that name found in the *Vulgate Cycle,* preserves the tradition of referring to Galahad only in prophecy. Only once, indeed, is there explicit mention made of him, and that at the very end of the work, when the author promises that in another book shall be rehearsed the exploits of Lancelot's son. There are, however, a few interesting allusions made to Galahad's coming, and in particular an account of the world-wide search for the Perfect Knight, quoted below.[12]

Chapter XXVII opens with the tidings spread through the

[11] Edited by H. B. Wheatley, E. E. T. S., Nos. 10, 21, 36, 112.
[12] P. 59.

realm of the Saint Grail and of the holy spear, which can be found only by the best knight in the world. The knights of the Round Table endeavor to discover this best knight, and when they hear of any good knight, they go in quest of him, and take him into their company.

This was the trouthe that tidinges spredde thourgh the reame of grete Breteigne of the seint Graal. In the which Joseph ab Aramathie hadde geten the holy blode that dropped oute of the side of oure blissed lorde Ieshu christ whan he henge on the gloriouse crosse, he and Nichodemus, and the holy vessell that com from heueue a-boue in the Citte of Sarras, in the whiche he sacrefied first his blissid body and his flessh by his Bisshoppe Iosephe that he sacred with his owene hande, and the holy spere, the whiche Ieshu the sone of marie his side was with opened, was left in the Cite of Logres that Ioseph thider hadde brought. But noon cowde wite in what place, he neuer ne shall, neuer be founde but by prophesie ne the merveiles of the seint graal, ne of the spere that thourgh the poynte of Iren dide blede. *Till that the beste knyght of the worlde com, and by hym sholde be discouered the merveiles of the seint Graal, and herde and seyn.* These tidinges were spredde all a-bout in euervy contrey, and so no man cowde neuer wite who sholde it bringe first forth, and whan the companye of the rounde table herde sey that thourgh the beste knyght of the worlde these thinges sholde be brought to fin. Thei entred in to many questes for to knowe whiche was the best knyght, and serched many a londe and many a contrey, and eche man hym peyned for to be the beste knyght; and whan thei herde speke that ther was eny gode knyght thourgh the contrey, then entred in to a quest hym to seche a yere and a day withoute soiour in a town more than oon nyght, and whan thei hadde hym founde, thei sholde bringe hym to court; and whan he was well preved of goode recorde that he was of high prowesse thei toke hym in to her companye, and than was his name writen a-monge the other knyghtes that were felowes of the rounde table; and as eche of hem com from his quest at the yeres ende, thei sholde telle the auentures that were hem befallen in theire traueile, and the clerkes that were therfore I-ordeyned it wrote worde for worde, euen as thei tolde. Now haue ye herde why the questes were stablisshed in the reame of the grete Breteigne. (Chap. XXVII, p. 502 f.)

The naïvely tender spirit of this work shows that no matter how pagan soever may be the origin of the stuff out of which the fair dreams of the medieval romances were made, it had become so thoroughly Christianized in concept that even the most pagan rendering of them all, the story of Merlin, cannot escape such tender religious touches as that which refers to the Holy Grail as the vessel in which Joseph of Arimathea " hadde geten the holy blode that dropped oute of the side of oure blissed Lorde Ieshu christ whan he henge on the gloriouse crosse," or that which alludes to " the holy spere, the whiche Ieshu the sone of marie his side was withopened," that spear " that thourgh the poynte of Iren dide blede."

The specific reference to Galahad occurs in the description of Nascien " cleped Nascien ffor love of the duke Nascien, that was so noble a knyght." (Chap. XX, p. 326.) The author of the *Prose Merlin* after enumerating the virtues of Nascien says: " This knyght hadde after Galahad, the sone of launcelot, many a day in his kepinge, wher-of the boke shall reherse here-after of alle thinges oon after a-nother as thei fill day be day." (Chap. XX, p. 326.) As V. D. Scudder says: " From the time the Grail reaches England predictions multiply; for the romance which carries us back to the foot of the Cross is also looking forward, and the reason for its peculiar quality is that it is concerned less with the present, than with what has been and what is to come. The future to which it points is the perfect Christianizing of the land. The Grail will vanish, through human sin, but it will come again; the ninth descendant from Nascien, the Good Knight Galahad, is he who shall restore it; and the romances continually prophesy his advent, in those coming days of Arthur when the mysteries of Britain shall be fulfilled." [13]

Two voluminous Arthurian romances came from the pen of Henry Lovelich (between the years 1450-1460), a metrical *History of the Holy Grail* and a metrical *Merlin*. Of the latter's 28,000 lines only 15,000 have been printed; and comparison of the first six thousand lines with the corresponding part of the French prose *Merlin* has shown that the two pieces agree in incident and vary but little in detail.[14] As in the *Prose Merlin* Galahad does not appear in person, though, as in the French original he distinctly seems to be the vessel of election hinted at, and as definitely hinted at in the Christ-like figure that dominates Lovelich's *History of the Holy Grail*.

In point of artistic literary achievement, his version is the least

[13] Scudder, V. D., *Morte Darthur of Sir Thomas Malory*, p. 96.
[14] Ed. by E. A. Koch, E. E. T. S., Extra Series 93 (1904), 112 (1913).

attractive of all the Grail romances, and most scholars agree that, as a literary monument or work of art, the *History of the Holy Grail* is valueless.　How far Malory's treatment of the same romance differed from that of Lovelich is seen by the subsequent popularity of their respective works: today, after nearly five centuries, Malory's *Morte Darthur* continues to be real and enjoyed, and quarried for new romance, while Lovelich's *Holy Grail* is practically forgotten.　The difference may perhaps be due to the fact that Malory possessed what Lovelich lacked, the touchstone of all true art—selectiveness.　Instead of following the beaten track of one single romance, as did Lovelich, Malory pried into a thousand tangled paths and followed up those which appeared most alluring.

Galahad is the implied chivalric hero of Lovelich's *Holy Grail* in the same sense as he is the hero of the *Estoire*.　It is he, the Christ-Galahad, who will accomplish the adventures of the Grail, of the bleeding lance, of the marvelous sword of David; it is he who will cure Mordrains of his wounds, and deliver Britain from the scourge of its afflictions; it is he to whom Joseph will turn his dying eyes in prophecy, and he to whom he will bequeath his famous red-cross shield.　Here, as in the *Estoire,* fulfillment is the watchword, and the Galahad-like protagonist, the Fulfiller.

It would be well-nigh impossible to give even a brief outline of Lovelich's voluminous work.　A resumé of the chapters pertinent to the subject in hand follows:

Chapter XVII.　After Nascien's sight has been miraculously restored by the angel, by means of the blood dripping from the lance, and Nascien, seeing the marvel, asks what the bleeding lance might be; Joseph tells him that when the lance shall again drop blood, the secrets of the " Sank Ryal," the Holy Grail, shall be revealed, and that the last of Nascien's line shall be the only man who shall see the wonders of the Holy Grail.　(Cf. ll. 197-199.)

Chapter XXVIII.　Nasciens on *Yl Torneant* (the Turning Isle) sees Solomon's ship approaching, but is warned against entering it unless he is full of faith.　He makes the sign of the cross, enters, and finds on a bed a crown of gold and a wonderful sword, the handle of which is covered with red cloth; on it is declared that no one shall draw the sword but the one worthiest of all men.　The scabbard is rose-red with gold and azure letters, and out of it issue a thousand filthy branches or hangings. The letters say that he who bears the sword and is girt with the branches will ever be safe.　(cf. ll. 259-274)

Chapter XXX. This tells the history of Solomon's ship. Solomon the wisest of all kings hearing that from him will in time far off be descended a knight, born of a virgin,[15] who will himself have no progeny (i. e. " schal ben of thy laste lyne," l. 191), a virgin knight who will deliver his people from all their ills, constructs a marvelous ship in which he places the sword of his father David, to which his wife attaches the mean hangings. Solomon having been himself deceived in a woman, then writes a letter to this unknown virgin knight, warning him against the wiles of women. One night in a dream Solomon sees angels sprinkle the ship with water and hears a voice saying that the last of his line shall enter the ship and draw the sword.

Up to this point, then, we have the prefigurement of a hero, the last of a knightly line, virginal in character and life, of the greatest prowess and grace of any man that ever lived, who accomplishes the quest of the Grail. In Chapter XXXIX he is mentioned by name Galaaz, or *Galahad,* who, under the more familiar form of the latter appelation, becomes one in the tradition of purity, and one in name, with the original hero of the twelfth century Cistercian monk.

Chapter XXXIX. Celidoyne appears to Nasciens in a vision accompanied by nine kings, one of whom is feeble and poor, another is like a lion; all kneel to Celidoyne. When Nasciens wakes, he finds in his hand a scroll on which are written the names of his descendants: they are Narpus, Nasciens, Elyan the grete (or Alains le Gros), Ysayes, Jonaanz, Lawnceloz, Baus, Lawncelot, like a hound, and Galath, like a flood, thick at the source, clear at the end, who shall pass all men in bounty, and end the adventures of Britain. Nasciens asks God to explain why his eighth descendant (Lancelot) shall be like a dog, and his ninth (Galahad) like a flood. From the lips of an old man he learns that the dog typifies a sinner, and the flood, thick at the outset but clear in the middle, a person begotten in sin, but renewed by grace into the greatest knight of the world.

> Of hym (*Lancelot*) Schal the Nynthe (*Galahad*) thenne Come,
> That is likned to a flood al & some,
> that Trowbled As A kanal schal be,
> and thikke atte Bogynneng, I telle it the;
> but In the Midwardis It schal be More Cler
> than to-forn it is In alle Manere;
>
> .   .   .   .
>
> and this same Man schal ben A kyng,

---

[15] See below, p. 63, 67.

And his Name Galath In vndirstondyng.
For he schal passen Of Bownte
Alle that Evere to-forn hym han be,
Oþer all that Ebere scholen hym sewe,
he schal hem passen; hold me for trewe.
This Man schal Enden alle Aventure
In that Iond, I the here Ensure. . . .   (ll. 241 ff.)

Nasciens meditates upon the words of the good old man, and chiefly upon the prophecy concerning Galahad, who will fulfill the great adventures of his race.

And that Galaaz it scholde be,
Ful Of Meknesse and of bownte,
Of knyhthod & of Chevalrye
Of Conqwest and Of Victorye;
" and this Man the Ende of thy lyne schal be
as I the telle ful Certeynle."   (ll. 275 ff.)

Galahad, Nasciens learns, is likened to a lion, for as the lion reigns over the other beasts, so does the wise man over the sinners.

For lik As the lyown Ouer Alle Other bestes
Is chef lord and þerto hath alle his hestes
and putteth hem vndir his Subieeciown,
Riht so doth the wyse Man be alle Manere Of Resown,—
he wil not In synne lyhtly falle,
thowghe þat be Entysment the devel to hym calle,
and ȝif it happe as be Mys-Aventure
that In dedly synne he falle, I the enswre,
ȝit he hopeth Into the Otterest degre
thorwgh Celastial thinges saved forto be;
and that be the holigostes Myht
synne to kepen hym bothe day and nyht.   (ll. 499 ff.)

In contrast to Galahad, Lancelot is likened to a hound that " for hunger Renneth to his vyawnde " (l. 519), and, unable to control his imagination, falls into temptation from which he has not the strength to rise. Galahad, it is true, was begotten in sin, but grows in virtue and grace and strength and remains a pure virgin all his life, ful of wisdom and prowess, and ends his days more wonderfully than any other man.

Of Chevalrye he schal passess Alle his fadris pleyn,
bothe of Erthly prowesse
Of bownte, and Of alle godnesse.
For a virgyne Evere schal he be
alle dayes Of his lyve Certeinle;
And the Ende of him More Merveillous schal be
thanne of Ony Other Man Certeynle.   (ll. 556 ff.)

The story then turns from Nasciens to Joseph of Arimathea describing how he and his company were borne miraculously across the sea on Joseph's shirt as on dry land; of how they arrived in the Promised Land (Britain) bringing the Holy Grail with them; and of how Joseph's company promised to keep God's law in this new country. Many other events are related which have no direct bearing on the Grail story. But in Chapter XLVI the Grail material and Galahad's connection therewith is resumed.

Chapter XLVI tells how Joseph and his disciples are imprisoned by King Crwdelx and later delivered by King Mordreins and Nasciens. In thanksgiving for their deliverance, the holy company kneel in player before the Holy Grail, and Mordreins through curiosity presses too close to the Holy Vessel, and, despite the warning he receives, loses his sight. He confesses himself a fool, but prays that he may live to see Nasciens' ninth descendant (Galahad):

> Tyl that þe goode knyht of þe Nynthe degre
> Of Sire Nasciens that I myht se,
> whiche þe Merveilles of Seint Graal schal do,
> that I mowe sen hym to-foren me go,
> that I myhte hym boþe Clippe & kisse,
> And that were mochel of my worldly blisse.   (l. 273 ff.)

A voice tells him that his prayers will be answered, and that he shall live until Galahad the Good Knight comes to restore his sight. King Mordreins then gathers his barons together, and tells them he desires to leave them and retire into an Abbey of White Monks (*Cistercians*), where many lords and barons later join him. Mordreins lives for two hundred years until the coming of Galahad.

Chapter XLVIII relates the story of the table constructed by Joseph of Arimathea in honor of the table at which our Lord sat at the Last Supper. It tells of Moys' presumption in attempting to sit in the vacant place, which Joseph tells his disciples means the place of Christ;

> and but þe holyere man he be þat I konne wit
> Elles schal there non Man here syt.   (ll. 35-36)

Seven burning hands reach from Heaven and destroy Moys " as a drye busch whanne it is On fere " (l. 178), and the event strikes terror into the hearts of the onlookers, who begin confessing their unworthiness.

Chapter XLIX. Joseph, when attacked by the Saracen's servants and cast into prison, is wounded in the thigh, half of the sword remaining in the flesh. Later Joseph heals the heathen Mathegrane with this same sword, and tells him that the pieces of the sword shall not be joined together till the hero of the quest (*Galahad*) comes to join them.

Chapters L and LI. Joseph passes through a valley where he finds a spacious house with the doors open, and in the hall of which there burns a great fire. A voice cries out from the fire asking Joseph's prayers; the voice is recognized as that of Moys, and when Joseph asks him how it is with him, Moys replies that he still hopes for grace through the mercy of God, but that he will remain in fire until Galahad comes to deliver him. God has ordained, he says,

> . this Sorwe An Ende to brynge
> thorwh an holy knytes Comenge,
> hos Name schal be Clepid Galaas
> here me schal visiten In this plas,
> and the Aventures Of þe seint Graal,
> To An Ende bringen he schal;
> and Alle the Aventures Of grete breteyne,
> In him schal ben Ended In Certeyne,
> and thanne slaken schal my dolour
> That I am here In this Owr.   (Ch. L, l. 467 ff.)

Joseph prays for him and a torrent of rain falls upon the fire, which Moys says greatly eases his pain. Moys begs Joseph to go through the country and convert the people and

> preche the name Of the Crucyfye,
> for it is ful gret Nede trewelye.   (Ch. L, ll. 481-482)

Joseph accordingly passes on to Scotland where some of his party fall into grievous sins. Chanaan, through envy, murders his twelve brothers, and Symen wounds Peers with a poisoned knife. Joseph prays for vengeance from Heaven, but is told from Heaven to do judgment on the sinners himself. He lets his company decide their fate, and they bury Chanaan and Symen in two pits " vp stondyng vene to the Chynnee." (Ch. L, l. 760.) From the realm of Gales (Wales) come two burning men flying through the air, and these carry off Symen. Chanaan begs for mercy. His twelve brothers are buried and when he dies he is buried beside them, but on Chanaan's tomb a fire burns continually which Joseph says will some day be extinguished by Lancelot, from whom shall be born the best knight of the world who shall end the adventures of Great Britain. His name shall be called Galahad and he shall also deliver Symen, Moys, and Chanaan out of their pains, all of which shall be done in the time of King Arthur.

> . Of hym (*Lancelot*) there schal sprynge
> The beste knyht That Evere Was levynge,
> to whom Oure lord schal schewen his Myht
> More thanne to Ony Othir Erthly knyht;
> For thorwh his Religious lyvenge
> hym schal befalle ful Many A thenge;

> For Alle the Aventures Of grete bretaynge
> In that knyht Schal behappen In Certayngne
> Passing Ony Othyr knyht,—
> sweche Aventures to hym ben dyht,—
> Hos Name, I telle ȝow, Galath schal be
> In baptesme I-Cleped ful Sykerle.
> whiche Galath deleveren schal Certayne
> bothe Symev and Moys Owt Of peyne,
> and Also Chanaam deliuered schal be
> Owt Of his peyne, As I telle the;
> And Alle these thinges schollen befalle
> In kynges tyme þat Arthour men schollen Calle.
>   (Ch. LI, ll. 239 ff.)

Chapter LIII. Josephes travels through Scotland, Wales, and Ireland, and, finally, after much wandering, comes back to the castle Galafort, which he has not visited in fifteen years. He finds his mother buried there, and many abbeys built about. His youngest brother Gales has grown into a brave young knight, and when the throne of Hotelise (Wales) is vacant, the people choose Gales as their king. After his death the land is called after him *Gales* (Wales),

> whiche Name Neuere Chongen schal,
> In this world whiche is Fynal.   (ll. 181 f.)

One evening Galaaz (*Galahad*), after hunting, comes upon a great fire in a dry ditch. Out of it comes a voice, which he recognizes to be that of his cousin Symen, who is burning there for his misdeeds, and who begs that a place of religion be founded to allay his pains. These, he says, will never be ended till Galaaz (*Galahad*), unstained by lust, comes to quench the flames.

> God with hym schal senden his grace,
> and In this diche stawnchen this feer,
> that thou here Sixt brennen so Cleer;
> and þat be Encheson Of On thing is this,
> that neuere with luxvre he was brend Iwys;
> and Into this lond Of his Entrynge,
> Alle the poyntes of seint graal scholen hauen Endynge.
>   (l. 278 ff.)

Galaaz promises to found an abbey, and to be buried there. The Abbey (called the Abbey of the Trinity) is built and endowed, and Galaaz is entombed there when he dies. Lancelot of the Lake removes his corpse from that place.

Chapter LV. Before his death Joseph of Arimathea gives the Holy Grail to Aleyn who carries it into strange lands. Together with his brethren he comes to a foolish people in the land of Foreygne, whose king

Galafres is a leper. Aleyn promises to cure him if he will believe in
Christ. The king professes his belief, and is cured by the power of the
Holy Grail. Out of gratitude he builds for the Holy Grail a magnificent
castle which is called *Corbenie* (Corvenie). The same castle is also called
the " Palace of Adventure," since no man is able to sleep in it without
meeting death. King Galafres gives his daughter in marriage to Joseph's
brother Josue. From this union is begotten Amynadappe who begets Car-
celois, and he Mangel, and he Lambor. Lambor engages in a duel with
his cousin Varlans, a pagan, and is slain with the sword of David which
Varlans finds in the ship of Solomon. From this act great misfortunes
visit the land: the trees cease to bear fruit, the fish die in the water,
and the whole country becomes waste and barren, for which cause it is
called the *Wastable Land*. Varlans is punished for his rash deed, for as
soon as he sheaths the sword of David, he falls dead in the ship, and the
sword remains sheathed until a maiden comes to draw it forth. Lambor
is succeeded by his son Pellean who is called the *Maimed King*.

> they cleped him kyng Mayham Euery Where
> For thorwgh bothe thyes Maymed was he.
>
> (ll. 488, 489)

Pellean's son Pelles has a daughter Pelle (Elaine) who surpasses in
beauty all women in Britain save Gonnore, Arthur's wife. Of Pelle
(Elaine) Lancelot begets Galaaz (*Galahad*), the blessed knight, who ends
all the adventures of Britain.

> vppon this damysele that was so faire,
> Engendered Lawncelot, Galas his Eyr,
> that ilke same Blessid knyht Certaigne
> whiche Endede Alle the Aventures of gret bretaigne.
>
> (l. 503 ff.)

Notwithstanding the fact that he was begotten in sin, Galaaz (*Galahad*)
by his own pure life and the virtuous lives of his ancestors is destined
to fulfill the promise of his race and to bring to a successful issue those
adventures.

> Wheche Alle Othere feillede Of Echon
> alle Browhte he to An Ende Alon.   (ll. 517, 518.)

Chapter LVI. Josephes and Nasciens die, and Nasciens with his famous
red-cross shield is buried in an abbey. Many knights come to Nasciens'
tomb and attempt to hang the shield about their neck, but are unable
to do so, and are punished for their presumption with death or some dire
misfortune; so the shield waits in the abbey for the coming of the good
knight Galaaz (*Galahad*).

> and thus In that Abbey lefte theke scheld stille
> tyl that worthy knyht Cam, As was goddis wille
> That hyghte worthy Galaaz, Lawncelottes sone,
> That Abowtes his Nekke henge it Anone.   (l. 34 ff.)

The final incident pertains to Galaaz' (*Galahad's*) paternal ancestor, the first Lancelot, who was the grandfather of King Ban, and therefore Galaaz' (*Galahad's*) great, great grandfather. This Lancelot I, though innocent, is accused by wicked men of illicit relations with the wife of a neighboring duke. On Good Friday Lancelot walks barefoot through the Forest Perilous, goes to a hermitage, confesses his sins and is absolved. After leaving the hermitage he pauses at a fountain to drink, and as he is stooping, the treacherous duke cuts off his head. It falls into the well, and when the duke attempts to pull it out, he discovers that the water which was ice cold has become boiling hot. The duke realizes that he has murdered an innocent man, and orders his followers to bury Lancelot's body where no one will find it. Each day, however, at the hour of his death, there are found on Lancelot's tomb, blooddrops which have the miraculous power of healing all manner of diseases, so that his tomb becomes a shrine for pilgrims. The water in the well continues to boil and will do so until the coming of Galahad.

Like the *Grand San Graal* from which it was taken, Lovelich's *Holy Grail* " creates that faint sense of ancient things and of spiritual mysteries which transforms the characters from flesh and blood champions of an earthly kingdom into instruments of a divine purpose deeply related to the larger issues of human destiny. Through all the reaches of the coming story, gay adventure, joy in fighting and comradeship,—it diffuses an awe, a sense of waiting expectation." [16]

If any one quality stands out more prominently than others in Lovelich's *Holy Grail,* it is the spirit of faith and reverence in the treatment of holy things. Nascien, on the Turning Isle, will not enter Solomon's ship (which signifies the Church) until he has signed himself with the sign of salvation; the angels sprinkle the ship with water, to signify it is holy unto the Lord; the Grail is the object of deepest reverence, and the writer referring to it as " that blessed Seint Greal," shows that he himself is humbly conscious of the dignity of this great mystery. " In the Grail is the founding of wisdom, the beginning of religion, the points of all gentry; and wherever ' that swete thing ' is, men are near to those secrets of the Most High which may not be approached too eagerly. Again and again worshipers seek to penetrate the arcana and suffer strange penalties—pierced by a spear, blinded by an exceeding glory; for the marvels of ' Christ's verray knights ' are not for

[16] Scudder, V. D., *Morte Darthur of Sir Thomas Malory*, p. 99.

earthly knights to savor. Thus Nasciens is struck blind, and Mordrains, lost in thanksgiving, feels of a sudden that his power is taken from him, not to return till Galahad shall come." [17]

There is a note of deep spirituality approaching mysticism in Lovelich's interpretation of Galahad. A messenger from heaven, having explained to Nascien why Galaaz (*Galahad*) has been likened to a flood, muddy at the source but clear and limpid at midstream, adds:

> and In that flood schal I bathen Me
> From top to too ful Sekerle.—(Chap. XXXIX, ll. 255-6.)

Elsewhere Galaaz (*Galahad*) is spoken of as a lion, because, " As a lion puts all other beasts under subjection," says Lovelich, " right so doth the wise man (subdue his passions) by all manner of reason "; and Galaaz, having obtained complete mastery over his passions, rules in the kingdom of his own soul. That Lovelich had a clear understanding of the Church's doctrine of sanctifying grace is seen in his simple statement, " the wise man prays that *by the Holy Spirit's power* he may be saved from sin both day and night." His words remind us of the admonition of the Apostle St. Jude writing to the first Christians: " But you, my beloved, building yourselves upon your most holy faith, *praying in the Holy Ghost,* keep yourselves in the love of God, waiting for the mercy of our Lord Jesus Christ, unto life everlasting." (I, 20, 21.)

The Galahad of Lovelich's *Holy Grail* is the pattern of the Perfect Man who, because he lives the life of Christ within himself, merits to be the leader and deliverer of men whose lives are built upon less supernatural lines. Because he sees with the eyes of faith, Galahad removes the scales from the eyes of the blind Mordreins; because he himself is firmly grounded in humility, he delivers the proud and presumptuous Moys from his torments of fire; because he is perfect in charity, he welds together the sword broken in Joseph's wound; because he is perfect in chastity, he bears upon his breast the red-cross shield of Nascien. Mighty in word and work, *Galahad accomplishes the marvels of the Grail because of the grace of God abounding in him.*

Lovelich's *Holy Grail* conveys a lesson similar to that taught by

---

[17] *Ibid.,* p. 95.

The Pilgrimage of the Life of Man, the contemporary Lydgate version from the French of Guillaume de Deguileville.[18] In both works, man's life on earth is pictured as a warfare, a time of trial, a place in which to prepare himself for the eternal joys of Heaven. That Lovelich's purpose was a high moral one cannot be doubted: the pity is that he wrote with a taste better than his capacity, and marred with his mechanical jog-trot one of the finest of mystical romances.[19]

Having examined Galahad's rôle in these earliest English pieces, we turn now to a study of his position in the work of a man whose genius built upon a mass of fragmentary medieval legends a colossal Arthurian epic, unparalleled in the history of our language; a work which delighted and inspired not only its own but succeeding gene-rations.   Malory's *Morte Darthur* is the fountainhead and source of much artistic expression—the poetry of Tennyson, Matthew Arnold, Swinburne, and Morris; the painting of Rossetti, Watts, and Burne-Jones; the music of Wagner; and Malory's *Morte* gives us the first clear picture of Galahad in English literature.

[18] Edited by Dr. Furnivall, E. E. T. S., Nos. 77, 83, 89.
[19] Scudder, V. D., *Morte Darthur of Sir Thomas Malory,* p. 148.

CHAPTER V

GALAHAD IN MALORY'S *Morte Darthur*

The few works in which Galahad's name was used or his rôle prefigured previous to Malory's *Morte Darthur* were, as pointed out in the last chapter, either too fragmentary to permit us to judge of their real literary worth, or else, when complete, too tediously long to suspect any great degree of popularity for them even in the age for which they were written, not to mention their persistent literary effect on later writers. Not until the redoubtable Sir Thomas [1] turned over the pages of his famous " Frenche booke " did Galahad come to occupy a permanent and conspicuous place in English literature.

" For the English reader, at least, no other record of chivalry will ever seem so noble. Malory wrote two centuries and a half after the close of the great creative epoch, and the lateness of his date well-nigh destroyed his value as a source. To the scholar he must probably remain a mere compiler who added little or nothing, and reduced his materials to one tenth their original bulk. But to the lover of romance, his book is the glorious consummation of a long development. It was written at the perfect moment." [2]

The *Morte Darthur,* was completed by Malory in 1469 or early in 1470, and was first published by William Caxton in 1485.[3] We

---

[1] To Professor Kittredge of Harvard belongs the credit of having, in 1896, identified the until then almost totally unknown author of the famous *Morte Darthur* with Sir Thomas Malory of Newbold Revell, Warwickshire. Malory succeeded his father at Newbold Revell in 1433. He was M. P. for Warwickshire in 1445, in the twenty-third year of Henry VI. Apparently he had fought when young in the French wars, under the Earl of Warwick, and later engaged in the War of the Roses. He died in 1471, and was buried in the Chapel of St. Francis at Grayfriars, with the epitaph " Valens Miles."—*Sir Thomas Malory* (1925).

[2] Scudder, Vida D., *Morte Darthur of Sir Thomas Malory and Its Sources*, p. 178.

[3] The next two editions were printed by Wynkyn de Worde in 1498 and 1529. There were other editions, made as follows: 1557 (William Copland); 1585 (Thomas East); 1634 (William Stansby); two editions in

have no exact information as to the method pursued by Malory, or as to the materials he used, but it is clear that a large portion of his book is taken from the great prose romances of *Merlin, Lancelot, Tristram,* the *Queste del St. Graal,* and the *Mort Artus.*[4] Concerning Malory's French source and the task of collecting material for this amazingly large work, Chambers says:[5] " There is no trace of any single French book which remotely resembles Malory's . . . Certain it is that he had some acquaintance with all the early French prose pieces. . . . However, the bulk was tremendous, and it was Malory's task to sift it down to a readable romance, without falling into the mistake of disproportion." Herein, undoubtedly, lies the secret of Malory's genius. Coming as he did at the last stage of the romantic era, he clearly saw the necessity of apprehending the whole scheme of the Arthuriad, and of concentrating its enormous expansions if any of the main lines of the structure were to be revealed. His task was to add order to beauty, and although the subject-matter of Malory's book belongs to the Middle Ages, still Malory himself, with his desire to preserve the literary monuments of the past, belongs to the Renaissance, and he deserves the lasting gratitude of English-speaking people for thus attempting to preserve the literary heritage of Britain while his contemporaries were busying themselves chiefly with the classics of Greece and Rome.

In bringing together and coördinating these scattered romances Malory often modified parts of the story, making use of extensive parentheses in recounting the adventures of Balin, Bors, Pelleas, and Tristram, his reason being evidently to enable the reader to

---

1816, 1817 (Southey); 1858 (Wright); 1866 (Wright); 1868 (Strachey); 1893 (Strachey). There were many abridgments of Malory's book since 1860. In 1889, 1890, and 1891, Dr. Oskar H. Somer edited, and Mr. Nutt published the best edition of Caxton's original text for scholar and student. Volume I is the text, Vols. II and III are commentary and critical matter. See Somer, *Malory,* Vol. II, for discussion of various editions of Malory's work.

[4] " No one can tell how far Malory's book is original," says Vida D. Scudder, " and how far it may lean on some intermediate source, now lost."—*Morte Darthur of Sir Thomas Malory and Its Sources,* p. 365.

[5] Chambers, E. K., *Sir Thomas Malory,* English Assn., Pamphlet 51 (January 1922), p. 3.

distinguish the lines of a dominant story—that of Arthur and earthly chivalry followed by that of Galahad and the chivalry of the Grail.

With regard to the Galahad-Grail motif, there was little difficulty in keeping the original material intact, as the French *Queste del St. Graal,* from which Malory drew, had undergone few changes at the hands of redactors. What is of greater interest to us, however, is the question as to whether or not Malory apprehended the real mystical significance of the Galahad-Grail story, and translated it in the same spirit in which the twelfth century Cistercian intended it to be understood. Eugene Vinaver is of the opinion that Malory was unable to explain and perhaps to understand the fundamental motif of the story, and that since Malory abolished the main purpose and sole reasonable justification of the Quest,—the substitution of Galahad the pure for Lancelot the sinner,—he had to be vague about its object. According to him, the Quest assumes the guise of a pageant full of strange adventures, and Galahad from being its mystical leader and inspirer becomes but a good and valiant knight. " Malory's quest," he says, " is a confused and almost pointless story, a beautiful parade of symbols and bright visions. It is deprived of its spiritual foundation, of its doctrine, and its direct object. The Quest is no longer an antithesis to the Round Table, but an ornament of Arthur's kingdom: the fortunes of Arthur and his fellowship do not decline with the coming of the Grail Knight, and the ultimate debate is not between the ideals of Camelot and the ideals of Corbenic. Faced with two main themes and forced to subordinate one, Malory made Corbenic a province of Camelot." [6]

Certain it is that Malory does not follow the *Queste* in repeatedly emphasizing the conflict that exists between the mystic symbol of the Grail and the sinful world; nor does he bring out so clearly the manner in which the Grail serves as a touchstone for the virtue of Arthur's knights. There is not the same heart-rending conflict between Lancelot and the Grail. Moreover, as Vinaver points out,[7] Malory in flat contradiction to his source insists on Lancelot's superiority to Galahad. " Malory," he says, " used it (the Grail theme) to deepen the background of romance, a background full

[6] Vinaver, Eugene, *Malory,* p. 84.
[7] *Ibid.,* p. 83.

6

of peace and beatitude. There is a serene light breaking from the Holy Vessel, and there is twofold rejoicing in chivalrous festivities. One is the feast of divine grace, the other is the pageant of beauty and love; but instead of being contrasted as in the Cistercian romance, in Malory they coalesce to form a powerful dramatic antithesis to the coming of the crisis. Malory, instead of stressing their antagonism, combines both for artistic effect. He is concerned with neither philosophy nor theology, and desires neither to teach nor to expound. His contribution is but a scenic arrangement laid for a play of light and shadow." [8]

There is no better way of proving the foregoing conclusions, and of showing Malory's treatment of the Grail, than by comparing parts of Malory's story with the corresponding portions of the original *Queste*. This E. Vinaver has done very carefully with Book XV,[9] his deductions being that the alterations are due either to carelessness or to over-condensation. The way in which Malory dismisses with brief resumés the elaborate theological treatises found in the French *Queste* illustrates his attitude towards the doctrine of the French source, and justifies the conclusion that he was little concerned with the mystical interpretation of the Quest.[10]

In all fairness to Malory, however, it must be stated, that while he does fail to grasp the deeper mystical interpretation of the Grail story, still his very condensation of it helps to preserve his *Morte* an integral work of art. His chief aim was to present, not one but three controlling interests of the Middle Ages—love, religion, and war—and in order to preserve their ideal symmetry, he sacrificed as much as he could of what he considered irrelevant detail. Malory's task was to tell of the rise and fall of chivalry, and chivalry, according to him, was built upon three loyalties—loyalty to the King, loyalty to the lady, and loyalty to God. It was upon these three pivotal points that Malory built a story which synthesizes the whole medieval civilization.

Because Malory failed to grasp the complete structural problem of the Galahad-Grail Quest, he treats the story of Galahad's birth as

[8] *Ibid.*, p. 96.

[9] Vinaver gives a complete collation of Book XV with ff. 540ʳ col. 2-545ᵗ col. 2 of MS Bibl. Nat. fr. 120 (MS O).

[10] *Ibid.*, p. 155.

an event of minor importance, relating the story in the most casual, objective manner, and investing it with little of the charm of mystery which surrounded it in the original *Queste.* Book XI, the first of the seven books which deal with Galahad and the Grail, opens with the hermit's prophecy concerning the Promised Knight (Galahad) who is one day to occupy the Perilous Seat at Arthur's table. An outline of this book and subsequent books here follows:

Book XI. Shortly after the hermit's prophecy concerning the Promised Knight, Lancelot visits Corbenic and there by the sorcery of Dame Brysen he mistakes Elaine for Guenevere, and Galahad is begotten. Furious at the deception, Lancelot threatens to slay Elaine, but she appeals to his nobility, telling him that she has but obeyed her father's command. Two years later Sir Bors comes to Corbin and is happy to learn that a son called Galahad has been born to Lancelot by Elaine. A mysterious old man appears to Bors and requests him to tell Lancelot about the coming Grail quest which Galahad will achieve, but from which Lancelot will be debarred because of his sin. Elaine visits Arthur's court with her two-year-old son Galahad, and is acclaimed the most beautiful woman of Camelot. Once again Dame Brysen arranges a nocturnal meeting between Elaine and Lancelot, and a second time Lancelot is deceived. The Queen infuriated at his apparent infidelity to her, banishes him from her presence, and for two years he wanders as a madman through the forests of Broceliande.

In this first of the Galahad-Grail books it is clearly evident that Malory not only did not fully appreciate the religious doctrine of his source, but that he only vaguely understood the mystical framework of the Cistercian's story. For Malory, Galahad's coming was not an act of redemption and purification through sin and repentance, but more than anything else an artistic device designed to bring into bolder relief the figure of his hero, Lancelot. What Malory saw in the Grail theme was not the apotheosis of a divine ideal in the sinless Galahad, but rather the personification of a human ideal in the sinful Lancelot. He lost no chance of increasing the desirability of making Lancelot as nearly as possible the hero of this quest, and since he realized that Lancelot's sinful love for Guenevere deprived him of the right to become the hero of a spiritual quest, he heartily agreed with the medieval mystic that the best solution was to give him a son, equal to him in wordly prowess but without his taint of sin, who could win the quest. Thus Malory gloried in the fact that the Grail winner could start on his quest with the matchless reputation of his father thrown as a resplendent mantle upon his shoulders, and the father, in turn, could become the protagonist of the romance by reaping vicariously the spiritual success of his son.[11]

In whatever light we view the matter, we cannot help being persuaded that throughout the entire story Malory's sympathies and affections are with Lancelot rather than with Galahad. We cannot, however, fully agree with Alfred Nutt [12] when he states that " Such human interest as there is in the story is supplied by Lancelot," and that " such moral teaching as the Quest affords is given us rather by sinful Lancelot than by sinless Galahad," for, as V. D. Scudder remarks: [13] " That can be no mean or casual art which created a figure (Galahad) whose beauty, when all is said, haunts men through the generations. Taken by himself, it is true that Galahad lacks human qualities; he must be taken in his setting. He is a pure symbol,—a rainbow apparition untouched by shadow, among the ruder passions that sway romance. He shines like a visitant from the world of Fra Angelico in the midst of the dusky chiaroscuro of Rembrandt or the rich tones of Titian. He wears the Pentecostal color of the Spirit, the flame-red of charity, like that of Dante's Love as she dances beside the chariot of Beatrice."

But there is something more. Mr. Nutt is correct in implying that to sin is human, in the sense that human beings *do* sin ; nevertheless, sin is *not* a part of human nature, and for this reason Lancelot himself was continually striving to be rid of it. Galahad's sinlessness does not exclude the idea of conflict, and his human interest lies in the fact that he is a moral champion never unhorsed. Galahad is human nature at its best.

Book XII, like Book XI, serves as a prelude to the main theme, and recounts the adventures of the half-crazed Lancelot after he has been banished by the Queen. Healed by the Holy Grail, Lancelot goes to live with King Pelles and Elaine at Joyous Garde where, after long searching, Ector and Perceval find him and persuade

[11] App, A. J., *Lancelot in English Literature*, p. 67.
[12] *Studies of the Legend of the Holy Grail*, pp. 239, 240.
[13] *Morte Darthur of Sir Thomas Malory and Its Sources*, p. 297.

him to return to the court. Galahad is now fifteen years of age, and is to be knighted at the approaching feast of Pentecost.

With the thirteenth book Malory begins the story of the Quest proper. " If anything can be claimed for England as distinct from France during the years of a united literature," says V. D. Scudder, " one would claim the latter forms of the Galahad Grail story." [14] It will be remembered that for a long period Percival was the Grail hero. But by the time the later redactions of Boron's poem were made and his ideas had passed into the main lines of growth, something else had happened: Lancelot had forced his way like a conqueror into the Arthurian circle, and Galahad, Lancelot's son, had supplanted Perceval as winner of the Grail. With the introduction of Galahad, the Arthurian story (if we except Wolfram's *Parzival* and its contrast between Gawain and Parzival) became a mixture of two chivalries, one earthly and the other divine—with the mysticism of the Grail enveloping both.

Book XIII. On the vigil of Pentecost as Arthur and his knights are gathered together at Camelot a damsel enters the hall and bids Lancelot depart with her to a neighboring abbey where, at the request of the nuns, he knights Galahad without, however, recognizing him.

The next day before the knights sit down to eat, they hear of a great stone which floats down the river. In the stone is a marvelous sword which only the best knight in the world shall be able to draw out, wherefore Arthur bids Lancelot try, but he answers with gravity that he is not that best knight who is destined to succeed. Gawain and Perceval try and fail. When the knights are seated at their meal, an old man clothed in white brings in Galahad clad in fiery red, and leads him to the Siege Perilous, which to everyone's amazement, he securely occupies. After the meal Galahad draws the sword out of the stone. A damsel now appears and says to Lancelot that he should no longer consider himself the best knight in the world, to which he replies: " I knowe wel I was neuer the best." That evening the Grail vessel passes veiled through the hall and Gawain vows to follow it for a year. The other knights make the same vow, and Arthur is grieved that his fellowship should so quickly come to an end.

Four days Galahad rides without any adventure. The fourth day he comes to an abbey where he finds, hanging behind the altar, a marvelous shield, " white as any snow, but in the midst a red cross." The keeper of the shield tells Galahad that only the worthiest knight of the world shall hang the shield about his neck. Bademagus, one of Arthur's knights,

---

[14] *Ibid.*, p. 82.

attempts to steal the shield, and carries it away from the abbey, but before he has ridden far he is overtaken by a mysterious White Knight who jousts with him, severely wounds him, and commands his squire to carry the shield to Galahad. Soon after Galahad meets the White Knight who tells him the story of the shield. Galahad returns to the abbey where in the churchyard he hears issuing from a grave such a noise that who that heard it should verily nigh be mad or lose his strength. Galahad lifts the stone, and from the grave there leaps the foulest figure that ever he saw in the likeness of a man. Galahad blesses himself knowing that it is a fiend.

Galahad then sets out for the Castle of Maidens whither a voice from Heaven has commanded him to go. Before the castle he meets a knight and seven damsels who warn him against the adventure, saying that the seven knights who guard the castle will overpower him. Galahad meets and conquers the seven knights, and is given the keys of the castle. He frees the captive maidens, and sets out upon new adventures. In a forest he meets Lancelot and Perceval, who, not recognizing him, offer to joust with him. Galahad unhorses both knights and rides swiftly away.

The more Grail literature is studied, the more intimate appear its affiliations with the vision and pilgrimage literature of the Middle Ages. The fighting, even against fiends, is dreamlike and unreal; the knights are often pilgrims in disguise; and their adventures can best be understood as phases of the Mystic Way on which contemplatives love to dwell: the Way of Purgation, the Way of Illumination, the Way of Unity. All this is especially true of the Galahad form of the Quest, as given in Malory.[15] " Light in these books is focused on Galahad. His grave and shining youth moves on a path gray with memories; he is called on to bring to a conclusion the episodes of a half-finished tale. It is the rôle of the Pure Knight so long awaited to atone for old wrongs, to achieve deferred feats of spiritual redemption; in thus fulfilling prophecy and satisfying the expectant generations, he accomplishes the patient purpose of God. Throughout his story, allusions are constant to earlier acts in the drama; vague parallels multiply, to awe and rouse. On every hand he encounters relics of former days. His first sword is that with which Balin had given the Dolorous Stroke to Pelles,—poor Balin whose faint capacity for spiritual things had harmed men rather than helped them. His second, the sword with the Strange Hangings, is most marvelous of all swords

---

[15] Scudder, V. D., *op. cit.*, p. 264.

in romance, not excepting Excalibur, for it is the authentic sword of David, and its scabbard is made from the wood of the Tree of Life. His white shield with the red cross has been awaiting him for centuries; it is the very shield given by Joseph of Arimathea to Mordrains, king of Sarras, whereon the Crucified appeared to convert that heathen king; and the cross is made with Joseph's blood. . . . Woe to those, whether Bagdemagus the good old king or Melias the untried knight, who seek to usurp the deeds of Galahad." [16]

Book XIV describes Perceval's search for Galahad and his eagerness to accompany the promised knight. Learning from a holy anchoress that the knight who lately unhorsed him is Galahad, Perceval sets out to find him. On the way he is accosted by twenty men who attempt to slay him. Galahad comes to his rescue, puts his assailants to flight, and quickly disappears.

Galahad achieves his marvels unconsciously, simply, nor is he ever seen long at a time. He is as it were always vanishing. . . . . The more worldly men seem to pursue him in their quest rather than the Grail,—their wish to behold Galahad being apparently as near an approach to heavenly desires as they can compass. In a sense, his chief function is to bring other personalities into clearer light by affording a fixed point for comparison and contrast.[17]

This is strikingly evident in the two books which follow. Book XV deals almost entirely with the adventures of Lancelot while Book XVI describes the exploits of Gawain in the quest of the Grail. Galahad does not appear, but Malory frequently finds occasion to contrast Lancelot's sin-blinded, irresolute course with Galahad's clear-eyed search for the Grail. "Lancelot's failure," says Vinaver,[18] " is as eloquent as Galahad's attainment. . . . Here, as with Gawain, the author implies his method of antithesis. He knows how to subordinate the secular to the divine, and how to develop the teaching of the Grail romance *a contrario*." At every turn hermits are waiting to expound to Lancelot and Gawain the cause of their failure. Thus a hermit explains to Gawain the mean-

[16] *Ibid.*, p. 296.
[17] *Ibid.*, p. 298.
[18] *Malory*, p. 75.

ing of his dream concerning the bridled hands bearing a lighted candle:

'Now will I tell you,' exclaims the hermit, 'What betokeneth the hand with the candle and bridle: that is to understand the Holy Ghost where charity is ever, and the bridle signifieth abstinence. And the candle which sheweth clearness and sight signifieth the right way of Jesus Christ. Knights of poor faith and of wicked belief, these three things failed, charity, abstinence, and truth; therefore ye may not attain that high adventure of the Sangreal.' (XVI, iv.)

Because Gawain lacks the virtues of charity, abstinence, and truth (signified by the bridled hand and the lighted candle), he is forbidden the secrets of the Grail; Galahad alone, girt with the sword of truth, clad in the armor of chastity, and wearing the robe of charity will attain the coveted treasure. Malory here senses quite clearly the purpose of the twelfth-century *Queste* in bringing romance into the service of religion, by showing how Galahad, as the protagonist of heavenly chivalry, serves as a foil for knights of earthly chivalry and worldly ambition.

Book XVII brings to its climax the drama of the Grail. Every adventure thus far related has been a remote preparation for the final episode—the finding of the Grail. From now on events sweep forward with breath-taking swiftness to a magnificent and colorful close. Galahad untouchable and aloof, has passed the first two stages of his mystical life and now awaits with quiet courage the third stage—consummation with Divine Love.

Malory enters upon the last book of the Grail story with a studied casualness which disappears as he proceeds, and he himself seems to be caught into the glory of his theme. " Merely from the point of style," says V. D. Scudder,[19] " Malory is at his best in this part of his work. His style is always his surest title to distinction, but it is seldom so nobly sustained and so full of lovely undertones; the rhythms, in their very simplicity cannot be forgotten. Often the rhythmic charm has a liturgical effect, and indeed the prose vibrates with echoes of the rich Low Latin of Breviary or Vulgate . . . Especially in the last scenes, then effects are constant; the prose has a depth of tone like the church sequence."

[19] *Ibid.*, p. 303.

Book XVII. Having freed Perceval from the twenty knights, Galahad goes into a waste forest where he brings to an end many adventures. One evening as he is resting in a hermitage near Corbenic Perceval's sister suddenly appears and summons Galahad to depart with her to the sea of Collibe where Bors and Perceval await him. Galahad obeys, and the three knights, following Perceval's sister, enter a ship which bears them far from Logris. After some time they are transported to a second and more stately ship which the damsel cautions them not to enter unless they be "perfect in belief." Galahad blesses himself and enters the ship, his three companions following. On the ship he finds a bed upon which is laid a sword "rich and fair" drawn half-way from its sheath. Perceval's sister tells the knights that this is the sword with which Nacien was wounded, and that King Pelles, Galahad's grandsire, had been smitten through both thighs for attempting to draw the sword from the scabbard. She explains to them other mysteries concerning the ship upon which they are sailing, telling them that it is called the ship of Solomon.

Having heard these wonders Galahad asks where they shall find the gentlewoman "that shall make new girdles to the sword," and Perceval's sister replies by taking from a box a precious girdle made of her own hair. This she girds upon Galahad, telling him that the sword is called the "Sword with the Strange Hangings." They depart from the ship of Solomon, and the next adventure brings them to the shores of Scotland, where Galahad delivers the aged Earl of Hernox from his three villainous sons. Then follows the adventure of the white hart and the four lions which Galahad and his companions discover to be figures of our Lord and the four evangelists.

An armed knight seizes Perceval's sister and attempts to slay her in order to cure with her blood the leprous lady of a certain castle. Galahad and his companions valiantly defend her until she, of her own accord, insists upon helping the stricken woman. Perceval's sister dies in the yielding of her blood, and the knights, acceding to her dying wish, lay her in a black barge, place in her hand a letter telling of her death, and set her adrift upon the sea. Lancelot comes upon the ship carrying the body of the dead maiden, and for a month he remains with her, sustained by "the grace of the Holy Ghost." Here Galahad finds him and father and son dwell together half a year until Galahad is summoned by a heavenly messenger and commanded to continue the adventures of the Grail.

He goes to the abbey where the blind King Mordrains awaits him, and as soon as Mordrains sees Galahad his soul departs from his body. Galahad buries him as befits a king and departs into a forest where he cools a mysterious boiling well. After five days he meets Perceval and Bors and goes with them to Corbenic where Galahad pieces the broken sword "wherewith Joseph was stricken through the thigh." While the knights are at meat Joseph of Arimathea appears clothed as a bishop and commands the three knights to go to sea, and he orders Galahad to take from its sheath the sword of David and to anoint with the bloody spear the legs and body of the Maimed King. Galahad does as he is commanded and the Maimed King is instantly healed. They again enter the ship of Solomon upon which they discover the Holy Grail covered with red samite. Then Galahad asks to be permitted to pass out of this world " at what time he should ask it," and God promises to grant his request. That night he sleeps in Solomon's bed, and in the morning he sees before him the city of Sarras, and near the shore the ship bearing the body of Perceval's sister. The knights bury the maid in a manner befitting a king's daughter, after which they carry the Holy Grail through the streets of the city. Many miracles are wrought by the power of the Grail, whereupon the pagan king orders the three knights to be cast into prison where they are sustained and comforted by the Holy Grail. Soon after the king falls dangerously ill and, repenting of his rashness, sends for the three knights and begs their forgiveness. The king dies and Galahad is chosen to succeed him. A year from the day on which he is crowned king of Sarras, as he is kneeling at Mass, he hears a heavenly voice bid him come forth to see that which he has so much desired to see. Straightway " he began to tremble right hard " when he " began to behold spiritual things." (XVII, 22). Then, having received Holy Communion, from the hands of Joseph of Arimathea, Galahad kisses Perceval and Bors, commending them both to God and bidding them remember him to Lancelot. " Salute me to my lord, Sir Lancelot, my father, and bid him remember of this unstable world." (XVII, 22). So saying he dies, and a great multitude of angels bear his soul to Heaven. Perceval and Bors see a hand come down from Heaven and take up the holy vessel and the spear, and bear them both away. After Galahad's death Perceval retires to a hermitage, and Bors returns to Arthur's court to relate the final adventures of the Grail.

In addition to the beauty of sound, this last of the Grail books abounds in beauty of pictorial detail, which, as Miss Scudder remarks,[20] goes far to compensate for the tenuous and abstract nature of the central theme. The very setting suggests the adventures of the soul. A few examples will suffice to show the compelling force of Malory's style, and to illustrate how his rhythmic prose serves as a perfect medium for his exalted theme.

The following passage describes the summons which Galahad receives from Perceval's sister before he achieves the adventures of the Grail.

And the good night, Galahad, rode so long till he came that night to

---

[20] *Ibid.,* p. 399.

the Castle of Corbenic; and it befell him thus that he was benighted in an hermitage. . . . When they were at rest there came a gentlewoman knocking at the door, and called Galahad. . . . Then the good man awaked Galahad and bade him: Arise, and speak with a gentlewoman that seemeth hath great need of you. Then Galahad went to her and asked her what she would. Galahad, said she, I will that ye arm you, and mount upon your horse and follow me, for I shall shew you within these three days the highest adventure that ever any knight saw. Anon Galahad armed him, and took his horse, and commended him to God, and bade the gentlewoman go, and he would follow. (XVII, 1)

No irrelevance of detail destroys the simplicity of the picture; the action is swift, direct, forceful; events sweep forward with surprising rapidity toward their mysterious and inevitable goal. The passage which describes the death of Perceval's sister is touchingly told.

Then Galahad and his two fellows start up to her, and lift her up . . . but she had bled so much that she might not live. Then she said when she was awaked: Fair brother Percevale, I die for the healing of his lady, so I require you that ye bury me not in this country but as soon as I am dead put me in a boat in the next haven, and let me go as adventure will lead me; and as soon as ye three come to the city of Sarras, there to enchieve the Holy Grail, ye shall find me under a tower arrived, and there bury me in the spiritual place; for I say you so much, there Galahad shall be buried, and ye also, in the same place. (XVII, 11.)

But the final quality of Malory's art lies deeper than cadence or dramatic narrative; it is in his power of suggestion. . . . It is conveyed largely through omens, prophecies, and hints of underrhythm in the events. The whole story seems to move to some unheard music from secret places.[21] The following passage telling how Galahad and his fellows prepared to receive the Sangreal, and of how our Blessed Lord, in the likeness of a Child, appeared to them is an illustration of this.

With that they heard the chamber open and there they saw angels; and two bare candles of wax, and the third a towel, and the fourth a spear which bled marvellously, that three drops fell within a box which he held with his other hand. And they set the candles upon the table, and the third the towel upon the vessel, and the fourth the holy spear even upright upon the vessel. And then the bishop made semblaunt as though he would

---

[21] *Ibid.*, p. 399.

have gone to the sacring of the mass. And then he took an ubblie which
was made in the likeness of bread. And at the lifting up there came a
figure in likeness of a child, and the visage was red and as bright as
any fire, and smote himself into the bread, so that they all saw it that
the bread was formed of a fleshly man; and then he put it into the Holy
Vessel again, and then he did that longed to a priest to do to a mass.
And then he went to Galahad and kissed him, and bade him go and kiss
his fellows: and so he did anon. Now, said he, servants of Jesu Christ,
ye shall be fed afore this table with sweet meats that never knights tasted.
And when he had said, he vanished away. And they set them at the
table in great dread, and made their prayers. (XVII, 20.)

From an artistic point of view, Malory's Grail story is in many
respects superior to its French source. Shorn of infinite allegorizings, it lacks the tediousness of the earlier romance, and at the same
time it presents a more composite picture of the main features of
the story. While Malory fails to comprehend the deeper religious
aspects of his story, he succeeds eminently in unfolding its artistic
merits. If Malory does not completely comprehend the religious
mysticism underlying the plot, it is, as we have pointed out, because he was merely a transcriber of a profound and beautiful
story, the depths of which he was incapable of sounding. "He
repeats his tale," says Emile Legouis, "like a marvelling child trying to tell faithfully what he has heard and not entirely understood." [22]

While mysticism may have been a closed road to Malory, the path
of natural virtue, so dear to the heart of chivalry, was not unknown
to him. Everywhere he stressed the importance of courtesy, courage, and that nobility of character which made Lancelot and
Galahad "the greatest gentlemen of the world." (XIII, 7.) Lancelot was, of course, Malory's hero *par excellence;* he possessed these
natural virtues in the highest degree, but Lancelot's son Malory
invests with a charm and nobility of character rivaled only by that
of his distinguished father. Indeed, the beauty of body and soul
with which Malory has depicted Galahad has accompanied him
down the ages, and finds few parallels in the history of literature.
From his very first appearance as an infant at Corbenic, there
lingers about him an atmosphere of other-worldliness and high

[22] *History of English Literature,* I, p. 126.

sanctity, which marks him not for earth but for the immortal chivalry of heaven. Bors, visiting Corbenic, sees him surrounded by doves and incense; Lancelot, summoned to knight him, finds him accompanied by nuns with whom he has spent his childhood. The peculiar circumstances attendant upon Galahad's birth, his mother's disinterestedness in the choice of a lover, her entire and unquestioning obedience to her father, Lancelot's ignorance of his part in the prophecy—all give to Galahad a certain aloofness and remoteness from things terrestrial. Severed from all fleshly ties, he appears as the high ideal of chastity moving among the passions of men.

Throughout Malory's *Morte* there is no mistaking the purity ideal with Galahad as its living embodiment. Lancelot, coming to knight him, sees him " fair of form and demure as a dove " (XIII, 1) and knows that the secret of his unearthly beauty is his translucent purity which shines like a star on his brow; the blind Mordrains, awaiting his coming through long and tedious years, begs to embrace him before he dies, for he sees in him " the flower of the lily in whom virginity is signified (and), the rose, that which is the flower of all good virtues." (XVII, 20.) Because of his spotless purity Galahad draws swords from enchanted scabbards, opens tombs, frees helpless maidens, restores sight to the blind, and health to the sick. So full is he of the pure love of God, which is the Holy Spirit, that a virtue goes out of him, and all who come in contact with him feel their spiritual youth renewed. " For the fire of the Holy Ghost is taken so in thee," says the aged King Mordrains, whose sight Galahad has restored, " that my flesh which was all dead of oldness is become young again." (XVII, 18.)

The companion virtues to Galahad's translucent purity are his meekness, his courage, his confidence in God, and his compassion for the weak and suffering. Vainly do we seek for an expression of Galahad's own feelings in the matter of his desires, his hopes, even his spiritual successes. His humility keeps him a silent man. When the Holy Grail appears the first time at the Round Table, Galahad, who of all knights present must have felt its tremendous power, speaks no word while he hears the boastful Gawain vowing boisterously to follow it. When the jealous Queen, wishing to convince herself that the young knight is really Lancelot's son, questions him artfully concerning his parentage, Galahad answers meekly but manfully, " Madam, sith ye know in certain, wherefore do ye ask of me?" (XIII, 8.) In the most climactic situations when Galahad is lifted to the very heights of spiritual exaltation, no word escapes his lips but the holy name of God. " In the name of God," says Galahad again and again as he goes upon his appointed way.

The spiritually courageous are not always the physically strong, but Malory could not have imagined the son of Lancelot any other than a physical as well as moral hero. Indeed he seems to go out of his way to describe those scenes in which Galahad's strong sword smites down offenders and redresses the evils of Arthur's kingdom. When Perceval is beset by twenty assailants Galahad rushes forward and

put a spear forth and smote the first that he fell to earth, and the spear brake to pieces. Then he drew his sword and smote thereas they were thickest, and so he did wonderful deeds of arms, that all they marvelled. (XVII, 1.)

When Perceval's sister would have been taken captive by the sixty knights of the leprous lady, Galahad

drew his sword and smote on the right hand and on the left hand, and slew what that ever abode him, and did such marvels that there was none that saw him but weaned he had been none earthly man but, a monster. (XVII, 10.)

But more than all else, the story of Galahad's quest is the story of a soul's boundless confidence in God and its unswerving devotion to an ideal. Once Galahad has set his hand to the plough, no power on earth can cause him to look back. His companion knights, Perceval, Bors, and Lancelot, all have their moments of temporizing, of doubt, and expediency; Galahad with the confidence of the perfect lover rides straight to the goal. Armed with purity, humility, and faith, he goes withersoever the spirit of God leads him. Yet there is no selfishness in his questing, nor is he contemptuous of those less favored than himself with spiritual gifts. For Lancelot, his father, he has only the deepest reverence, affection, and compassion. Malory has expended some of the finest touches of his art in depicting the relation existing between "the greatest lover of the world" and his stainless son. Throughout the history of the quest Lancelot, like another Tantalus, is ever near the fount of grace, the Grail, but because of his sin is never able to slake his thirst. Willing in spirit but weak in flesh, Lancelot sleeps before a wayside chapel, and is despoiled of his arms and his horse; Galahad, kneeling in vigil before another altar, watches and prays and gathers fresh courage to carry on divine commands. The thought of Galahad is a constant inspiration to Lancelot. When a hermit chides him for his infidelity to grace, and contrasts his course with that of the good knight Galahad, Lancelot replies in all humility: "Well, meseemeth that good knight should pray for me unto the High Father, that I may not fall into sin again." (XV, 4.)

One of the most pathetic touches in all of Malory's work is Galahad's meeting with his father on the ship which carries Perceval's dead sister to the city of Sarras. Lancelot has been in the ship a month, and one night becoming "somewhat weary of the ship" he goes to "play him by the water side." Here Galahad finds him, and greets him with the words, "Sir, be ye welcome, for ye were the beginner of me in this world." And, says Malory, "there was great joy between them, for there is no tongue can tell the joy that they made either of other." "Few relations in fiction," says V. D. Scudder, "are more touching than those between the mature, sinning, repentant Lancelot, and the one to whom he has transmitted that spiritual capacity innate in his own heritage but obstructed by his sin. It is a tender imagination which grants them long quiet intercourse before the end, and right sweetly and nobly does each bear himself. . . . A fine artistic instinct holds the two a long time apart. Their meeting when it comes is full of human beauty. . . . It is a lovely human interlude in the sternness of the Holy Way. Galahad is perfect in reverent tenderness toward his father, Lancelot bears himself with a hushed awe." [23]

During the half year in which Galahad remains with his father they have many adventures, which Malory tells us "were with wild beasts, and not in the quest of the Sangreal." A less objective-

[23] *Ibid.*, p. 293.

minded narrator than Malory might have made much of the " wild beast " episodes as signifying Lancelot's purification from his passions before attaining to the vision of the Grail, but Malory passes this over in silence and describes Galahad's leave-taking in what are perhaps the most touching lines of the whole story. A White Knight comes to tell Galahad that he must leave his father and start out again on the adventures of the Grail.

> Then he went to his father and kissed him sweetly and said: Fair sweet father, I wot not when I shall see you more till I see the body of Jesu Christ. I pray you, said Sir Launcelot, pray ye to the High Father that He hold me in His service. And so he took horse, and there they heard a voice that said: Think for to do well, for the one shall never see the other before the dreadful day of doom. Now, son Galahad, said Launcelot, since we shall depart, and never see each other, I pray to the High Father to conserve me and you both. Sir, said Sir Galahad, no prayer availeth so much as yours. And therewith Galahad entered into the forest.   (XVII, 14.)

Never once during the entire story does Galahad rebuke his father; never, by the slightest hint or insinuation does he fall short of the filial reverence which he owes him. When Lancelot bestows his parting benediction Galahad says, " No prayer availeth so much as yours." And when Galahad, having achieved the wonders of the Grail, is dying, his last words are a legacy of love to his father: " Commend me to my Lord, Sir Launcelot, my father," he says to Bors, " and bid him remember of his unstable world." (XVII, 22.)

One last characteristic of Galahad must be noted before concluding this study of his rôle in the *Morte Darthur,*—his entire and unquestioning obedience, his complete surrender to divine commands. To Galahad the pilgrim path had been one of union from the outset; he had laid himself a victim upon the altar of divine love, and there was to be no rapine in the holocaust. With the Apostle of the Gentiles he could exclaim: " I live, now not I; but Christ liveth in me." [24] Whether seated at the tables of kings or resting with humble hermits, whether in the heat of battle or alone on solitary seas, Galahad's heart was ever attuned to the whisper-

[24] *Galatians*, ii, 20.

ings of divine grace. Like Samuel of old he could say, "Speak, Lord, for thy servant heareth." [25]

The Galahad of Malory is perhaps some distance removed from the popular hero of the Cistercian story, but he is far more accessible to the humbler ranges of human understanding. Had Malory presented him otherwise it is difficult to say whether the English mind would have accepted him so readily and given him so exalted a place in the ideals of its people. Standing upon the threshold of a departing civilization, Malory's Galahad carries the burden of a whole era; he is the crystalization of the beliefs, the practices, the ideals of medieval mysticism, seen through the clear, dispassionate, beauty-loving eyes of a fifteenth-century Warwickshire knight.

[25] *I Kings,* iii, 10.

7

CHAPTER VI

GALAHAD FROM MALORY TO TENNYSON

The century immediately following Malory witnessed a steady decline in the popularity of Arthurian literature. Several causes conspired to bring this about, the most important, without doubt, being the revival of classical learning. Renaissance culture looked askance at the pseudo-historical romances represented prominently by Geoffrey of Monmouth, and offered in their stead the long neglected masterpieces of Homer, Vergil, and Cicero. In his *Angliae Historiae* (1534),[1] Polydore Vergil, an Italian residing in England, voiced the generally prevailing scepticism towards the historicity of Arthurian material, and particularly towards the many fantastic details that had engrafted themselves upon the ancient chronicles. Such matters were felt to belong to romance rather than to history,[2] and despite the stout defense of the romantic conservatists led by John Leland,[3] the romances were destined to a long period of oblivion.[4]

---

[1] Published, Basel, 1534; second edition, Basel, 1570. An English translation was made soon after 1534. This translation was later edited by Sir Henry Ellis, Camden Society, 1846.

[2] Mead, William, *Chinon of England*, E. E. T. S., London, 1925.

[3] John Leland, *Assertio Inclytissimi Arturii*, edited by William E. Mead, E. E. T. S., 165 (1925). The *Assertio* was first translated and edited by Richard Robinson in 1582.

[4] The controversy over the historicity of Arthurian material continued for half a century; the stoutest defenders of the old romances were Stow, Price, Leland, and Robinson, while Ascham, Polydore Vergil, and Holinshed held the opposing field. In order to offset some of Holinshed's rather daring modifications of Arthurian legend, and to reinstate the tradition in the hearts of the people, Robinson, in 1583, brought out a pamphlet entitled *The Ancient Order, Societie and Unitie Laudable of Prince Arthur and His Knightly Armorie of the Round Table*. The members of the society conceived the idea of assuming the names of various knights of Arthur's Round Table. Among the sixteen kings, one duke, and forty-nine knights inscribed above the escutcheons, Galahad's name does not appear, probably in view of the fact that no one would arrogate to himself the title of perfect knight.

Nor were the Arthurian the only national romances affected by this prevailing attitude of mind. "Of the main streams of medieval poetry," says George McLean Harper, "three were so seriously checked by the Renaissance that they are only at the present day beginning to flow again as literary influences. They are the Norse Edda, the German Heldensaga, and the Celtic national cycle. From these abundant sources the literature of Europe during the sixteenth, seventeenth, and eighteenth centuries drew but little." [5]

Although the Renaissance brought Greek ideas and Greek culture to England, opened the doors of numerous universities, and flaunted great and significant names, still it added no names of importance to the history of English literature. Whether or not the recently discovered classics which flooded the newly-invented printing presses discouraged native talent, the fact remains that until the last quarter of the sixteenth century, no native literary genius appeared. England's poets were prosaic and her prose writers were, for the most part, awkward and dull imitators.

When England concluded the inglorious treaty with France, however, and the wealth of the Spanish Main was turned into English coffers, conditions suddenly changed. The nation's industries grew, discovery gave new impetus to the activity of the people, and immediately literature began to flourish. The modern era had begun.

Unfortunately for the medieval romances, the change from medieval to modern thought which marked the period gave rise also to a new system of philosophy (the outgrowth of Luther's religious doctrines), which found its expression in psychological dualism, and attempted to supplant the principles of medieval Scholasticism. Wherever the influence of the reformers asserted itself, medieval philosophy and literature were discouraged. The humanists, too, claimed the privilege of ridiculing and attacking Scholastic philosophy, and since the Galahad-Grail story, with its elements of mysticism, was inextricably bound up with the philosophy of the Schoolmen, it is scarcely to be doubted that these two powerful movements, the Renaissance and the Reformation, working together, were chiefly responsible for the temporary disappearance

---

[5] *Legend of the Holy Grail*, p. 3.

of Galahad and the Grail. For three hundred years after Malory,
no mention is made of Galahad.

The principal Arthurian works of the sixteenth century approach
neither in beauty nor depth the simple grandeur of the early
romances. Among the best known are: the Scottish metrical
romance, *Lancelot of the Laik,* composed about the year 1478,
by an unknown author; Thomas Hughes' *Misfortunes of Arthur*
(1587) ; William Warner's *Albion's England* (1586) ; Christopher
Middleton's *Chinon of England* (1597) ; and added to these are
a few ballads preserved in the *Percy Folio Manuscript* (1645),
chief among which are: *Arthur and the King of Cornwall, The
Boy and the Mantle, King Arthur's Death,* and the ballad Shakespeare knew, *Sir Lancelot du Lake.*[6] The quaint little ballad, *The
Boy and the Mantle,* reflects some of the characteristics of Galahad, but the resemblance is too remote to argue more than a passing influence. There is, however, a very significant work of the
sixteenth century which unmistakably shows the impress of the
Galahad ideal, and this work, the greatest of its age, and the
greatest after Chaucer, is Spenser's *Fairie Queene.*

Drawn largely from Arthurian tradition, this magnificent allegory, with its rich and varied picturization of medieval society,
is nearer the spirit of the Galahad *Queste* than any other work of
its time. The adventures of Gloriana's knights, each representing some particular virtue—the Red Cross Knight, *Holiness,* Sir
Guyon, *Temperance,* Britomart, *Chastity,* and so forth, find many
counterparts in the adventures of the Cistercian Grail story. Why
Spenser should have invented an entirely new galaxy of names and
adventures for his knights is difficult to understand, especially
since the work is admittedly Arthurian;[7] however, Dr. App offers
the suggestion that since Spenser's purpose was to write a moral
and political allegory, it was necessary that each of his main characters should symbolize goodness or badness in one form or another.

[6] King Henry IV, Part II, Act II, iv, 11. 38 ff.; Act III, ii, 1. 300;
King Henry V, Act II, iii, 11. 8 ff.

[7] " I labor," says Spenser, " to pourtraict in Arthure the image of a
brave knight perfected in the twelve morall vertues." Spenser's letter to
Sir Walter Raleigh, Introduction to *The Fairie Queene,* edited by William
Trent, p. 3.

" But none of the familiar Arthurian figures," he says, " excepting perhaps Galahad, was so wholly good or bad as to fit into such an unequivocal category." [8]

Galahad, however, who stands nearest the purpose of allegory, finds no place in Spenser's stately pageant. Instead, the poet prefers to assign the rôle of Chastity to a lady knight, Britomart, whose sole claim to the part seems to be her " warlike puissaunce " and her constancy to a single lover. Evidently Spenser, in thus summarily dismissing the traditional chastity hero, wished to flatter the " glorious person " of his " souveraine the Queene " for whose worship the entire allegory was written.[9] Not to the militant lady, however, but to the Red Cross Knight, representing Holiness, does Galahad find his closest resemblance in the *Fairie Queene*. The " bloodie crosse " which the Red Cross Knight wears upon his breast is similar to the bloody cross Galahad bears upon his shield, and the story of the Red Cross Knight's conquest of the pagan Sarazin is strikingly reminiscent of the story of King Evelak's victory over the pagan Tholomer, as told to Galahad by the White Knight in the *Queste*. Galahad espouses the cause of Perceval's virgin sister from whose pure hands flows strength to aid him in the adventure of the quest; the Red Cross Knight champions the lovely Lady Una, whose purity is symbolized by the snow-white mule and the spotless lamb which accompany her.

> So pure and innocent, as that same lambe
> She was in life and every vertuous lore.[10]

Like Galahad, the Red Cross Knight rests with hermits whose pious stories furnish him with fresh courage for his high adventures; like Galahad, he easily conquers the most formidable foes,— a dragon, a pagan Sarazin, and the seven deadly sins in the guise of enemy knights,—and finally, like Galahad, he follows through

[8] App, A. J., *Lancelot in English Literature*, p. 104.
[9] Spenser's purpose is clearly set forth in the following lines:

> Of warlike puissaunce in ages spent
> Be thou, fair Britomart, whose prayse I wryte;
> But of all wisdom bee thou precedent,
> O soveraine Queene! whose prayse I would endyte.
>
> (Bk. III, Canto II, 3.)

[10] *Fairie Queene*, Bk. I, Canto I, 4.

the varying vicissitudes of fortune the one ideal to which he has dedicated his life, and in the end is rewarded by the attainment and the possession of that ideal.

While the Red Cross Knight bears the closest resemblance to Galahad, points of similarity exist between Galahad and the other knights as well; thus, Sir Calidore reflects his courtesy; Sir Guyon, his modesty and dignified bearing; Sir Artegall, his justice, and so forth. In fact, throughout the poem the virtues of the Grail knight are everywhere conspicuous, and since Spenser's purpose was, as he tells us, to construct an allegory that would give us the picture of a gentleman " fashioned in vertuous and gentle discipline," we may well conclude that in drawing this picture he borrowed, not from the traditional Arthur alone, but more noticeably and more generously from the traditional Galahad whom Malory called with Lancelot " the greatest gentleman of the world." [11]

Although Spenser formed his ambitious masterpiece upon the fanciful plan of Ariosto, yet, as Warton observes,[12] it must be confessed that the adventures of his knights are a more exact and immediate copy of these which we meet in the old romances, or books of chivalry, than those which form the *Orlando Furioso*. And although the poet was acquainted with most of the Arthurian material from Geoffrey to Malory, still it can not be doubted that " we owe to Malory the transmission from the earlier romances of all that was worth preserving in these to the generation which should give birth to the *Fairie Queene*." [13]

Spenser, however, differs widely from Malory in his treatment of the original legend. Experiencing none of the reverence with which Malory approached the shores of the old romance, Spenser, with the characteristic scepticism of his age, feels free to abridge, expand, retain or reject traditional material at will; indeed, as far as fidelity to his sources is concerned, the poet, in looking about for the picture of a perfect gentleman, might as consistently have chosen Charlemagne or Richard *Coeur de Lion,* or any other medieval king for his hero. For, while he admitted that Arthur had

[11] *Morte Darthur*, Book XIII, Chapter 7.

[12] Warton, Thomas, *Observations on the Fairy Queen of Spenser*, p. 17.

[13] Strachey, Sir Edward, Introduction to Malory's *Le Morte d'Arthur*, p. xxiv.

been made famous by " many men's former works," he evidently
was not sufficiently impressed with these works to retain Arthur in
his traditional setting.   Commenting on this departure, Legouis
says : [14]

> He empties it (Arthurian romance) of its human interest, of the drama
> of occasions and of play of character, which are perceptible even in the
> work of a compiler like Malory, and are so obvious in Tennyson's *Idylls of
> the King.* Spenser introduced us to an Arthur without a Guenevere, with-
> out a Lancelot.   From that marvelous storehouse of passionate love-
> adventures, he has taken only names and accessories.   The characters are
> so superficially drawn that they are for the most part interchangeable.
> When allegories are married, we remain unmoved.

While much of Legouis' criticism is true, while Spenser does
rob Arthurian romance of its human interest, still he accomplishes
his purpose of making a romantic pageant a veil for ethical truth [15]
and in so doing gives to the English language an allegory without
a rival.   " At the same time that Spenser was striving to carry
forward the national life of his countrymen by presenting the
noblest ideals of chivalry under the old forms of romance, Shakespeare was embodying them in the new form destined thenceforth
to take the place of the old, and showing us in a Ferdinand, a
Prince Henry, or a Hamlet, the ideals of the Gentleman, while
the Sydneys and the Raleighs were presenting the counterpart in
actual life.   Ben Jonson, too, though he makes fun of ' the whole
sum of Errant Knighthood ' in his *Execration upon Vulcan,* elsewhere describes the training of pages and squires in chivalry, as
' the noblest way of breeding up our youth in all the blazon of a
gentleman.' " [16]

It is significant that with the passing of Spenser " the poets'
poet " in the last year of the sixteenth century, we close the door
upon our literature's greatest poetic age, and turn to the less
romantic seventeenth century.

Before turning to the next century, however, a word must be
said in regard to Shakespeare's rather noticeable neglect of Galahad and Arthurian themes.   It can scarcely be doubted that Shake-

---

[14] Legouis, Emile, *Spenser,* p. 138.
[15] MacCallum, W. M., *Tennyson's Idylls and the Arthurian Story,* p. 129.
[16] Strachey, Sir Edward, *Introduction to Le Morte Darthur,* p. xxiv.

speare was thoroughly conversant with at least the broad outlines
of the Arthurian story, and that the fortunes of Galahad, Lancelot,
Gawaine, and Tristram, were as familiar to him as were those of
Romeo, Antony or Bassanio.   To ascertain the cause of Shakespeare's complete silence on a subject dear to the heart of his contemporary Spenser and dear to the heart of the English people,
one must understand the psychology of Shakespeare's romanticism.
Romanticist he certainly was, but of an order entirely different
from that of Spenser, for whom Arthur was the embodiment of
all those virtues which go to make a perfect gentleman.   Shakespeare's romanticism was, if we may use a paradox, of the realistic
sort; his heroes were borrowed, not from the misty land of faery,
but from the marts of living men—from the huts of beggars and
the thrones of kings.   Shakespeare, like Chaucer, was a combination of poet and man of affairs.   Though dealing largely with
themes foreign to Elizabethan England, he had a curiously modern way of viewing life.   Through his "small Latin and less
Greek" he knew the classics, and he knew the medieval romances
as well, but he lived wholly in his own time, studied the men and
women who moved about him every day, and wrote of them as they
were.   Shakespeare's genius did not lend itself to the dimly-seen,
half-understood visions of medieval mysticism; he was content
to hold the mirror up to nature, to show virtue her image, and
vice his proper form.   Unlike his friend and contemporary, Ben
Jonson, he does not ridicule "the whole sum of knight errantry,"
but (except for passing reference to Lancelot) gives to Arthur and
his knights of the Round Table the gracious tribute of silence.

This reticence concerning Galahad is continued in the period
following Shakespeare.   Nowhere is Galahad mentioned in the
principal Arthurian works of the seventeenth century.   This century, which terminated the long and disastrous Civil War, was in
the main not particularly favorable to literature, nor could men
be expected to cultivate letters during the broils that agitated the
nation.   Militant Puritanism, under the Commonwealth and the
Protectorate, was no patron of poets, wits, and artists; and the
Restoration, with its looseness of manners and its servile imitation of French tastes and ideas, was even more dangerous to literature than the exaggerated rigidity of the Puritans.   The stage was

the chief offender, openly sneering at virtue and winking at immorality. The whole period was one of transition and the breaking up of old ideals. Medieval standards of chivalry were no longer held; the impossible romances, of which Spenser had furnished types, were relegated to oblivion, and a general spirit of gloom prevailed. The Elizabethan Age, with all its diversity, had preserved in literature and politics a marked unity in spirit—the outgrowth of a national feeling of patriotism. The Puritan Age, on the contrary, divided by religious and political struggles, presented a literature as divided as its various parties; it was an age of gloom and drab pessimism. In vain one searches the literature of the Puritan period for that romantic ardor which characterizes the preceding age. Although there were a number of exquisite minor poets, even their love lyrics lacked the spontaneous overflow of emotion which marked Elizabethan utterances. Both prose and poetry were characterized by artificial conceits and fantastic adornments epitomized in the metaphysical poetry of Donne and the sombre prose of Burton's *Anatomy of Melancholy.*

Nor did the rationalistic philosophy of the seventeenth century contribute in any sense to the alleviation of this spirit of universal gloom. The critical and empirical philosophy of Locke (grounded in Cartesian materialism), the natural philosophy of Newton, and the theological doctrines of the Deists, held no ultimate solution for the baffling problem of existence. It was little wonder, then, that dissatisfied and restless, some men looked backward for their golden age, and sighed for the glories of the past. Thus, Michael Drayton's *Polyolbion* attempted to wrest from the ravages of time the fragments of England's departed glory, and Percy's *Reliques* sought to preserve the monuments of a departed civilization.

Naturally, Galahad is nowhere mentioned or dealt with in the works of this century; but there was one writer who caught at least the spirit of the Galahad ideal perhaps more clearly than any other, one who from his earliest years felt drawn to " the sage and serious doctrine of virginity," and who gave expression to his thought in some of the sublimest flights of poetic genius. This poet, the greatest of his age, and one of the greatest of all times was John Milton.

Deeply impressed by the Arthurian story, especially as he found it in the chronicles of Geoffrey, Milton himself at early age projected an Arthurian epic,[17] but was never so completely drawn to the subject as to cast his life work in that direction. Men of letters have frequently speculated as to what might have resulted if the poet of *Paradise Lost* had turned his eyes towards Caerleon instead of Eden; and Sir Walter Scott harbored a perpetual wonder as to what Milton would have made of the Ruinous Chapel, the Adventurous Castle, the Perilous Seat, the Dolorous Wound, " and many other (things) susceptible of being described in the most sublime poetry." [18]   However, Milton's temperament and training being what they were, one is safe in concluding that he made a much happier selection of the story of the Fall.   Unlike Spenser, Milton refused to be shackled by the conventions of pure poetic allegorizing; his was too serious a mind to see life through the mirror of fanciful conceits; virtues on horseback had no attractions for him. And although there is an ethical and religious content in all his great works, still his chief purpose in writing was not a didactic one.

The tendency of the later seventeenth century writers was toward the factual and historical rather than the romantic, and John Dryden, who stands as the literary exponent of the Restoration period, exemplifies in his one Arthurian work, a drama entitled *King Arthur,* the popular attempt to use Arthurian romance merely as a framework upon which to build a national reputation.   Admittedly political in purpose and intent, Dryden's *King Arthur,* except for its name, has no claim in the authentic Arthurian tradition.   Other Arthurian works of the century are: Richard Johnson's *Tom a Lincolne* (1607), a highly fantastic piece written in the euphuistic style of Middleton's *Chinon of England;* Michael Drayton's *Polyolbion* (1613-1622), a huge work attempting to

---

[17] In January, 1638, Milton wrote to Giovanni Battista Manso Marquis of Villa, friend of Tasso and of himself, " May I find a friend like thee when, if ever, I shall recall to song our native kings . . . or shall sing the great-hearted heroes of the unvanquished Table in their bond of fellowship, and when (if only inspiration give me aid) I shall break the Saxon bonds beneath the prowess of the Britons."—*Mansus,* 80.

[18] Scott, Introduction to Dryden's *King Arthur,* p. ix.

reclaim for posterity all the glorious traditions of Britain; [19] Thomas Heywood's *Life of Merlin* (1641), a colorless history of England down to the reign of Charles I; *The Percy Folio Manuscript* (1645-1650), which contained several authentic Arthurian pieces, and which, because of its influence on eighteenth century romanticism, is one of the most important Arthurian works of this century; William Rowley's *Birth of Merlin* (1662), a tedious and terrible drama [20] based on Geoffrey of Monmouth's story; John Dryden's *King Arthur or the British Worthy* (1691), which has already been mentioned; and Richard Blachmore's two pretentions epics, which Addison praised,[21] and Dr. Johnson ridiculed.[22]

In none of the foregoing works do we find even indirect mention of Galahad. Drayton's *Polyolbion* refers to the Round Table and the " Pentecosts prepared at Caerleon . . . that Table's ancient seat," [23] but says nothing of the Promised Knight who should make one of these Pentecostal feasts immortal. Drayton, however, draws his account chiefly from Geoffrey of Monmouth, and Galahad was unknown to Geoffrey.[24]

Nor is Galahad found in *The Percy Folio Manuscript,* which exerted so profound an influence on eighteenth century romanticism. At the time of its publication in 1645, this important work (which included about a dozen Arthurian pieces, all of which

[19] Drayton's Polyolbion confirms the fact that " in the old age of a literary period the desire of great things outlives their performance."— Oliver Elton, *Michael Drayton: a Critical Study,* London (1905).

[20] It is interesting to note that this drama, first published by Kirkman in 1662, bears on the title-page the names of William Rowley and William Shakespeare. Fortunately for Shakespeare, internal evidence has disproved the possibility of his collaboration, and " the whole tone, style, thought, and expression," says A. F. Hopkinson, " negatives the assertion at once."— Introduction to Rowley's *Birth of Merlin or The Child Hath Found His Father,* p. v, London (1901).

[21] *Spectator,* No. 339.

[22] In his life of Blackmore, Dr. Johnson says: " Of his four epic poems, the first had such reputation and popularity as enraged the critics; the second was, at least, known enough to be ridiculed; the two last found neither friends nor enemies."

[23] *Polyolbion,* Book IV.

[24] *Complete Works of Michael Drayton,* edited with Introduction and notes by Richard Hooper, London (1876).

faithfully retained the flavor of the old romances) apparently received little attention; but when, a century later, Bishop Percy
accidentally chanced upon the precious manuscript, it suddenly
sprang into fame, and from that day forward Arthurian romance
began slowly to revive until it found its glorious flowering in the
age of Tennyson's *Idylls.*

Thomas Percy, much to the annoyance of contemporary anti-
quarians and scholars, set himself the task of revising and enlarging
many of the selections in the original *Percy Folio Manuscript,* and
in 1765 he published, under the title *Reliques of Ancient English
Poetry,* "the most important collection of poems and ballads in
the whole eighteenth century." [25] The importance of the book lay
in the fact that it familiarized readers with the ancient stories
which were the most authentic Arthurian material that had appeared since Malory's second edition in 1634. "For a hundred
and thirty-one years in which time Arthur had appeared as Dryden's
hero and Blackmore's . . . scarcely any Arthurian pieces had been
published faithful to the old legends in substance and spirit. . . .
And so it meant something that now there should appear six
Arthurian pieces, true for the most part to the old spirit and
matter." [26]

Indirectly the *Reliques* tended to stimulate interest in medievalism generally, and thus to pave the way for the ultimate return of
Arthurian romance. The publication of Bishop Percy's volume
profoundly affected eighteenth century literary tastes, and the influence of his *Reliques* extended even to the nineteenth century, to Sir
Walter Scott, whose *Minstrelsy of the Scottish Border* was due
chiefly to the influence of Percy's work.

Percy's popularizing of Arthurian romance, moreover, gave new
impetus to the ballad strain. After the publication of the *Reliques,*
a number of collections made their appearance, among which Ritson's *Ancient English Metrical Romances* (1802) and Ellis' *Specimens of English Romance* (1805) are the best known. Half a
century before these came *Some Specimens of the Poetry of the
Ancient Welsh Bards* (1764) by the Reverend Sebastian Evans,

[25] Maynadier, H., *Arthur of the English Poets,* p. 320.
[26] *Ibid.,* p. 328.

and in 1777 appeared Evans' *Old Ballads, Historical and Narra tive.*

The questing motif figures quite prominently in the ballad poetry of this period, as is shown in such poems as *Sir Guy the Seeker,* written by Matthew Gregory Lewis, and first published in his *Romantic Tales* (1808). " It is founded," he says, " upon a tradition current in Northumberland. Indeed, an adventure nearly similar to Sir Guy's is said to have taken place in various parts of Great Britain, particularly on the Pentland Hills in Scotland, where the prisoners are supposed to be King Arthur and the Knights of the Round Table.[27] How far the medieval Grail quest was responsible for stimulating an interest in this kind of literature, and how closely Galahad is related to Sir Guyon, one can only conjecture, but it appears that Malory, rather than tradition, is the source of these later accretions to medieval romance. Besides the spell, there is also the lifting of enchantments by means of a particular word, sign, or question. In *Sir Guy the Seeker,* the spell of the imprisoned lady can be broken only by the seizure of either the sword or the horn. It is Sir Guy's fate to seize the horn—and to search for the sword forever after. The ballad ends:

> But still he seeks, and aye he seeks
> And seeks and seeks in vain;
> And still he repeats to all he meets,
> " Could I find the sword again! "

The *Luck of Muncaster* appears to have at least an indirect connection with the Grail theme. Taken from Roby's *Traditions of Lancashire,* the ballad tells the story of a curiously wrought glass cup studded with gold and white enamel, which was given by King Henry VI on his departure from Muncaster Castle[28] where he had found shelter from the pursuit of his enemies in 1461, to Sir John Pennington, the then possessor of the castle. The king accompanied his present with the following blessing: " The family shall prosper as long as they preserve it unbroken." The cup was buried till the cessation of hostilities had rendered further care and concealment unnecessary. Unfortunately, the box was let fall, and for

---

[27] More, J. S., *Ancient Ballad Poetry of Great Britain,* p. 741.
[28] Then called *Mealcastre.*

forty years the family feared to open it lest they should find their
"luck" shattered. At the expiration of that term, a Pennington
more courageous than his predecessors, unlocked the casket and
found the luck of Muncaster intact.

The sacred quality of the cup is its outstanding characteristic;
it is a "hallowed thing," and a "cup of grace," from which martyrs
and saints have been refreshed, and so great is its potency that the
wealth of an empire cannot purchase it. As the Grail was a spiritual talisman of Heaven's good will toward Britain, so the "luck
of Muncaster" was a token of prosperity to those who had it in
their keeping. The allusion to the church of the Holy Sepulcher,
in which the "luck of Muncaster" was supposed to have been
found, furnishes the suggestion that the story perhaps originated
in the tales of the Crusaders.

Whatever may have been its origin, *The Luck of Muncaster,*
like many other anonymous songs and ballads whose themes were
unearthed from medieval lore, met an enthusiastic and responsive
audience in this century of growing medievalism, but in no one
did such tales find a more ardent champion than in that highly
gifted exponent of nineteenth century romanticism, Sir Walter
Scott.

Born in an atmosphere redolent of knight errantry, Scott's
fervid imagination seized upon every stray leaf of traditionary lore,
and his *Minstrelsy of the Scottish Border* (1802) published when
he was scarcely twenty-one, attests to the profound study he had
made of medieval institutions and customs. At twelve he had read
Percy's *Reliques,* and this book with Malory's *Morte Darthur* was
responsible for enkindling Scott's love for medievalism. In 1804
he edited and completed the unfinished thirteenth century poem
Sir Tristrem, the concluding lines being written with such faithful-
ness to the original that it is difficult to tell where Scott begins
and the old romance ends.

Galahad is not mentioned in Scott, nor indeed do any of the
Arthurian knights figure conspicuously in his works. For, despite
his early apprenticeship to Malory and Percy, Scott was not content
to spend his years in the narrow confines of Broceliande nor to
satisfy his genius in the glittering pomp of Carlisle. His romanticism demanded a broader sweep, a more extensive horizon; and
instead of "pealing proud Arthur's march from Fairyland," Scott

preferred to paint "with deathless lustre in romantic lay" the knights and ladies of a later England.

After concluding the medieval *Sir Tristrem,* Scott produced one other Arthurian poem, *The Bridal of Triermain,* which "is not so much an Arthurian poem as a poem that contains an Arthurian episode." [29] The work is of special interest in that it bears a striking resemblance to the theme of Wordsworth's one and only Arthurian poem, in which Galahad is the hero.

Although Wordsworth disclaims any Arthurian connections except for the names and places in this poem,[30] there is reason to believe that his *Egyptian Maid,* written twenty-two years after Scott's *Bridal of Triermain,* was at least unconsciously influenced by the latter poem. Scott's fanciful story, which deals with the enchanted sleep of a beautiful maiden and her awakening by the kiss of her lover, is, of course, the common property of European folklore; it is the tale of Sleeping Beauty, of Brunhilde, of Grimm's Dornröschen, and even of the German Ulrich's Guenevere. But that the treatment of the theme by the two poets was more than remotely analogous is seen in the incidents of the sleeping maiden, the trial of the knights to rouse her, the kiss or touch of the successful knight (who in each case must be proved the best knight in all the world), and finally in the bestowal of the maid as bride upon the favored knight. There is, however, one essential difference: Scott's poem emphasizes no moral teaching, while Wordsworth's is frankly didactic.

Recognizing Galahad as the traditional chastity hero, Wordsworth assigns him the most prominent part in his highly allegorical poem, the purpose of which is to extol the virtue of purity. Galahad's rôle is similar to that of Gawain in the medieval *Marriage of Sir Gawain* and that of Sir Roland in Scott's *Bridal of Triermain.* Although the *Egyptian Maid* has neither the naïvete of *Sir Gawain* nor the elusive charm of Scott's *Triermain,* still there breathes through some of the strange stanzas more of the

[29] MacCallum, W. M., *Tennyson's Idylls and the Arthurian Story,* p. 186.
[30] " For the names and persons in the following poem," Wordsworth says in the Introduction to the work, " see the *History of the Renowned Prince Arthur and His Knights of the Round Table.* For the rest the author is answerable."—*Complete Poetical Works,* p. 672.

old romantic feeling than can be traced in many professed imitations." [31] The story is briefly told.

Merlin pacing the Cornish sands, sees the ship, " Water Lily," making for British shores, and possessed of a fiendish desire to work his magic, causes a terrific storm to dash the ship to pieces. The Lady of the Lake rebukes him for his rashness, and goes in search of the victims. She finds only the Egyptian Maid, who, apparently dead or in a trance, is washed ashore. The Lady of the Lake then commands Merlin to take the maid to Caerleon. The ancient seer places her in his ebony ship and bears her to Arthur's Court. Awesomely the knights and ladies gaze upon the face of the dead girl, while Arthur explains that the maid is daughter of a king whom he once had defended, and who in gratitude had offered to bestow his child in marriage on the knight whom he (King Arthur) should choose for her. Thinking himself responsible for her untimely death, the king orders the knights to bury her (though " her birth was heathen ") with due observance of Christian rites; but Merlin intervenes, telling the King that he knows the secret of restoring the maid to life.

> . . . One by one
> Thy knights must touch the cold hand of the Virgin;
> So for the favored One, the Flower may bloom
> Once more. . . .

The King assents, and the trial begins. Sir Agravaine, Sir Kaye, Sir Dinas, all touch her hand and turn away. Even Sir Perceval is unable to rouse her though " full thrice he had crossed himself " before he reached the bier. Next Sir Gawaine, armed for the tournament, softly touches her hand " with high expectancy," but no sign is granted. Sir Tristram, casting aside his harp, is likewise unsuccessful, for

> . . . the fair Izonda he had wooed
> With love too true, a love with pangs too sharp.

Then the great Sir Lancelot, " tired slave of vain contrition," comes seeking a sign from Heaven, but is rebuked with failure, and Guenevere is passing glad when his touch fails. Finally Galahad tries his skill.

> Next came Sir Galahad;
> He paused and stood entranced by that still face
> Whose features he had seen in noontide vision.
>
> .   .   .   .
>
> Now, while his bright-haired front he bowed,
> And stood, far-kenned by mantle furred with ermine,
> As o'er the insensate body hung
> The enrapt, the beautiful, the young,

---

[31] MacCallum, W. M., *Tennyson's Idylls and the Arthurian Story*, p. 212.

Belief sank deep into the crowd
That he the solemn issue would determine.

Galahad touches with hesitant hand and

> . . . a tender twilight streak
> Of color dawned upon the damsel's cheek
> And her lips, quivering with uncertain red,
> Seem from each other a faint warmth to borrow

and

> . . . to the mouth, relenting death
> Allowed a soft and flower-like breath,
> Precurser to a timid sigh. . . .

The King, gazing in silence upon the girl brought back to life by the touch of his stainless knight, exclaims:

> . . . " Take her to thy heart
> Sir Galahad! A treasure that God giveth,
> Bound by indissoluble ties to thee
> Through mortal change and immortality;
> Be happy and unenvied, thou who art
> A goodly Knight, that hath no peer that liveth! "

The poem ends with the song of angels as King Arthur leads the Egyptian Maid to the altar to bestow her in marriage upon his purest knight, Sir Galahad.

Such, then, is Wordsworth's one Arthurian poem. As in the older romances, Galahad, because of his singular purity, achieves the adventures from which the other knights are debarred. Neither Tristan who " loved with a love too fond," nor Lancelot, the " tired slave of vain contrition," can rouse the girl from the sleep of death. Galahad alone can span the abyss separating the world of sense and spirit, and perform the miracle of bringing the dead girl back to life. That such a theme should have attracted the eminently spiritual-minded Wordsworth is not at all surprising, nor is it to be wondered at that his purpose should have been moral instruction. One of Wordsworth's favorite sayings was that " Every poet is a teacher," and he himself wished to be considered a teacher or nothing.[32]

While Wordsworth's *Egyptian Maid* in itself contributed only slightly to the revival of interest in Galahad and the Arthurian

[32] Morley, John, Introduction, *Wordsworth's Complete Poetical Works*, p. xviii.

8

story proper, still it represented the trend of literary thought toward that freedom of utterance and action characteristic of romanticism, whose apostle Wordsworth was. The publication of *Lyrical Ballads* (1798) had marked the triumph of romanticism over eighteenth century classicism, a triumph in which Scott, Coleridge, Byron, Shelley, Keats, Lamb, Landor, and many others shared. Wordsworth opened the door upon nineteenth century romanticism, and heralded the Augustan Age of English Arthurian literature.

Before examining Galahad's position in the works of the nineteenth century, a word remains to be said of the various editions of Malory's *Morte Darthur.*

The return of romanticism meant the return of Malory, and with Malory came Galahad. The *Morte Darthur* has frequently been called the touchstone of English romanticism. Whether or not this be true, it is interesting and curious to note that throughout the history of our literature, with its cyclic movements and changes, this unique compilation—a veritable encyclopedia of medieval romance—comes and goes, rises and falls, is condemned and honored concommitantly with that vaguest and most difficult to define of all literary movements, romanticism. Just why this should be, has never been determined, but the fact remains that it is so.

Shortly after Caxton's first printed edition in 1485, Wynkyn de Worde brought out a second edition in 1498; but from this time until 1634, Malory's book gathered the dust of two centuries in neglected corners of libraries. Now, however, at the beginning of the nineteenth century, the sun of romanticism raised its diminished head. In rapid succession, between 1816 and 1817, two editions of *Morte Darthur* were brought out.[33] A power had gone

[33] Of the editions of 1816, one, in three volumes, was by F. Hasselwood; another, in two volumes, was in Walker's British Classics. Both follow the edition of 1634, in which there was a division into chapters, but not into books. To the edition of 1817 Robert Southey gave his name, but in point of fact he did little more than write an introduction; the real editing was done by Upcott. This edition followed the division into books, as well as chapters, of Caxton's first edition. It seems to have been based, however, not only on that edition of 1485, but on Wynkyn de Worde's edition of 1498, and perhaps on other earlier ones.—H. Maynadier, *Arthur of the English Poets*, p. 343.

forth from Otranto which set fire to the lips of Ossian, and caused the medieval hero to leap from his grave. By the beginning of the nineteenth century the high tide of medievalism had set in, and on the crest of the wave came Galahad bearing the Grail.

CHAPTER VII

GALAHAD IN TENNYSON'S CONTEMPORARIES

Between *The Lady of Shalott* (1837), Tennyson's first Arthurian poem, and *Merlin and the Gleam* (1889), his last, lie the golden years of English Arthurian romance. While Scott, Heber, Warton, and Keats, had done much for the revival of medievalism, it was not until the first quarter of the nineteenth century had passed (after the publication of Peacock's *Misfortunes of Elphin,* Wordsworth's *Egyptian Maid,* and Tennyson's first three Arthurian lyrics [1]), that popular interest in the old romances revived, and the period became one of pronounced Arthurian activity. Nor was this activity confined to England alone. On the Continent after Wieland, came the Schlegels, Görres, Immermann, Tieck, Uhlland, and Tcheffel. Wagner turned to the Arthurian heroes and set to immortal music the story of *Parsifal, Lohengrin,* and *Tristan und Isolde,* while Lowell in America gave his version of the Grail story in *The Vision of Sir Launfal.* It was during this period also that Lady Guest made her remarkable translation of the Welsh *Mabinogion.*

Galahad enjoys a greater prominence during this period than ever before in the history of English literature, nor does it seem strange that this should be so, since the revival of medievalism meant the bringing back of medieval ideals, and Galahad is in a peculiar sense the highest expression of the medieval ideal. Chivalrous, courteous, pure, he reflects all those virtues which made for the perfection of knighthood. Curiously, however, each age of English literature which has adopted these medieval heroes has made them expressive of its own traits and ideals. Thus, the nineteenth century, with its ideas of democracy and its philosophy of individualistic and natural expression, attempted to give these shadowy knights and ladies, and in particular Galahad, a more

[1] *The Lady of Shalott, Sir Launcelot and Queen Guinevere,* and *Sir Galahad.*

108

realistic and human character. The Arthurian pieces of this century resemble in this respect the Canterbury Tales of Chaucer, with their story interest and their characters drawn to reflect life as it is.

And English life in the nineteenth century, being an age of democracy, was an age of popular education, of political enfranchisement, and an age of common striving to ameliorate economic and religious conditions. But it was also an age of profound social unrest. True, the nation after the Napoleonic wars was at peace; commerce was thriving; the arts, sciences, and industries, were making vast strides. But the England which had freed the slaves in all its colonies, in 1833, saw as a result of its growing industrial system, a far more terrible slavery fastened upon even women and children. Thinking men began to turn in serious reflection upon the moral problems that confronted the nation, and literature dropped its maxim " art for art's sake " and began to be actuated by a definite moral purpose. The didactic note is seen in all the great writers of the period—Tennyson, Browning, Ruskin, Carlyle—in the humor and pathos of Dickens' novels, and the careful satire of Thackeray's. The Victorian Age strove to attack moral irregularities by holding up spiritual ideals, and hence it was inevitable that Galahad, who stood as the highest expression of spiritual ideals and who, traditionally, exemplified the outward mold of inner perfection, should have held a potent fascination for all Victorians, but particularly for that group of painters and poets who called themselves Pre-Raphaelites, and who, in the face of doubt and materialism, strove to express the " wonder, reverence, and awe " which characterizes medieval thought and art. How profoundly Galahad influenced the writings of one of their chief exponents, is seen in the work of William Morris.

In 1858, when but twenty-four years of age, this literary man and artist, friend of Rossetti, and one of the most colorful figures among the Pre-Raphaelites, published the four Arthurian poems upon which his fame as a poet rests. These are: *The Defense of Guenevere, King Arthur's Tomb, Sir Galahad: A Christmas Mystery,* and *The Chapel in Lyoness.*

Sir Galahad (the alternative title of which might have been *A*

Study in Temptation) represents a hitherto untouched aspect of the Grail hero. Neither the author of the *Queste* nor Malory had portrayed Galahad as subject to the temptations which beset Lancelot, Bors, and Perceval, in the quest of the Grail. For the first time in literature (and significant enough for the trend of thought of this time), Galahad is the object of critical analysis; his motives are questioned; his secret thoughts are laid bare; Morris shows him struggling with doubt and almost despair at the futility of the quest he has undertaken, and turning with wistful eyes to the pleasures of sense he has vowed to forego. Aloof, untouchable, infallible,—the medieval mystic Galahad cannot escape the scrutiny of this shrewd psychologist, whose philosophy was to pierce the artificial accoutrements of flesh, and find beneath the struggling soul. To the nineteenth century romanticist, the only subjects of permanent literary interest were those which shared the common life,—the general heritage of joys and sorrows, hopes and fears, labors and loves. And thus Galahad, though breathing the sweet, pure airs of Heaven, must walk on feet of clay, and feel the sting of those temptations to which all flesh is heir. In bringing out this new phase, the writer violates the traditional concept of the Grail hero, but since his fanciful version is not altogether irreconcilable with the others, Morris by no means destroys his hero. In this departure Morris illustrates a characteristic of nearly all the writers of the Victorian Age, namely, a strong intellectual tendency to analyze the problems of life, and at the same time to explain to men the method by which these problems may be solved. In *Sir Galahad* his aim seems to have been to show that even the elect have their moments of doubt and darkness, and that to the victor in the spiritual combat, not to the still untried, go the rewards of divine love. In so doing, he has injected the element of realism into the character of Galahad, and established between this medieval mystic and modern men of flesh and blood a deep and understanding sympathy.

On Christmas eve, "the longest night in all the year," Galahad, overcome with weariness, sits in a chapel and muses on the rapid flight of time and the seeming futility of his quest. He thinks how night after night his horse treads alone the sere damp fern, and how night after night he sits dismal and unfriended holding his bridle "like a man of stone" wondering what good will come of it. He compares his lot with that of the other questers, remembering that each of these has his human compensation—Palomydes, his Ieult, and Lancelot, his Guenevere. When Lancelot rides out, can he not think of Guenevere's arms, lithe and warm about his neck? For himself there is nothing to expect but the loneliness of the grave, when some knight shall find him dead in his armor in the half-melted snow. Then men will sigh a sigh of pity, not for his death but for his deluusion.

> ". . . this Galahad
> If he had lived, had been a right good knight.
> Ah! poor chaste body! "

No lovely maid will come to sit on his tomb to mourn for him, and the very night of his burial, the court, forgetful of him, will laugh at the gay-dressed minstrels in their scarlet sleeves. He recalls with a pang the picture of a knight kissing his lady good-by when the quest began. Suddenly, he is roused from his half-dreams by the sharp clang of a bell, and some mysterious Presence passing by him.

> . . . Still half blind
> I staggered after, a great sense of awe
> At every step kept gathering on my mind,
> Thereat I have no marvel, for I saw
> One sitting on the altar as a throne,
> Whose Face no man could say he did not know,
> And though the bell still rang, He sat alone,
> With raiment half blood-red, half white as snow.

Galahad falls prostrate upon the chapel floor and " feels the first time what a thing is perfect dread," until he hears the gentle voice of Christ bidding him

> " Rise up, and look and listen, Galahad,
> Good knight of God, for you will see no frown
> Upon My Face; I come to make you glad."

Comfortingly Christ assures him that he is not alone; that God's love is ever with him, and that, though no maid will mourn above his tomb, still he will be rewarded with a love greater than the world has ever known. Lancelot, the Voice tells him, will in good time through penitence become God's servant, but meanwhile his sin wounds the Divine Lover. A day will come when Lancelot will dismally hang his head, and so also will poor Palomydes fretting out his soul for lovely Iseult. But Galahad has so far fought the good fight, and Divine Love is to be his reward.

> " O good son, Galahad, upon this day,
> Now even, all these things are on your side,

> But these you fight not for; look up, I say,
>   And see how I can love you, for no pride
>   Closes your eyes, no vain lust keeps them down.
> See how you have *Me* always; following
>   That holy Vision, Galahad, go on,
> Until at last you come to *Me* to sing
>   In Heaven always. . . .

The Voice ceases, and Galahad looks up to find the chapel deserted. Then two scarlet-winged angels clad in white enter, and after them four ladies, in gowns of red and green, bearing a bed, which they set down beneath the altar step, and disarming Galahad, gently persuade him to sleep. Towards morning an angel commands Galahad to hasten to the sea, to King Solomon's ship, wherein he will find the sword " that no man draweth without sin, but if he be most pure." Thereupon the four ladies, who are Saint Margaret, Saint Cecily, Saint Lucy, and Saint Catherine, arm Galahad with hauberk, sword, spurs, and basnet, the angel finally putting on him the surcoat with the red cross. The four heavenly ladies remove the bed from the chapel, and the angel announces the arrival of Sir Bors, Sir Perceval, and Sir Perceval's sister. Galahad rceives them joyfully, asking eagerly for news of Lancelot and the Holy Grail. Bors informs him that an hour before they had seen a great light glide through the forest, accompanied by sweet singing, but that everywhere

> " The knights come foil'd from the quest in vain;
>   In vain they struggle for the vision fair."

With this significant line Morris abruptly concludes his poem. The inference is that, had Galahad yielded to the temptation, he too would have struggled for the vision in vain, but now he sees, from the failure of others, the secret of virginity's strength.

Although the tone and spirit, as well as the material of the poem are traditional, the temptation theme is largely Morris' own invention. *Sir Galahad* is really a magnificent allegory of every soul's struggle with temptation, especially with temptations against chastity. The drowsiness and weariness which Galahad experiences at the outset show that he is perilously near the slough of despond, through which the tempter finds easy access to the soul. "Watch and pray" is the divine admonition, and Galahad, in Morris' conception, is nodding. Weariness in the pursuit of virtue is often harbinger to that most subtle of spiritual foes, self-pity; and Galahad, vowed to stand on the lofty heights of chastity, commiserates his lot as he senses the warmth and beauty of human love

in the lives of those about him. Has he perhaps been cheated by
a Vision? Is the Vision worth it all? Divine grace enters at
the perilous moment, and the voice of God, conscience, assures him
that sin, which appears so alluring, must inevitably meet its retri-
bution; that the wages of sin is death; that life passes quickly,
and that, after this life, there is the recompense of eternal love.
Assurance comes to Galahad when he sees exemplified in the lives
of those about him the futility of sin; and when Bors tells him that
many knights come " foil'd from the quest," Galahad knows it is
because they have failed to keep faith with their spiritual vision,
and have turned a deaf ear to conscience, which is the voice of God.

Had Morris written a sequel to *Sir Galahad,* bringing to its
glorious climax the finding of the Holy Grail, it is doubtful whether
the second poem could have surpassed in artistic value this first
quaint lyrical narrative of fifty quatrains. He did, however, give
Galahad a conspicuous place in another of his poems, *The Chapel
in Lyoness,* which is not a story after the metrical romances, but
rather a vivid painting of a romantic mood. Executed in true
Pre-Raphaelite fashion, it exhibits all the characteristics of that
school. The dreamy, half-heard undertones of the poem create
an atmosphere of exotic beauty strongly akin to that of Rossetti's
Blessed Damosel, whose haunting charm it strives to emulate.

The main interest centers about a wounded knight, Sir Ozana le
Cure Hardy, whom Malory merely mentioned in passing, but whose
name, because of its musical quality, had always held for Morris a
peculiar fascination.

All day long Galahad watches beside the dying knight with the tenderness of a brother, smoothing the fevered pillow, cooling the parched lips,
and lulling the wounded man to rest. When Ozana sinks into his last
stupor, and Galahad is unable to rouse him by singing, he plucks a rose
and lays it across the dying man's mouth. Ozana revives, but only long
enough to gaze upon a treasured lock of his lady's golden hair.

> The sparkling drops seem'd good for drouth;
>   He smiled, turned round toward the south,
>   Held up a golden tress.
> The light smote on it from the west;
> He drew the covering from his breast,
> Against his heart that hair he prest;
>   Death him soon will bless.

Ozana dies, and Galahad gazing at him dreamily, exclaims:

> Ozana, shall I pray for thee?
> Her cheek is laid to thine;
> No long time hence, also I see
>   Thy wasted fingers twine
> Within the tresses of her hair
> That shineth gloriously,
> Thinly outspread in the clear air
>   Against the jasper sea.

Beautiful and intangible as a dream, *The Chapel in Lyoness* displays the dominant qualities of the Pre-Raphaelite poets: a love of sensuous beauty, a touch of pessimism (as seen in Galahad's closing speech), a half-pagan conception of human love, and a strong individualism.

Who the lady of the golden tresses is, Morris does not say, and since Malory knew Ozana merely by name we have reason to suppose that the lady, as well as the episode, grew out of the poet's imagination. In the introduction of the lady, but more especially in the wistfulness expressed in Galahad's closing speech, Morris shows himself a faithful disciple of his master Rossetti, for whom the delights of human love are the apex of all happiness, the *summum bonum* to which man can attain. In *Sir Galahad,* it matters not that the hero overcomes his temptation and preserves his purity intact; the poet's chief concern is in showing that even the purest of knights could be tempted, and his sympathy inclines rather to the temptation than to the mastery of it. His hero changes from one who blazed his unfaltering trail in intimate union with God, to one who put aside a pleasure or two now in hope of more enduring joys to come. However deeply he felt the divine afflatus, Morris never quite fathomed the light that is Galahad.

Nor did his contemporary, Thomas Westwood, come nearer to the Cistercian conception of Galahad, when, a few months before the appearance of Tennyson's Idyll of the *Holy Grail,* he published *The Quest of the Sancgreal.*[2] In six cantos or books, which are

---

[2] Westwood was born in 1814, the son of a well-to-do tradesman who had retired to Enfield and there established himself as a country gentleman. Through the friendship of the family with Charles Lamb, the young man

somewhat marred by a looseness of construction, Westwood tells again the story of the Quest, with Galahad as his hero. The story in the main is traditional, but there is that freedom from the more or less canonized incidentals and that penchant for unique and fanciful situations which marked this new Arthurian revival.

Galahad here, too, as in the works of William Morris, is not immune from violent temptations, and there is no assurance in the mind of the reader that he will come through the trials unscathed. Although he conquers these temptations ultimately, they are hard fought battles, and a very human hero of flesh and blood stands in the armor which had clothed an absolutely impeccable Galahad through the centuries.

Still, here as with Morris, the change is not a radical one, nor does it basically alter the character of the good knight. From his earliest conception in literature, Galahad had been meeting villainous knights in public joust or private combat and always overpowering them. Sometimes implicitly, often explicitly, they were said to have come from the castles of the Powers of Darkness. The whole allegorical structure of the battles fought in search of the Grail made it unnecessary to introduce into his story the actual temptations which try men's souls. His entire course was rather a flight from the perfumed bowers which held such allurements for his father into the wilds where phantoms in burnished armor tried to bar his path.

With Galahad's renaissance in the nineteenth century, however, the allegory resolved itself into something more complicated. The more personal and human phases of romanticism were dominant, and in order to offer Galahad the Chaste to the world, it was considered the correct procedure to strike directly at his vow of Chastity. He still stood out a valiant man in combat, but the later authors insisted on peering more searchingly into his soul, blinding his eyes with the most seductive temptations of sense, and only saving him from a fall by signs and distractions from Heaven. The white-heat of divine love and the single-mindedness of the traditional Galahad are tempered, and his final triumph is that of

had the use of the latter's library. His interest in Isaak Walton led him to collect an unrivalled library of works on angling.

a man who thought well on the passing pleasures of the flesh, and chose to mount above them.

The six divisions of Westwood's poem are: *The Vow, The Legend of King Evelake, The Legend of the Enchanted Shield, The Legend of the Syren Isles, Corbenek,* and *The Sancgreall.* The poem opens with a picture of Galahad seated in the Siege Perilous.

> Sir Galahad, the flower of knights, the pure;
> Sir Galahad, that, kneeling at the cross
> In Carlisle minister on All-hallow-eve,
> Was caught up, in the spirit or the flesh,
>
> .   .   .   .
>
> And drank the odour of the blooms of heaven.

Seated in the Siege Perilous, Galahad beholds, as in a vision, far down the vista of the years, " beyond the cloud of conflict, shock of fate . . . the issue and the end of all." Arthur tells his knights of the evil days that have come upon the country since the disappearance of the Grail, and begs for a sign from heaven. No sooner has he spoken than the Sancgreall suddenly appears in their midst, " flushing each upturned and transfigured face with rosy radiance," but in Galahad's eyes " the mystic splendor burned with deeper flame." Galahad springs to his feet and vows to follow the Sancgreall through all the world, while the knights echo his cry.

> " Ours be thy vow!   By Mary Mother too
> We'll seek the sovran Sancgreall through
>   all the world! "

The next day the questers bid farwell to Camelot. After three years of unsuccessful striving, the knights return one by one, with tales of fiends and dragons and demoniac dreams and

> . . . worse than all,
> A glamor of the senses, vehement
> And irresistible, that drew them on
>
> .   .   .   .
>
> To isles of syrens on the summer seas.

Only Galahad, Perceval, Lancelot, and Bors, continue the quest. Finally the whisper spreads through the court that Galahad has found the Grail. A hoary anchorite of the hills had seen in his midnight watch a stately knight climb the precipitous pass that leads to steep Tintagel and the sea, and the knight was Galahad.

> Snow-white his steed, snow-white his armour all
> From helm to heel; his visage pale, but pure

As holy angels! . . .
He scaled the steep—the curtain of the mist
Shimmered like silver, as he entered in,
And from the perilous summits, pealed a cry
Reverberate, echoed back by cliff and scaur,
" Ho! for the Sancgreall, blessed blood of God! "

The Second Canto recounts the story of King Evelake and his famous shield, foreordained to Galahad. It tells of how Joseph, when he lay dying, commanded his attendant to convey the shield to Nacien to be stored up in trust until Galahad should come. . . .

. . . Galahad,
A faithful knight and pure, ordained to win
Much worship, and achieve a sacred quest—
His should the shield be, and no other man's.

The Third Canto describes Sir Galahad's journey to the abbey wherein hangs the famous shield. A monk delivers the shield, and as Galahad with wonder gazes upon its " brands and bosses," he seems to hear " the thunders of old battles roll o'erhead," and to behold " hot plains that sweltered under skies of brass." Sir Galheron, Galahad's companion on this journey, begs leave to wear the marvelous shield, but the monk Anselmus rebukes him sternly, saying:

" The truest, purest knight in all the world
Shall wear the shield, no other. . . ."

But Galheron seizes the shield and, spurring his steed down the rocky path, is hidden in a hurricane of dust. A giant knight, " black-armoured and black-plumed," rides after him with furious haste, and with a mortal stroke lays Galheron in the dust. The Black Knight then returns to the abbey with the shield which he hangs around Galahad's neck and vanishes.

Then Galahad saw that solemn sight of old
Vouchsafed to Joseph in his dying hour:
He saw the summer night break out in stars,
Myriads on myriads, as if God were there,
With all the hosts and hierarchies of heaven.

.   .   .   .

And in the silence, with the silver dew,
Came down a voice that said, " Fair knight of Christ,
The end is nigh . . . be faithful to the end! "
All night before the altar Galahad knelt
In vigil, and at sunrise rode away.

The Legend of the Syren Isles, the Fourth Canto, is Westwood's fanciful conception of the temptations which beset Galahad and his father in their search for the Sancgreall.

Borne along in their shallop, the two knights are lost in dreams, while at the stern, unseen by them, sits a woman with weird and steadfast face, and "eyes inscrutable as the stars of heaven." Through fen and fallow tract, through pasture, plain and limitless expanse, this silent creature steers them, while ever and anon the Neck and the Kelpy wail from the marshes, "Woe for Sir Galahad! Woe for Sir Lancelot!" When the rosy morning flushes with splendor the syren seas, Lancelot falls beneath the spell, and is lured into forgetfulness by a golden-haired syren. Not so Sir Galahad. For although "the lucious air rained sweetness on him and his senses swam" when a syren transforming herself into the lovely image of his betrothed Isonde (whom the Norsemen had carried off in a raid when Galahad was but a boy), tempts him to sin; still Heaven's strength is with him, and he withstands the tempter's wiles. As he is about to step ashore with the maiden, a snow-white bird chased by a hawk flutters across his path, and Galahad watching the bird's upward flight, suddenly has a vision of "angels innumerous shining tier on tier,"

> And floating in their midst, half-seen, half hid
> By flicker of white vans, the rosy cloud
> That round the Sancgreall burned at Camelot!

And Sir Galahad knew

> Each angel face looked down on him from heaven
> And every face was sad.

Conscience-stricken, and filled with shame and self-contempt, the pure knight

> Uttered such a cry as must have reached
> To God the Father, for a sudden night
> Fell on the golden land and sapphire sea,—
> And he dropped stark and senseless on the deck.
> Nor heard the winnowing of the angelic wings
> Nor saw the shining multitude descend.
>
> .   .   .   .
>
> But when his swoon was over, Galahad knew . . .
> A sense of peace and pardon filled his soul.

The Fifth Canto tells of Galahad's return to Carbonek after many years of questing. Changed was the Flower of Knights from him that sat in the Siege Perilous at Pentecost

> Still in his eyes the mystic splendor burned,
> And still his lips were lit with smiles of heaven;
> But wan his visage, withered as with fire,
> And wasted all his strength—like Christ's true knight
> Of Tarsus, much had he endured and known.

His grandsire King Pelles, holding vigil on Christmas eve, sees Galahad coming, " like a white wraith across the wizard plain," and knows now the end is near.   Galahad recounts to the assembled knights the story of his adventures.

The Sancgreall, the last and Sixth Canto, brings the cycle to a close. Galahad at Corbenek has a vision of the Grail which Joseph of Arimathea and four angels bring from Heaven.   At the Mass which Joseph celebrates, Christ appears first in the image of a Child, then as the Crucified.   An Angel communicates the knights, and a voice tells them that this very day the secrets of the Grail shall be accomplished at Sarras " in the spiritual place."   That night they set out from Logres, and reaching Solomon's ship, find therein the Holy Grail.   When he sees it, Galahad prays with uplifted arms that whensoever he should ask the Lord to let him pass out of this world his wish should be granted, and a voice replies that his prayer shall be answered.   When Perceval questions him concerning this strange petition, Galahad replies:

> " When this morn mine eyes beheld
>   The cup unveiled, and o'ver my lips had passed
>   The savour of His flesh and of His blood,
>   Such bliss possessed me as I ne'er have known.
>   Wherefore, my travail o'er, I would have leave
>   To quie my mortal coil and be with Him. . . .
>   . . . and all day long
>   Worship the majesty of Christ, my King."

The ship moves swiftly over the sea, and on the seventh day, the Sabboth morn, they reach the city of Sarras.   As they bear the Holy Grail through the streets, a virtue goes out from it whereby the maimed are healed, the blind receive their sight, and the dumb break out in praise. The pagan king, enraged at these strange events, causes the knights to be cast into prison.

> . . . but nor rack, nor chain
>   Nor fire, nor any anguish of the flesh
>   Had power against them, evermore they saw
>   The Vision of the Grail; their dungeon shone
>   With splendour, as of Paradise . . .
>   They said, " This place is Heaven! we cannot fail;
>   The everlasting arms do hold us up."

Before a year has passed the King falls dangerously ill, and moved by fear or remorse, he orders his satraps to bring the imprisoned knights before him.   He marks with speechless awe the glory in their faces, and touches their hands to assure himself they are not angels in disguise. Then, with a muttered prayer for pardon, he dies, and Galahad is unanimously acclaimed king.   The nobles bring the crown and set it on Galahad's head and place him upon the throne hailing him king of Sarras, and the throng around the palace gates shout with joy, "Long live the knight of Christ! Long live the King!"

A year from that very day, before the dawn of Christmas morn, Joseph of Arimathea appears to Galahad telling him to make strong his heart for now the hour is at hand when those things which he has seen darkly as in a glass he will now see face to face. And Galahad exclaims, "Dear Lord, I thank Thee; Thou hast heard my prayer." He then receives his last Communion from Joseph's hands

> And all his face grew bright, until it shone
> With a pure glory, past belief of men,
> As God were gazing through his mortal eyes.

Turning to his companions, he kisses each of them thrice, telling them to carry to Arthur's court the wonderous story of the Holy Grail, and he bids them say to his sire Sir Lancelot, "Remember this unstable world."

> Then suddenly he fell asleep in Christ
> And a great multitude of angels bore
> His soul to Heaven. And out of Heaven there came
> The semblance of a Hand, that, reaching down,
> Caught up the Grail, and no man saw it more.

In spite of the looseness of construction, there is a stately delicacy which bears the burden along to its goal, and in spite of the humanizing process which makes Westwood's work kin to that of Morris, the goal is union with God. With Westwood, as with the others Galahad stands as a man apart, and it would be surprising if this tradesman's son (whose collection of books is more famous than his own literary contributions) were to have known Galahad so slightly that he could have left him a creature of common clay. Although he introduces a more turbulent rebellion of the flesh into his hero, he still sees the face of the dying knight "as God were gazing through his mortal eyes."

In striking contrast to the treatment and style of Morris and Westwood, is *The Quest of the Sangraal* by Robert Stephen Hawker. Sometimes classed among the Pre-Raphaelites, Hawker, in spite of his instinctive medievalism, possesses little in common with their school.

The Quest of the Sangraal, published in 1863, six years before Tennyson's *Holy Grail,* is the first notable work on the theme since Lovelich.[3] That the subject should have attracted the stalwart

[3] *The Quest of the Sangraal* was written during the days which followed

vicar of St. Morwenna is not surprising, since he spent his life in an atmosphere of medieval belief, amid the Cornish fastnesses which helped to give these legends being. Moreover, the theme itself with its mystic symbolism had a direct and satisfying appeal to the intensely religious nature of the man who a few hours before his death was received into the Catholic Church. The pity of it is that Hawker, through diffidence perhaps, or because he recognized in Tennyson a poet better fitted for so sublime a theme, gave us only a fragment of scarcely five hundred lines, which for the most part consists of an introductory chant.

Galahad, "whose chosen hand unbars the gates of day," is Hawker's hero, and the picture the poet paints of him is worthy of the old tradition. The poem opens with a sort of battle cry which suggests the clash of a thousand spears:

> Ho! for the Sangraal! vanish'd Vase of Heaven!
> That held, like Christ's own heart, an hin of blood! [4]
> Ho! for the Sangraal!
> How the merry shout
> Of reckless riders on their rushing steeds
> Smote the loose echo from the drowsy rock
> Of grim Dundagel, thron'd along the sea!

Outstanding in this host is Galahad, and with him are Tristan, Perceval, and " the sad Sir Lancelot," all " battle-shouldering men, massive in mould, but graceful, thorough men."

Arthur, " in whose pulses beat a thousand kings," and, " whose eye ruled them like a throne of light," addresses the questers in a lengthy hortatory speech, magnificent in its dignity, and in parts reminiscent of Henry's before Agincourt. He urges the knights to remember that it is no ordinary quest they undertake, wherein they may " quench their thirst of love in ladies' eyes "; they ride forth to a mightier, holier cause; their goal is the " vanish'd Vase of God." He recounts the history of the vase which Joseph of Arimathea " the vassal of the Vase " brought into England. He tells of how Herod " that yellow Jew " and Pilate " the earth-wide judge and doomster for all lands " had bound Jesus to " the world's tallest tree, slowly to die," and of how Joseph had caught in a vase the ruddy drops from the great tree of life, and taken it to orient Syria, " God's own land, the ladder foot of Heaven," where

---

Mrs. Hawker's death in February, 1863. It is to be regretted that the poem was never completed.

[4] The *hin*, says Hawker, was a Hebrew measure used for the wine of the Sacrifice.

9

> Young men that no one knew went in and out
> With a far look in their eternal eyes

while the Sangraal, as though it clung to some ethereal chain, " brought high Heaven to earth at Arimathea." Finally, evil days set in, and wicked men " tainted the land with the garbage of their sin," and the Sangraal disappeared. But Merlin's prophecy, that the curse should not last forever, but that some day a king should arise from Keltic loins who should call a quest, is about to be fulfilled. A chosen knight, the ninth from Joseph in the line of blood, " clean as a maid from fleshly sin . . . he with the shield of Sarras " is about to achieve the Holy Grail. The king ends his speech with the opening cry: " Ho! for the Sangraal! Vanish'd Vase of God! " The knights take up the cry, and Gawain, " a man of Pentecost for words that burn," proposes that the questers separate by lot to the four winds of heaven in order to " search the regions one by one and pluck this Sangraal."

Accordingly, Merlin brings forth the silver arrows upon which their separate fates are engraved. Lancelot draws the North, Perceval the South, Tristan the West, and Galahad the East.

> Sir Galahad holds the Orient arrow's name:
> His chosen hand unbars the gate of day.

Each of the questers bears on his banner an appropriate device: Lancelot's is a lily with a broken stem, and beneath it the words, " Stately once and ever fair." Perceval's shows a turbaned Syrian wrestling for mastery with a stately foe, and coiled in rich tracery around the shield are the words: " Whoso is strong with God shall conquer men." Tristan's bears a rainbow with the words: " When toil and tears have worn the westering day, behold the smile of fame! So brief, so bright! " A vast archangel floods Sir Galahad's shield, and beneath it the words as in graven fire:

> " I thirst, O Jesu! let me drink and die! "

The questers depart, and that same night Arthur has a vision of Galahad, and in his hands—the Grail.

> Forth gleamed the east, and yet it was not day!
> A white and glowing horse outrode the dawn;
> A youthful rider ruled the bounding rein,
> And he, in semblance of Sir Galahad shone.
> A vase he held on high; one molten gem,
> Like massive ruby or the chrysolite,
> Then gushed the light in flakes, and flowing, fell
> As though the pavement of the sky brake up,
> And stars were shed to sojourn on the hills.
>
> .   .   .   .
>
> Then saw they that the mighty quest was won!

The Sangraal swooned along the air. . . .

. . . .

Whole ages glided in that blink of time,
While Merlin and the King looked wondering on.

The last thirty lines of the poem are directed against the horrors of war
and are an exhortation to England to turn from temporal gains to things
spiritual.

The clarion call which opens this poem never quite dies out but
echoes again and again to the accompaniment of pounding hoof-
beats and the clang of steel on steel. Hawker's Galahad is one in
whom there could be not even the slightest flaw, the most fleeting
hesitation or looking back. In this he is utterly different from the
Galahad of the other two poets treated in this chapter. Half of
Morris' charm lies in the dreamy uncertainty of half-told things;
Westwood with a fine brush paints new and unfamiliar settings;
Hawker, his eyes full of the glamor of the past, has no delays for
doubts and temptations, no time for dalliance among sensual allurements and self-pity. His song suggests a straining at the leash
which the other two never sought to attain. Their hero sighed
deeply, and with a tinge of melancholy took his way, while Hawker's
with unbounded rein outrode the dawn. With Hawker, the Galahad
of old, that half-ethereal creature who was more the incarnation of
what Lancelot might have been than a child of flesh, is born again,
thirsting with a thirst unslakable for things divine. It is all
summed up in the inscription on the arrow offered him by Merlin,
which expresses his single-mindedness in a single sentence, " I
thirst, O Jesu, let me drink and die."

The Galahad of Tennyson's contemporaries, though not radically
different from the Galahad of Malory and the Old French romancers, illustrates quite clearly the manner in which this medieval
hero may be made to express the psychological tendencies of the
period in which he is reborn; and at the same time shows how
writers of one period may vary in their attitude towards the same
character.

Besides the poets, two prose writers entered the field of nineteenth century Arthurian romance, each of whom did much to
revive interest in Malory's *Morte Darthur* by presenting it in new
and attractive style.

The first to undertake this arduous and comprehensive task was James Knowles, who in 1862, brought out *The Legends of King Arthur and His Knights,* a work which, as he himself admits in the preface to the eighth edition, is little else than an abridgement of Sir Thomas Malory's compilation, with a few additions from Geoffrey of Monmouth and other sources. The work is dedicated to Lord Tennyson, with whom Knowles enjoyed a long and intimate acquaintance. The author's purpose, to arrange the many tales in a more or less consecutive story, has proved eminently successful, as the many editions through which the book has passed shows, and the style in which the stories are told renders them as enjoyable as any in the field of Arthurian romance.

Like Tennyson, Knowles, in true Victorian fashion, omits the story of Galahad's conception, birth, and infancy, and although Galahad is referred to as Lancelot's son, we are not told how this relationship came to be. The author thus robs the story of much of its mystical and spiritual significance, since the peculiar circumstances of Galahad's birth were by the old romancers bound up in the story of the Dolourous Stroke and the rehabilitation of *La Terre Foraine.* This neglect is less noticeable in Knowles than in Tennyson, however, since the former following Malory is content merely to tell the stories as plain objective facts. Tennyson, with keen insight into things spiritual, might have found a solution for the baffling Grail problem had he utilized rather than neglected this important part of the original Galahad story. The adventures of Galahad in the quest of the Sangreal are told in Chapter XII of Knowles' work, and correspond more or less closely with Books XIII to XVII of Malory.

Another version of the Galahad story is told in Books X and XI of Henry Frith's *King Arthur and His Knights of the Round Table,* a juvenile rendering of Malory's *Morte Darthur.* Here also, as in Knowles' *King Arthur,* the account of Galahad's conception and birth is omitted, and the relationship between Lancelot and Guenevere is modified, as might be expected in a book prepared expressly for the young. Without destroying the consistency of the narrative, the author gives the principal episodes and adventures in the life of Galahad, beginning with his appearance at the Round Table in his fifteenth year to claim the Siege Perilous, and ending with his death in Sarras after he has enjoyed for a year the kingship of that city. Frith's Galahad is the Galahad of Malory, and the same virtues of modesty, courtesy, and valor which accompany him in the older story, everywhere accompany him here.

Having examined at length the rôle of Galahad in the works of Tennyson's contemporaries, we now turn to a consideration of the part which Galahad plays in the works of the man who throughout the entire Victorian period stood at the summit of poetry in England, whose voice was for nearly half a century the voice of a whole people, expressing in exquisite melody their hopes and fears, their joys and sorrows, their griefs and triumphs; a poet who combined in himself, to a marked degree, the simplicity of Wordsworth, the elusiveness of Blake and Coleridge, the music of Keats and Shelley, the manliness of Scott; a poet who, because of his own devotion to high spiritual ideals, was admirably fitted to interpret to a modern world the medieval ideal, Galahad.

CHAPTER VIII

GALAHAD IN THE POETRY OF TENNYSON

The picture of Galahad, like the vision of Arthur, came to Tennyson early in life. "The vision of Arthur as I have drawn him," the poet said to his son Hallam,[1] "had come upon me when, little more than a boy, I first lighted upon Malory." Like the youthful Scott with his *Reliques,* Tennyson found in the *Morte* of Malory a casket of precious gems which needed only the critical eye of the artist to separate and classify, and place in settings designed to accentuate their beauty. That this early acquaintance with Malory was a happy event not only for Tennyson, but for the whole literary world, no one who has thrilled to the exquisite *Idylls* will deny, and although Tennyson lacks somewhat of the rugged epic grandeur of the fifteenth century romancer, he rivals him in spiritual beauty and power.

As early as 1832, when scarcely twenty-three years old, Tennyson produced his first Arthurian poem, *The Lady of Shalott,* "a mystical and more fanciful version of Malory's beautiful story of Elaine of Astolat,"[2] and thereafter for upwards of fifty years continued to ferry new treasures from the shores of the old romance. In 1843 appeared the well known lyrics *Sir Launcelot and Queen Guenevere* and *Sir Galahad,* each of which foreshadowed in its way the glorious work to which he was to dedicate his genius. Wanting none of the warmth and color of the true medieval mood, these last two poems, together with *The Lady of Shalott,* sang their way into the heart of nineteenth century romanticism, and heralded the approach of the stately *Idylls of the King.* Although written twenty years before the advent of the Pre-Raphaelite movement, these first Arthurian pieces have much in common with that school, but, as Maynadier points out, while they share its tone and spirit they borrow none of the Pre-Raphaelite oddity.[3]

[1] Hallam Lord Tennyson, *Alfred Lord Tennyson: A Memoir,* Vol. 3, p. 128.

[2] Maynadier, Howard, *Arthur of the English Poets,* p. 411.

[3] *Ibid.,* p. 411.

126

Sir Galahad, which some critics pronounce the purest and high-est of all Tennyson's lyrical pieces, is a simple ballad of seven twelve-line stanzas, less elaborate in structure than the other two lyrics, but possessed of a peculiar haunting melody all its own. Its theme " anticipates the exaltation of the virtue of purity which constitutes the principal motive of the *Idylls,*" [4] and there is not in our literature, with the possible exception of *Comus,* a more sublime expression of the godlike figure of Chastity. Permeated with the consciousness of his soul's high destiny, and filled with that deep humility which is grounded in truth, Galahad in a trans-port of joy exclaims:

> My good sword carves the casques of men,
>   My tough lance thrusteth sure,
> My strength is as the strength of ten,
>   Because my heart is pure.

Purity is his magic talisman, the spiritual sesame with which he discovers the secrets of the Grail. Other knights may perform deeds of prowess to win worship from fair ladies' eyes, but for Galahad there is another and a higher recompense; and though he is willing to fight to the end for the honor of all women " to save them from shame and thrall," still he cannot permit his own heart to become a captive to human love. One vision burns within his soul, and to that vision he has dedicated his life, his strength, the sum of his affections. Not disdaining earthly love, he realizes that, in God's eternal plan, it is not meant for him. His is the virgin heart in work and will, and to that higher voca-tion he dedicates his being.

> How sweet are looks that ladies bend
>   On whom their favors fall!
> For them I battle to the end,
>   To save from shame and thrall:
> But all my heart is drawn above,
>   My knees are bow'd in crypt and shrine:
> I never felt the kiss of love,
>   Nor maiden's hand in mine.
> More bounteous aspects on me beam,
>   Me mightier transports move and thrill;

---

[4] App, A. J., *Lancelot in English Literature,* p. 153.

> As keep I fair thro' faith and prayer
> A virgin heart in work and will.

Once he has tasted the delights of divine love, nothing earthly can satisfy him; desire for union with God becomes the consuming fire that sweeps him along over bridge and ford, through hostel, hall and grange, until the world of sense and reality becomes a world of shadows; and the unseen world of the spirit becomes the real world in which his spirit lives and moves and has its being.

> When down the stormy crescent goes,
>   A light before me swims,
> Between dark stems the forest glows,
>   I hear a noise of hymns:
> Then by some secret shrine I ride:
>   I hear a voice but none are there;
> The stalls are void, the doors are wide,
>   The tapers burning fair.
> Fair gleams the snowy altar-cloth,
>   The silver vessels sparkle clean,
> The shrill bell rings, the censer swings,
>   And solemn chants resound between.

But he who seeks shall find, and Galahad's quest is at last rewarded.

> Sometimes on lonely mountain-meres
>   I find a magic bark;
> I leap on board; no helmsman steers;
>   I float till all is dark.
> A gentle sound, an awful light!
>   Three angels bear the holy Grail;
> With folded feet, in stoles of white,
>   On sleeping wings they sail.
> Ah, blessed vision! Blood of God!
>   My spirit beats her mortal bars,
> As down dark tides the glory slides,
>   And starlike mingles with the stars.

It is clearly evident, from his early treatment of Galahad, that Tennyson accepted the Grail hero in much the same allegorical sense as did the author of the Old French *Queste;* with this difference, however, that while the author of the *Queste* created his Grail hero to fill a definite place in a definite romance, Tennyson's Galahad is independent of time and historical setting; he is any soul striving after a divine ideal, a mystic living in a material

world, translating all experience in terms of the spirit.   For such
a soul there is no loneliness, no sorrow, no physical pain, no mental anguish; death itself has no power to quench the invincible
spirit.   Every event of life is but a stepping stone to the attainment of its divine destiny; through the darkest of life's forests,
it sees the light of Heaven; through the roughest storm of circumstances, the glory of the stars.   Tennyson's *Sir Galahad* is a beautiful allegory of the soul's journey towards God, and its final
possession of Him in the Beatific Vision.   It is not, however, in
this exquisite lyric that we find Tennyson's fullest conception of
Galahad; for that we must turn to *The Idylls of the King.*

Tennyson's greatest work was not the spontaneous outpouring
of the inspired moment; the *Idylls* represent fifty years of patient
labor, mirroring the experience of the poet's youthful dreams, his
manhood's clearer vision, and the mature wisdom of old age.   In
1859 he brought out his first four *Idylls: Enid, Vivien, Elaine,* and
Guenevere.   These, his son tells us, aroused as much enthusiasm
as *Maud* had provoked resentment.[5]   Ten thousand copies were
sold the week of publication.   Some of his friends, however, like
Ruskin, objected that "so great power ought not to be spent on
vision of things past, but on the living present."   Swinburne,
although he disliked the scheme of the *Idylls,* had great admiration
for their "exquisite magnificence of style." [6]   In spite of the critics, the popularity of the *Idylls* steadily increased, and in 1869,
after an interim of ten years, another volume appeared, containing
The Coming of Arthur, The Holy Grail, Pelleas and Etarre, and
The Passing of Arthur.   In 1871 *The Last Tournament* was privately printed and subsequently published in the *Contemporary
Review;* the same Idyll was republished with *Gareth and Lynette*
in 1872.   These, with *Balin and Balan* (1885), made up the entire
cycle of the *Idylls,* a work which, as Hallam Tennyson tells us,
gives us more fully than any other the innermost being of the
poet.[7]

The complete epic as finally arranged consists of a *Dedication
to Prince Albert,* an epilogue *To the Queen,* and the *Idylls* in three

[5] Tennyson's Poetical Works, edited with notes and introduced by Hallam
Tennyson, p. xxxix.

[6] *Ibid.,* p. xl.   [7] *Ibid.,* p. xl.

parts: *The Coming of Arthur, The Passing of Arthur,* and *The Round Table.* The last consists of ten *Idylls,* the names of which have already been mentioned.

Galahad's rôle in the Idylls can best be understood by a sympathetic study of the spiritual elements which underlie the framework of the poem. While it is true that the sinful love of Guenevere and Lancelot working to undo the unsuspecting goodness of the blameless King furnishes the main theme of the Idylls, still beneath all this purely human story there is, as Tennyson himself admitted, a deeper and more subtle meaning, one which is the essence of all dramatic art—the eternal conflict between sense and soul. " The personal drift of the *Idylls,*" he says, " is clear enough. The whole is a dream of man coming into practical life and ruined by one sin—the guilty love of Lancelot and Guenevere. Birth is a mystery and Death is a mystery, and in the midst is the table-land of life, and its struggles and performances. It is not the history of one man or of one generation, but of a whole cycle of generations." [8]

Here, then, we have Tennyson's own explanation of the real meaning of the *Idylls.* The historicity of the legends was a matter of secondary importance to him. " I believe," he is quoted as saying, " the existence of King Arthur is more or less mythical." But that the legends held a deep significance for him he left us no room for doubt. " My meaning in the *Idylls of the King,*" he says expressly, " is a spiritual one. I took the legendary stories of the Round Table as illustrations. Arthur was allegorical to me: I intended to represent him as the Ideal of the Soul of Man coming in contact with the warring elements of the flesh." [9]

While the poet himself thus refers to Arthur as allegorical and his poems as allegories, Van Dyke prefers to treat them not as allegories but as parables, since, as he says, they are not merely personifications of abstract virtues and vices, but living men and women whose lives show forth in a parabolic way the virtues and vices that dominate them.[10]

[8] *Memoirs,* Vol. 2, p. 127.

[9] *Tennyson's Poetical Works,* edited with notes and introduction by Hallam Tennyson, p. xl.

[10] " The distinguishing mark of an allegory," says Van Dyke, " is per-

There are, of course, as Van Dyke points out, many purely allegorical figures, the Lady of the Lake, Excalibur, the three Queens, and the various visions, but these are to be distinguished from the characters which, possessing the quality of probability, belong in the plane of parables.

If we are to accept Van Dyke's distinction, we might say that as Arthur's life is a parable of a just man, Lancelot's of a sinner who finally repents, so Galahad's is a parable of a pure man whose reward even in this life is a foretaste of the vision of God. This parable of purity runs like a golden thread -through the entire cycle, uniting and vivifying the whole, while Galahad, who stands as the champion of this virtue, deserves in this sense to be called the protagonist of the tale. No mention is made of Galahad in the first five Idylls, and Tennyson seems purposely to keep him hidden from view until, in the natural evolution of the drama of Sense and Soul, the stage is cleared for him. Unlike the old romancers, the poet does not allude to him even through the lips of Merlin, but all the while we are conscious that he exists somewhere and that his coming will be the climax of the drama. When, in the *Coming of Arthur,* we hear the Ideal of the Soul of Man (Arthur) expressing the wish to be joined with Sense (Guenevere) in a union such as only pure spirits enjoy, we realize how mercilessly that hope will be blighted by the dark storm of passion; how the order for which the King yearned will be plunged into wildest confusion; how his kingdom will " reel back into the beast." But at the same time there comes the hope that some day a deliverer will appear, a Promised Knight who, because of his perfect mastery over sense, will fulfill the wish for which the Ideal of the Soul of Man sighs, and will

---

sonification. It does not deal with actual persons, but with abstract qualities which are treated as if they were real persons . . . It moves, therefore, altogether in a dream-world; it is not only improbable but impossible . . . A parable is just the reverse of this. If instead of a virtue representing a person, the poet gave us a person embodying and representing a virtue; if instead of the oppositions and attractions of abstract qualities, we had the trials and conflicts and loves of real men and women in whom these qualities were living and working—then we would have a parable."—Henry Van Dyke, *The Poetry of Tennyson*, p. 170.

Have power on this dark land to lighten it
And power on this dead world to make it live.
                    The Coming of Arthur.

Tennyson had long dreamed of executing a Grail poem, but the fear of incurring the charge of irreverence had kept him from carrying out his design. " It would be too much like playing with sacred things," he said, and he added by way of argument, " the old romancers *believed* in the Sangreal." [11] But the vision persistently haunted him, and finally, in 1869, *The Holy Grail* was given to the world. Until this time the poet's plan for the Idylls had not yet assumed definite shape; now, however, Tennyson recognized the possibility of making this new Idyll the unifying principle of the cycle; this parable of purity would become the touchstone by which he would test the knights of the Table Round.

In the complete allegory or cycle of the spiritual life, as Tennyson conceived it, *The Holy Grail* holds the highest place. " It is," says Tennyson, " one of the most imaginative poems. I have expressed there my strong feeling as to the Reality of the Unseen." [12] And Henry Van Dyke considers this Idyll in some respects the richest and most splendid of them all.[13] He says: " It shows us the strife between superstition, which is a sensual religion, and true faith, which is spiritual . . . Out of the mystical twilight which envelops the action this truth emerges: that those knights who thought of the Grail only as an external wonder, a miracle which they fain would see because others had seen it, ' followed wandering fires '; while those to whom it became a symbol of inward purity and grace, like Galahad and Percivale, and even the dull, honest, simple-minded Bors and the sin-tormented Lancelot, finally attained unto the vision." [14]

Though much of Tennyson's *Holy Grail* is entirely underived, a good part of this Idyll is based upon Malory's translation of *La Queste del Saint Graal*. It is often, however, the portions which have no traditional antecedents that are the most beautiful. Instead of telling the story directly, the poet puts the tale upon the lips of

[11] *Memoir*, Vol. 2, p. 126.
[12] *Memoir*, Vol. 2, pp. 89, 90.
[13] Van Dyke, *The Poetry of Tennyson*, p. 184.
[14] *Ibid.*, p. 184.

Perceval, who, having " passed into the silent life," relates to a
brother monk Ambrosius the marvels of the quest. " What is it? "
asks the monk of Perceval, " the phantom of a cup that comes and
goes? " Perceval's answer precludes all doubt as to the reverence
in which the Grail was held, not only by the medieval knights, but
by the nineteenth century laureate as well:

> " Nay, monk! what phantom? . . .
> The cup, the cup itself from which our Lord
> Drank at the last sad supper with His own."

The knight then relates how the cup was brought to England
by Joseph of Arimathea and deposited in Glastonbury where daily
miracles were wrought by it; how the times grew evil so that " the
holy cup was caught away to Heaven and disappeared; " how
his own sister, a nun, was the first to see it again; how it appeared
to her at midnight in her cell " rose-red with beatings in it, as if
alive; " and how she charged him and all of Arthur's knights to
fast and pray, as she had fasted and prayed that they might also
see the blessed Vision.

Here a word may be said, in passing, concerning Perceval's sister,
one of the most beautiful characters in all Arthurian romance, a
character whom tradition closely associates with Galahad. The
Conte del Graal of Chrétien de Troyes does not mention her, nor
is she found in Wolfram von Eschenbach's *Parzival*. One of Chrétien's continuators, Gautier de Doulens, mentions her as conveying
to Perceval the story of his mother's death. Malory's account of
her, from which Tennyson drew, is practically the same as that
found in the Old French *Queste*.[15]

When the white-armoured Galahad, the youngest of Arthur's
knights, to whom the King had said when he dubbed him knight,
" God make thee good as thou art beautiful," hears of the vision,
Perceval notices that his eyes take on a striking similarity to his
sister's.

> His eyes became so like her own, they seem'd
> Hers, and himself her brother more than I.

---

[15] For the Gautier de Doulens version, see Nutt, p. 16. Also Potvin, iv,
ll. 25745-25944. A similar incident to that found in Gautier occurs in the
so-called Didot *Perceval*. (See Nutt, p. 30; Hucher, Vol. 1, pp. 446, 447.)

It is in delicate touches such as this that Tennyson reveals the deeply spiritual meaning of the *Idylls*. United by the mystical bond that is Christ, the soul of the nun and Galahad are transformed, so that they live, now, not they, but Christ lives in them; and, as in *The Coming of Arthur,* Queen Bellicent had noticed, upon the taking of the vows, that there flashed through the faces of Arthur's knights the momentary likeness of the King, so now Galahad and the nun, vowed to the same divine quest, mirror the image of Christ Whom they follow. This spiritual union is further symbolized by the sword-belt which Perceval's sister weaves from her hair and girds upon Galahad.

> But she, the wan sweet maiden, shore away
> Clean from her forehead all the wealth of hair
>
> .   .   .   .
>
> And out of this she plaited broad and long
> A strong sword-belt . . .
> . . . and bound it on him
> Saying, " My knight, my love, my knight of heaven,
> O thou, my love, whose love is one with mine,
> I, maiden, round thee, maiden, bind my belt.
> Go forth, for thou shalt see what I have seen,
> And break thro' all, till one will crown thee king
> Far in the spiritual city." And as she spake
> She sent the deathless passion in her eyes
> Thro' him, and made him hers, and laid her mind
> On him, and he believed in her belief.

In the Old French *Estoire* and the *Queste,* the belt so mysteriously fashioned and girded upon Galahad was the proof, or one of the proofs, of his predestined position as Grail knight. Tennyson neglects the prophetic significance of the belt, and prefers to let it stand as a symbol of the spiritual love existing between Galahad and Perceval's sister. The " spiritual city " of which the nun speaks is also a slight innovation of Tennyson's, since the earlier versions speak of a " spiritual palace " in the city of Sarras.[16]

Perceval then goes on to describe for Ambrosius the year of miracles. He tells of how Galahad, hearing the story of the Siege

---

[16] In the *Grand Saint Graal* it is called *li palais esperiteus.* Hucher, 11, p. 128. Malory, Book XVII, chapters 11, 21 and 22.

Perilous, which Merlin had fashioned, and in which "no man could sit but he should lose himself," suddenly cried,

> If I lose myself, I gain myself

and forthwith seated himself in the Perilous Siege. Then all at once, amidst a cracking of roofs and peals of thunder, there appeared

> A beam of light seven times more clear than day:
> And down the long beam stole the holy Grail
> All covered with luminous cloud

and the knights were struck dumb with wonder and " every knight beheld his fellow's face as in a glory."

In Tennyson's version it is Perceval who first vows to follow the Grail, while in Malory and in most of the earlier versions it is Gawain who takes the initiative. Because Perceval has not *seen* the Grail he vows to ride a twelve-month and a day in quest of it, and so it is with Bors, Gawain, and the other questers. Still weak in faith, they must *see* in order to believe; they are not content with merely the outward manifestations of inward grace. Galahad alone possesses the faith that pierces the veils of sense and transcends the bonds of space and time. Galahad alone *sees* the Grail.

> " But I, Sir Arthur, saw the Holy Grail,
>   I saw the Holy Grail, and heard a cry—
> ' O Galahad, and O Galahad, follow me! ' "

Some critics find here a strange discrepancy in Tennyson's allegory, in view of the fact that the old romances considered *seeing* the Grail as tantamount to the achievement of the Quest. As Gurteen points out,[17] not even Galahad is allowed to *see* the Grail until the quest is virtually at an end. He says: " If Galahad had *seen* the Holy Grail, there was no longer any need of a vow, for to him, the Quest was achieved." Thus he believes Tennyson has somewhat confused the point at issue, and substantially detracted from the purity of the original story. In Wolfram's *Parzival,* it is interesting to note that only the baptized can see the Grail. Thus, Parzival's half-brother Feirefiz, who is a heathen, is not permitted a vision of

---

[17] Gurteen, *The Arthurian Epic,* p. 258, 259.

the Grail, even in the hall of Monsalvat, until he has received baptism.

In the Old French *Queste,* King Arthur's reaction to the vow comes in the form of a reprimand to Gawain: " Ha, Gawain, thou hast betrayed me! This day hast thou deprived me of the most loyal company that ever I have found!" Arthur's grief is the natural outcome of his sense of loss and departed glory.

" Never had any Christian king so many good knights as myself this day nor when they part shall ever they be gathered at one table, as up to this time they have been." [18]

Tennyson's Arthur has a deeper spiritual insight; his lament is not for himself but for his knights, to whom he foresees the Grail will be as a sign that will be contradicted. Like the ancient Simeon holding the Light of the World in his arms, and prophecy-ing that this Child shall be set for the resurrection and the fall of many in Israel, Arthur, standing sorrowful in the midst of his knights, warns them against following " wandering fires " of doubt, and losing themselves in the quagmire of sin. Too well he knows that for Galahad alone the vision is, and for the nun, Perceval's sister. These have seen a sign, says Arthur,

" A sign to main this Order which I made."

The discerning king, knowing that presumption is grounded in pride, asks his over-confident knights whether they consider them-selves all Galahads. He reminds them that, in a quest such as they have sworn to follow, even Lancelot's skill will little avail. But now it is too late; the knights are foresworn, and Arthur is power-less to prevent them. The next day, after one last tournament, in which Galahad and Perceval distinguish themselves, the quest begins.

Perceval's presumption is soon turned into despair, when he remembers his sins.

" And every evil thought I had of old,
And every evil deed I ever did,
Awoke and cried, ' This quest is not for thee! ' " [19]

---

[18] Newell, Vol. 2, pp. 165, 167.

[19] An interesting comparison might be drawn between the Perceval quest in Tennyson's *Holy Grail* and the quest of the Soul in Francis Thompson's

One morning in a vale, "low as the hill was high, and where the vale was lowest" (the description of the place is significant of the truth Perceval is to learn), he hears from the lips of a hermit that what he lacks most is the virtue of humility, that "highest virtue, mother of them all." With the loss of humility, Perceval has lost the singleness of purpose which would have enabled him to follow the vision unhesitatingly. Instead of the Grail, he has been thinking of his sins and past failures. Unlike Galahad, he has not "lost himself to save himself," and therefore his quest has been fruitless. Scarcely has the hermit finished speaking, when Galahad in silver armor suddenly appears, and kneels with Perceval at the "sacring of the mass." After mass, Perceval tells Galahad that he saw nothing during the sacred ceremony but the elements of bread and wine. But Galahad, from whom the vision of the Grail has never departed since first he beheld it at Camelot, in a transport of joy exclaims:

> "Saw ye no more? I, Galahad, saw the Grail,
> The Holy Grail descend upon the shrine;
> I saw the fiery face as of a child
> That smote itself into the bread and went;
> And hither am I come; and never yet
> Hath what thy sister taught me first to see,
> This holy Thing, fail'd from my side, nor come
> Cover'd, but moving with me night and day,
> Fainter by day but always in the night
> Blood-red, and sliding down the blackened marsh
> Blood-red, and on the naked mountain top
> Blood-red, and in the sleeping mere below
> Blood-red . . .
>   But my time is hard at hand,
> And hence I go; and one will crown me king
> Far in the spiritual city; and come thou, too,
> For thou shalt see the vision when I go."

Armed with a spiritual strength which flows from this constant vision of the Grail, Galahad rides through the world shattering all evil customs, subduing pagan nations, and, as Perceval's sister

Hound of Heaven. Some of the passages are strikingly similar, and the scheme of the two is nearly identical. Perceval, like the Soul in Thompson's poem, looks to many things for happiness,—nature, human comforts, children, fame, wealth,—all crumble into dust at his touch.

prophesied, breaking through all till he come forth victor. One thing alone is wanting—the kingship of the Spiritual City, perfect union with God, the ecstasy of the Beatific Vision. To the great ocean that divides time and eternity Galahad speeds; across the thousand piers extending into the open sea he swiftly runs, and, as he crosses the countless bridges made of dead kings' bones, each bridge is quickly burned behind him—a symbol of the perfect soul's complete detachment from earthly ties. Perceval, powerless to follow, stands on the shore and sees the heavens suddenly open and "blazed with thunder such as seemed shoutings of all the sons of God." Over Galahad's head hangs the Holy Grail, "clothed with white samite as a luminous cloud," while the boat in which he moves seems to become a living creature clad with wings.[20] And now Perceval knows the veil has been withdrawn, and he has been permitted a vision of the Grail. He says:

> "I saw the spiritual city and all her spires
> And gateways in a glory like one pearl—
>
> .   .   .   .
>
> Strike from the sea; and from the star there shot
> A rose-red sparkle to the city, and there
> Dwelt, and I knew it was the Holy Grail [21]
> Which never eyes on earth again shall see."

---

[20] These lines recall the passage in the *Purgatorio* of Dante, where the poet sees the boat with its angelic pilot approaching over the mystic sea. "And . . . appeared to me . . . a light along the sea coming so swiftly that no flight equals its motion. . . . Again I saw it brighter become and larger. Then on each side of it appeared to me a something I know not what, white, and beneath, little by little, another came forth from it. My Master still said not a word, until the first white things showed themselves wings; then, when he clearly recognized the pilot, he cried out, "Mind, mind thou bend thy knees. Lo! the Angel of God: fold thy hands. . . . See how he scorns human means, so that he will not oar, or other sail than his own wings between such distant shores."—Dante, *Purgatorio* 11.

[21] Compare Milton's description of the celestial city, *Paradise Lost*, Bk. II, ll. 1047-1050. All through the *Idyll of the Grail* Tennyson's use of color is most noticeable. Galahad's armour is white or silver, which, of course, is a symbol of purity. Medieval symbolism took red for the symbol of this virtue; red also signified burning love and zeal. Perceval's sister sees the Grail as rose-red; to Bors it appears as a rosy glow like that of a taper held to the fingers of a hand; Galahad on mountain, marsh, or mere, sees the Grail in blood-red color; Perceval beholds it above the head of

In the account of Galahad's passing, Tennyson has differed radically from the old romancers. While emphasizing the spiritual, Tennyson has neglected one of the most touchingly human episodes of the Galahad's quest, his farewell of his brother questers Bors and Perceval, and his last message to his father Lancelot. This latter relation, however, Tennyson never seriously regarded; in fact, he seems deliberately to avoid the matter of Galahad's parentage. In one sweeping rhetorical question, in the early part of the *Idyll,* he summarily dismisses the suggestion of Lancelot's parenthood:

> " For when was Lancelot wanderingly lewd? "

" He thereby removes the (to him) distasteful Galahad conception incident related by Malory (XI, ii) . . . but he thereby also reduces the human interest of the Grail story. The touching meeting of Lancelot and Galahad and their living together for a half year . . . loses its point if Galahad be not Lancelot's son, and Tennyson correctly omits it. But his omission, nevertheless, robs the *Idyll* of much of its interest. It also robs Lancelot of the glory of participating vicariously in Galahad's successes." [22]

One after another the questers return to court and relate to Arthur their several adventures, but, of all the knights who started forth, only three, Sir Bors, Perceval, and the penitent Lancelot, are successful. When the worldly Gawain, drawn aside by the allurements of his merry maidens, openly voices his contempt for all such future quests, saying that henceforth he " will be deafer than the blue-eyed cat to holy virgins and their ecstasies," the king hurls at him this sharp rebuke:

> " Deafer . . .
> Gawain, and blinder unto holy things
> Hope not to make thyself by idle vows,
> Being too blind to have desire to see."

Galahad redder than any rose. Although its light to Lancelot is as of a furnace seven times heated, he sees it covered with crimson samite. Dante, in his *Paradiso* thus describes the angelic host: " Their faces were all of living flame, and their wings of gold; and the rest so white that no snow reaches that extreme."—*Canto XXXI.*

[22] App, A. J., *Lancelot in English Literature,* p. 170.

Lancelot, conscious of his deep-rooted sin, is for a long time held
back by despair of ever attaining the quest. Finally, with heroic
effort, he resolves to tear this sin from his soul. Like Galahad he
cries, " I will lose myself," and " in the great sea (I will) wash
away my sin." This magnificent trust, coupled with true repentance, gives Arthur's mightiest knight a distant glimpse of the
Grail.

> " And but for my madness and my sin,
>   And then my swooning, I had sworn I saw
>   That which I saw; but what I saw was veiled
>   And covered."

"Yet the veil was not the ' luminous cloud ' that shrouds it from
the knights; it is of deeper hue than the Grail itself as it appeared
to the eyes of Perceval or Bors. In the agonized glimpse, of which
he cannot be sure, Lancelot comes next to Galahad not in clearness, but intensity of vision; though in his remorse he is not aware
of his success and concludes sorrowfully, ' This Quest was not for
me ! ' " [23]

Tennyson's purpose in all the *Idylls,* but particularly in *The
Holy Grail,* is an ethical and spiritual one, and he fashions his
various episodes and characters to serve this end. Those who
would accuse him of having wandered too far from the original
story,[24] must remember that his intention was not (as was often
the case with the old romancers) merely to entertain; he realized
with a kind of religious awe that the poet's function is chiefly to
instruct, to warn, to inspire, to be in a sense the interpreter of God
to men. Like all the great writers of his age, Tennyson was
emphatically a teacher, and a teacher conscious of the sac-
redness of his calling. Out of the chaos produced by the French
Revolution in the preceding age, he sought to bring order, particularly order in the spiritual world, working out the perfect man.
This was the theme of all his works: the orderly development of
law in the natural and in the supernatural world. Certainly this
was a new philosophy in poetry, but Tennyson's message does not
end here. He gives this law an infinite and personal source, and

[23] MacCallum, M. W., Tennyson's *Idylls of the King and the Arthurian
Story,* p. 394.
[24] Weston, J. L., *Sir Lancelot du Lac,* p. 114.

shows that the supreme purpose behind all law is a manifestation of divine love. In the light of his doctrine, all earthly love becomes an image of heavenly love, and faith is the only reasonable attitude toward death and life and all life's baffling problems, even though man understands them not. " Perhaps," says Chesterton,[25] " he might have been something more of a poet, if he had not sought to be something more than a poet." And he adds, " But there are some things that are greater than greatness: there are some things that no man with blood in his body would sell for the throne of a Dante, and one of them is to fire the feeblest shot in a war that really wants decision, or carry the meanest musket in an army that is marching by." This Tennyson did in his defense of " the ordered life," as opposed to the revolutionary theories that arose with the advance of the new science. To him, " the lame hands of faith " were far more powerful than the skilled hands of science, and in his philosophy, faith always takes precedence over the highest reaches of intellectual attainment.[26] In spite of his fanciful wanderings from the beaten paths of traditional lore, Tennyson at least remained true to his inner vision, and had the fine courage to report that vision faithfully to men.

Tennyson's Galahad is his own conception of the highest ideal of a spiritual manhood. " What matters it how much a man knows and does," he wrote,[27] " if he keep not a reverential looking upward? He is only the subtlest beast in the field." Galahad, more than any of Tennyson's characters, represents this " reverential looking upward," this striving towards the goal as the Apostle expresses it.[28] " Never," says Galahad to Perceval, " hath this holy Thing failed from my side." And Jowett tells us [29] that

---

[25] Chesterton, G. K., *Tennyson*, p. 8.

[26] The following lines illustrate the poet's philosophy, and show his fear of advancing materialism:

> Hold thou the good: define it well:
> For fear divine Philosophy
> Should push beyond her mark, and be
> Procuress to the Lords of Hell.   *In Memoriam*, LIII.

[27] To Emily Sellwood, who later became his wife. The letter is quoted in the *Works of Tennyson*, edited by his son, Hallam Lord Tennyson, p. xxvii.

[28] *Corinthians* ix, 26.

[29] *Works of Tennyson*, edited by Hallam Tennyson, p. xxiii.

Tennyson's habitual thought of Christ was that of an old saint or mystic rather than of a modern rationalist. " My most passionate desire," wrote the poet shortly before his death, " is to have a clearer vision of God." An on the day of his death he said, " What a shadow this life is, and how men cling to what is after all but a small part of the great world's life." [30] A man of such high ideals and deep spirituality was eminently qualified to interpret the Galahad character, and no doubt his success in delineating the Grail hero lay in his ability to experience vicariously Galahad's exalted spiritual emotion. What our hero lacks in the quantity of Tennyson's poetry he gains in most exquisite quality. The Galahad of Tennyson is a challenge to a world of increasing materialism, a symbol of the spirit in combat with the flesh,—the expression of the divine law working out the Perfect Man.

[30] *Ibid.*, p. lv.

CHAPTER IX

GALAHAD AFTER TENNYSON

By the last quarter of the nineteenth century Tennyson had completed his epic of Arthur, and the popularity he had given the legends tended greatly to an increased productivity in Arthurian fields. No one, however, attempted to rival Tennyson in his epic treatment of the legends, and the inclination of writers was either to dramatize the story [1] or to center their interest upon themes more or less neglected by the Victorian laureate. Thus Swinburne in 1882 published his *Tristram of Lyonesse,* and fourteen years later his *Tale of Balen,* both of which works gave their respective heroes a prominence not enjoyed in the *Idylls.* Moreover, the tendency of the nineteenth century writers was to modernize the story, either by changing the nature of the characters, as Heber did, or by making them point contemporary morals, as did Matthew Arnold in *Tristram and Iseult,* James Russell Lowell in *The Vision of Sir Launfal,* and above all Tennyson in the *Idylls.* These writers, in their efforts to bring the age-old legends in conformity with contemporary feeling, did not, however, destroy the spirit and incident of the original stories; they merely gave to them more vivid coloring and a more human appeal.

The most radical departure from Arthurian tradition since the days of Bulwer Lytton's *King Arthur* (1848) came from the pen of an American, Richard Hovey, whose treatment of Galahad is perhaps the best illustration of modern thought, and of his own general attitude towards the old romances. Before his early death,

---

[1] In 1895 was enacted J. Comyns Carr's play, *King Arthur.* Perceval is the Grail hero, and Galahad is not mentioned. Elaine of Astolat occupies the place of prominence usually accorded Galahad's mother, Elaine of Corbin. In the same year was published Henry Newbolt's play, *Modred.* In recent years the best known plays dealing with the Arthurian story are: Martha Kinross' *Tristam and Iseult* (1913), Thomas Hardy's *Tragedy of the Queen of Cornwall* (1923), Laurence Binyon's *Arthur* (1923), and John Masefield's *Tristan and Isolt* (1927). Galahad is mentioned in none of these.

143

in 1900, this young Dartmouth graduate, projected under the title *Lancelot and Guenevere, A Poem in Dramas* a whole series of masques and dramas dealing with the Arthurian story. Four parts of this work, two lyrical masques, *The Quest of Merlin* and *Taliesin,* and two plays, *The Marriage of Guenevere* and *The Birth of Galahad,* were published during his lifetime. Fragments of his unfinished *Holy Graal,* together with outlines and plans for other unexecuted works, were published by Mrs. Hovey after her husband's death.[2]

Galahad occupies a unique place in the works of Hovey in that he is here the child of Guenevere and Lancelot instead of the child of Lancelot and Elaine. In thus violating the traditional story Hovey is as unscrupulous as Bulwer Lytton, and no two nineteenth century writers were more anachronistic in their treatment of Arthurian themes. His *Poem in Dramas,* Hovey maintained, was a retelling of the central drama (the Lancelot-Guenevere theme), about which the other legends of the cycle are grouped. " The version of Malory has been followed as a basis," he says, " but in many details other authorities have been preferred, nor has the author thought it beyond his privilege to alter and invent largely for himself." [3] Indeed, as Bliss Carmen observes, " Hovey was not primarily interested in the legends merely for their historic and romantic value. He chose the story of Guenevere and Lancelot for the sake of the psychological problem it involves and illustrates. It was the inward significance of the old tale, so apt and familiar a case in point, that formed its supreme value in his considerations. . . . He had at heart and in mind some frank solution of perplexing human relationships, and needed an adequate plot to make his solution clear." [4] The problem which Hovey attempted to solve

[2] Richard Hovey was born in Normal, Illinois, May 4, 1864. His early years were spent chiefly in Washington, D. C., and at his mother's home in Andover, Mass. He was graduated from Dartmouth College in 1885, and in 1886 entered the Theological Seminary of the Episcopal Church at Chelsea Square, N. Y., but remained in that institution only a year. Towards the end of his life he was a professor of English Literature at Barnard College, New York. He died in that city in the spring of 1900.

[3] Hovey, Richard, *The Holy Graal,* p. 20.

[4] Carmen, B., *Introduction to Hovey's Holy Graal,* p. 8.

was the age-old problem of squaring the ethical code of men with
the exemptions which the frailties of supermen have demanded that
their self-expression may be unhampered. " He was not attempting
a comedy of manners but a harmonody of ethics, and the Arthurian
story afforded a modern instance stripped of modern dress." [5] Here
is a clear example of the subjectivism prevalent in our modern
literature, an outgrowth of the rationalism of the sixteenth and
eighteenth century. It is based upon the principle that morality
is what it is conceived to be subjectively, and accordingly whatever
the author touches upon he colors with his individual moods. How
well Richard Hovey succeeded can be seen by a brief examination
of Galahad's rôle in the poet's works.

The Birth of Galahad, a well-rounded drama in five acts, has
for its central theme the love of Lancelot and Guenevere, with its
flowering in the birth of their son Galahad.

Act. I. Ylen, daughter of King Pelles, and the lifelong friend of Guenevere, agrees to claim the parentage of the latter's child by Lancelot, in order
to shield the lovers from the wrath of the King. In a garden of Lyoness
the two young women discuss the birth of Guenevere's child, when a messenger arrives with reports of Launcelot's success in arms, and a message
from Merlin, in which he intimates his knowledge of Guenevere's secret.
Launcelot, fighting Arthur's wars, is torn between loyalty to his King and
love for his King's Queen.

On Easter Sunday Guenevere's child is born, and the third day after is
christened Galahad, for Launcelot who was named Galahad in baptism.
The day of Galahad's christening, Guenevere dispatches a letter to Launcelot, informing him of Galahad's birth, and of her intention of coming to
Rome. Merlin, present at the child's baptism, rebukes Guenevere for trying
to deceive him, and Guenevere, knowing it is useless to hide anything from
Merlin, admits that she is prouder of her child than of her crown. Merlin
advises Guenevere for the good of the state to continue her policy of
secrecy, and prophesies great things concerning the child. He says:

> " I behold this child
>   Grown to a man; the armor that he bears
>   Is silvern pale; he stands among the knights
>   Like a white birch among grim-visaged pines;
>   He is like a moon-lit pillar in the night;
>   And angels float unseen above his head,
>   Bearing the Holy Graal."

---

[5] *Ibid.,* p. 9.

Merlin tells the Queen that her child has been foretold in prophecy since King Evelac's time; that it was of Galahad the seers spoke when they said there should come a knight without peer, a stainless knight set apart unto the Lord. His arm, they said, should be like David's, and his sword like Michael's when he leads the seraphim.

> "None shall withstand him; the immaterial fiend
> Dare not affront the flame along his blade.
> So shall he pass across the twilight world
> Like a white meteor and disappear
> None knoweth how or whither."

Guenevere says she knows her child is strange and holy, for in the still hours she has heard the footfalls of celestial visitants. Bitterly she laments the fate that keeps her from acknowledging Galahad as her son.

> "Never to call him son, never to feel
> His little arms about my neck, never
> To hear his wakening spirit turn to mine. . . .
>   . . . and even now
> To leave him! "

But bravely she resolves to watch him from afar, and "Though great gulfs of silence lie between us," she says, "his glory will be trumpets in my heart."

Act II. Dagonet, the court Jester, bearing Guenevere's letter, is captured by the Romans, and in spite of his clever maneuvers to conceal it, is unsuccessful. The Roman generals seize this opportunity of weakening Arthur's forces by setting up a bitter feud between the British king and his bravest soldier. Moreover, Lucius the Roman emperor plans to have Guenevere for himself. Dagonet escapes and tells Launcelot of the captured letter and its contents. Launcelot's one thought now is to get the letter and to save the Queen. The second act closes with Launcelot's soliloquy over Galahand.

> "Yet to have a son!
> That's worth an agony. Born of such a mother!
> How his achievements will keep life a joy!
> The day he puts his armor on, unblazoned,
> And goes to his first victory, what pride
> To see his helmet glittering in the sun!
>
> . . . .
>
> A son's accomplishment is ours for triumph
> Not ours for selfward shame."

Act III. Dagonet, in order to keep in touch with Roman affairs, attaches himself as scribe to the court poet Vaconius. The latter, ambitious for the emperor's favor, prepares an elaborate entertainment in the imperial gardens. In the midst of the performance the doors of the palace suddenly open, and Guenevere as a captive appears before them. Struck by her amazing beauty, the emperor is more than ever resolved upon winning her love, but all his advances are met with contemptuous scorn.

Act IV. Launcelot, eager to ascertain the whereabouts of Guenevere's letter, enters the Roman camp by night. Publius and Bursa, two scheming Roman generals, promise to give it to him if he will renounce his allegiance to Arthur and espouse the Roman cause. Launcelot spurns their traitorous suggestions, declaring that he loves his King howsoever his life belies it. Publius then endeavors to win him through a consideration of the Queen's honor. He pictures what may happen should gossip touch her fair name; how that "miracle of flesh" may be consigned to the flames, if Arthur's eyes should light upon the letter. Still unable to shake Launcelot's fealty to the King, Publius finally discloses the fact that even now the Queen is within the Roman lines, and that at any moment she is at the mercy of the emperor. Unless Launcelot yields, the Queen will suffer one of two fates—the funeral pyre or Caesar's arms! The Queen is then brought forth, and the two lovers are left to decide their fate. When they are alone Launcelot inquires eagerly for Galahad. "He is watched over," Guenevere assures him. "Where he is, one is brushed by the unseen, and the air thickens with the hush of shadows." When morning dawns Publius finds Launcelot more than ever resolved to remain faithful to his King.

Act. V. Guenevere, held a captive in the imperial palace, persistently spurns the emperor's passionate advances. In a last desperate effort to win her love, Lucius produces the letter which she had written to Launcelot. Seeing her startled but still inflexible, he threatens to send the telltale document to Arthur, and Dagonet the scribe is commanded to make a copy of the letter. At last the little jester has his long-hoped-for advantage. Holding the letter above the burning taper prepared for the royal seal, Dagonet destroys the evidence, and before the frenzied emperor has time to speak, Dagonet has disappeared. At the same moment a messenger reports that the enemy has burst the Roman gates. Launcelot, fighting his way to the palace to rescue Guenevere, is severely wounded, and Lucius orders Launcelot to be bound, and in his very presence approaches Guenevere with malign intent. Launcelot bursts his bonds, springs upon Lucius, grapples with him, and finally throws him to the pavement below. The populace in wild excitement clamor for Arthur to be made king; the bells ring out a joyous *Te Deum*, and the Pope himself comes to place the crown of Rome upon Arthur's head. A messenger arrives from Cameliard with letters for Arthur and the Queen. The latter's is from Merlin, and reading it silently apart she whispers to Launcelot, "All is well with him (Galahad)."

Thus the play closes as it opened with a reference to Galahad, who serves as an invisible cord binding together the action of the whole, and is the hero of the play which bears his name only in so far as he is the concrete embodiment of Launcelot and Guenevere's love.

In justification of this entirely new conception of the Grail hero Mrs. Hovey says: [6] " We have the creation of a Galahad who could be to the thought of our time what the Galahad of the legend was to the knightly thought of the Middle Ages. He was no witchcraft-engendered abnormality. He was a spirit engendered in the highest love, and his purity was ultimation, not elimination. He is to the modern mind what the Galahad of Malory or the Parsifal of Eschenbach and Wagner is to the medieval-minded Christian. Galahad's pure soul grew as the form of blessing which only the miracle, the mystic love can bring to earth. It belongs to the realms that are above the social order."

Thus, the Galahad who came into the world centuries ago to incarnate " chastity," the protecting virtue of the social order, is offered to us as one belonging to the " realms which are above " and incidentally opposed to it. Pauphilet took pains to show that the virtues of the first Galahad were less personal than social. He freed castles of their enchantments, relieved the entombed knight from his tortures, restored soundness to the Maimed King. His zeal for the social order being to him but part of the Divine Plan in the universe, makes him a dull, uncomprehending creature indeed in the light of Hovey's thesis. This " miracle of mystic love " was throughout the ages a reproach to his father, not because he had been born but because he possessed in himself a restraint, a mastery of self which Lancelot could not command. At least so thought the benighted medieval writers. And that mystic love is a beautiful thing taken in itself, because love is a going out to that which is good, but when it works an injustice on another of God's creatures (as it certainly did on Arthur), it becomes a bit less mystic, and we are less sure that it has the special exempting sanction of the God Who watches over the lives of every one of His creatures. Moreover, the attempt to justify Launcelot's and Guenevere's guilt destroys to some extent the artistic value of the story, since it is precisely this conflict which constitutes the matter of the drama.

[6] *Introduction to Hovey's Holy Graal*, p. 12.

Without the consciousness of their wrong, there is no need of the breathless suspense, the tragic climax, the heartbreaking close.

No nearer the original conception are Hovey's references to Galahad in *Taliesin,* a masque of three movements, with scenes laid respectively: (1) in the forest of Broceliande, (2) in Helicon, and (3) in the Chapel of the Graal. Taliesin the poet and Perceval are the principal characters, although Merlin, Nimue, and King Evelac have prominent parts.

Galahad is not mentioned until the third movement when, in the Chapel of the Graal, the aged king Evelac relates to Perceval the story of the Graal.

He (Evelac) was a king at the time of Christ's birth, and after Christ's death the Arimathean Joseph came to Evelac in the " wild North " where he reigned, and with him he brought " the Cup of Mystery men call the Graal." Evelac rashly attempted to touch the sacred vessel, and for his presumption was sorely wounded. Centuries pass while Evelac waits for Galahad to come to heal him of his wound, and " lift the Graal up like a vasty torch blazing God's beacon in the gulfs of sky." The Grail knight will be born of Launcelot, the aged king tells Perceval. And since he (Perceval) is not Launcelot's son, the Graal is not for him. As he is speaking, the golden doors behind which the Graal is concealed open noiselessly, and the soft splendors of the Graal fill the place. But Perceval does not see the Graal, for seven angels all in gold stand before it, and in their midst, Uriel, who holds in his hand a flaming sword. He warns Perceval to approach no nearer, " until the pure light of perfection burns about him like an aureole." When Taliesin asks Uriel why the sinless Perceval is denied the gift of vision, the angel replies that Perceval's own soul bars him from God's bliss, and that he should " go back among his fellow men and learn to love and learn to give, forgetting the white beauty of his soul." When Galahad comes, he will teach Perceval the secret of perfect renunciation and perfect love.

> Let him await another who shall come, and sit in
>   the Siege of Perilous
> And live. In him he shall behold how light can
>   look on darkness and forgive;
> How love can walk in the mire and take no stain
>   therefrom.

The poet Taliesin then sees through a diamond sphere, which Uriel holds high above his head, the glory hidden behind the angels' golden wings, and the masque closes with the chant of the angels before the Graal.

Hovey's unfinished *Holy Graal* bade fair to be one of the best of the poet's Arthurian pieces. Unfortunately, we have nothing more than the first two acts, which Mrs. Hovey published together with a digest of the poet's notes, and a general plan of the entire play.[7]

[7] The following is an outline of Richard Hovey's unfinished Graal drama: The play opens at the Castle of Morgause, Queen of Orkney, with a scene of evil counsel between Morgause and Morgana her sister. Lamoracke, the lover of Morgause, comes to bid her good-by, saying that he has sworn a vow since he left her three days before; that a great wonder has happened at the Court of King Arthur, namely, that Galahad, the son of Launcelot, has taken the Siege Perilous at the Round Table; that a vision of the Holy Graal has appeared to the knights assembled, and that all have sworn an oath to follow it a twelvemonth and a day. Morgause lures Lamoracke from the idea of the quest, and wins him back to herself again. Thus he is the first knight to fail in the performance of his vow.

Launcelot before going on the quest confesses to Dubric, Archbishop of Canterbury, and receives his blessing. Arthur does not wish his knights to leave the court, but seeing Launcelot determined to go, he bids him Godspeed. Galahad then enters the hall and is presented by Launcelot to the king.

In the garden of Camelot we are introduced to Madelon, the saintly sister of Sir Perceval, and Sendal the temptress. The influence of these two women follows Galahad throughout the play, and from the notes it appears that Madelon dies, as in Malory's story, and that Sendal repents on realizing the purity and strength of Galahad, who releases her from her own evil nature. Before leaving the court, Launcelot and Galahad bid Guenevere good-by, and with this scene the first act ends.

At Tintagel, Morgause, Lamoracke, and Agravaine, plot together to send Sendal and Guimere, disguised in men's clothes, to meet the Graal knights on the road, pretending to be desirous of joining the quest and then to seduce them from the performance of their vow. Galahad and Perceval on their journey arrive at a beautiful garden, which turns out to be the courtyard of a brothel, and there they meet Sendal and Guimere.

In the next act there is an attempt to carry out the plan. The Graal knights meet the women in their masculine disguise. The women, being attacked in revenge for their treachery, are saved by Galahad. Sendal confesses the plot, which implicates Morgause and Lamoracke. Gawaine, Morgause's son, furious at his mother and Lamoracke, goes to Tintagel and kills them both, and gives up the quest of the Graal.

In another scene we are at Camelot again with King Arthur and Guenevere. A note for the last scene of the fourth act shows it to have been between Galahad and Launcelot at Glastonbury Abbey whither Launcelot

In her notes Mrs. Hovey remarks that Richard Hovey in his *Poem in Dramas* could not have intended to show that Galahad, the typical knight of purity, ·should have attained his height through any ascetic or otherwise morbid ideal of life. " Not by living less than the best," she says, " but by living all things better than the best is the whiteness of the soul attained." [8] In proof of this she quotes the lines from *Taliesin*:

> In him ye shall behold how light can look on darkness and forgive,
> How love can walk in the mire and take no stain therefrom.

Thus, Hovey's conception of Galahad shows how the spirit of rationalism in literature invariably tends to break away from the moorings of tradition, and to substitute the untrammeled expression of the individual which inevitably leads to bizarre conclusions and often to moral rebellion. If carried to its logical conclusions, the thesis would end in that extreme individualism and chaos which makes every man his own dogmatist, every writer his own moralist, and divides mankind into multitudinous sects without any fixed law or principle. Every man his own dogmatist means ultimately everybody his own moral code; and art for art's sake, interpreted in an individualistic sense, would be destructive of the very foundation of true art. While this Galahad may be an attempt to teach " how love can walk in the mire, and take no stain therefrom," still, as Maynadier remarks, " if love walks in the mire too often, it is likely to get smirched." [9]

Richard Hovey's use of the Arthurian story as " a modern instance stripped of modern dress " is exemplified in the work of his contemporary John Davidson, who, ten years after Tennyson's

comes on the miraculous ship which brings also the body of Madelon after her death. Here Galahad attains the Graal. From here Launcelot, broken in spirit, wanders away and is, in the next play (which was never written), cared for by Elaine. Finally restored to strength, he goes to Camelot, only to pass through new sufferings in the experience of the death of Elaine and the jealousy of Guenevere, and the death of Arthur.

The last act is at Camelot. The Court is assembled in the garden when Bors and Lancelot return. The play closes with a scene between Launcelot and Guenevere.—*Notes from Richard Hovey's Holy Graal*, p. 63 ff.

[8] *Notes on Hovey's Holy Graal*, p. 57.

[9] *Arthur of the English Poets*, p. 404.

last Arthurian poem [10] added one more brilliant production, *The Last Ballad* (1899), to the richest century of English Arthurian romance. Unique in conception and rich in poetic expression, this ballad of eighty-four iambic tetrameter quatrains, which tells the story of Lancelot's madness during the period of his self-imposed banishment from Arthur's court, and of Galahad's rescue of his half-crazed father, rivals in beauty and depth any work of the period. Here, as in Malory, the method of antithesis is employed in the portrayal of Galahad's success and Lancelot's failure in the attainment of an ideal.

Tortured with visions of Guenevere whose beauty stands between him and his loyalty to the King, Lancelot wanders through the wide spaces of the world, seeking redress for his outraged conscience in deeds of helpfulness to his King. But though he strives to forget her, everywhere her beauty haunts him.

> From heaven she bent when twilight knit
> The dusky air and earth in one;
> He saw her like a goddess sit
> Enthroned upon the noonday sun.

Irresolute of purpose, he turns once more towards Cameliard, towards " the sky that canopied, the tide that girdled Guenevere," but is scarcely ashore when he curses himself for his weakness, and doffing his armor dashes into the darkness of the forest. For a year he wanders like a madman, feeding upon berries, efts, and snails, and always and everywhere bemoaning his sin and his broken trust. At Easter when " the hyacinth and violet empurpled all the russet ways," he leaves the spell-bound wood and climbing to the top of a hill stands " alone above the prospect of the world." Here his memory begins to struggle vaguely for some guiding star

> Dimly he groped to see
> What star, what sun, what light should break
> And set his darkened spirit free.

Galahad is the star, the sun, the light that now appears to set his wretched father free.

> Afar he saw a horseman speed,
> A knight, a spirit clad in flame
> Riding upon a milkwhite steed.

The sun fires Galahad's golden arms as he advances, and Lancelot seeing him approach dimly remembers his days of departed glory and cries, "A

---

[10] *Merlin and the Gleam* (1889).

horse! a lance! to arms!" And weeping, he fingers Galahad's jeweled
bridle and handles Galahad's spear.

> The golden knight dismounting took
> Sir Lancelot by the hand and said,
> "Your voice of woe, your lonely look
> As of a dead man whom the dead
> Themselves cast out—whence are they, friend?"

For a moment Lancelot stands as though in doubt, then kneeling "makes
an end of all his madness," as he recognizes in the "spirit" before him
the face of his own son Galahad. Tenderly Galahad embraces his father
and, "Now I shall be your squire," he says, as gently he leads him to a
nearby castle and "clothed his body, clothed his heart in human garniture
once more."

But no matter how intense his love for his father, Galahad must follow
the Holy Grail, whose presence is as insistent to him as is Lancelot's vision
of Guenevere. He says to his father,

> "Afar or near, at noon, or night
>   . . . it fills
> My soul with peace, as heaven with light
> O'er flows when morning crowns the hills.
>
>   . . . through every veil
> And mutable device I know
> And follow still the Holy Grail."

And bidding his father farewell, like a spirit in flame, he departs.
Lancelot feels that from henceforth the bitterest of his struggle is past,
and now he too resolves to seek the Holy Grail, saying, "the very purpose
shall avail my soul."

Instead of taking Galahad's father at his word, the poet concludes by throwing over Lancelot's manly resolution the dark
shadow of cynicism and doubt. In vain, he says, does Lancelot
fight for the vision of the cup, and the poem ends where it began,
with the lonely figure of a man still plagued with desires he can
never fulfill, and tormented with hopes to which he can never
attain.

There is in Davidson's philosophy a note of fatalism entirely
foreign to the mind of the medievalists, who conceived the will
as free. With them it was not the Greek idea of necessity but the
Christian idea of responsibility which lay at the foundation of
all morality. With Malory, too, these characters do not find themselves enmeshed in hopeless circumstances; "the web which en-

11

tangles them is of their own weaving, and the doom which overtakes them, the destruction of the aims they have cherished, is the
solemn witness to the freedom they have enjoyed.   If the whole
nexus of events reveals unrelenting law, the individual characters
are never conceived as victims, for their choice shapes the events." [11]
Davidson, on the contrary, shows a suppression of the individual
will, which is almost Oriental in its fatalism, and suggests Schopen-
hauer in its mixture of fate and pessimism.   Although he knows
that following Galahad will avail his soul, Lancelot has not the
strength of purpose to carry his resolution into action.   The episode
of Lancelot's meeting with Galahad the poet uses to prove his thesis,
namely, that those who love are fated to love forever, and that
even the holiest contacts must minister to love's bitter-sweet
tyranny.   Instead of seeing in Galahad the spiritual resurrection
of his dead hopes and ideals, Lancelot beholds in the boy's eyes
" the darkling orbs of Guenevere," of her who claimed his thought
when Galahad was begotten.   It is but another phase of a theory
as old as Sophocles, and as melancholy as some of his heartbreaking
tragedies.

Beautiful in its lyric quality, *The Last Ballad* contains one of the
saddest stories ever told, and it is doubtful whether Malory or
Tennyson would have considered Lancelot had either thought, as
Davidson appears to do, that a man's moral conflict—the greatest
to which he is called—depends upon fate or the folly of the gods.

Diametrically opposed to Davidson's, is Conde B. Pallen's conception of Galahad's effect upon his sinful father Lancelot in the
latter's declining years.   In *The Death of Sir Launcelot* Dr. Pallen
pictures the erring knight after seven years as a monk in Canterbury, wasted with penance and self-denial, but filled with spiritual
peace and joy, his face transformed by prayer and union with God
into the likeness of Galahad.

> . . . the shining spirit burned and glowed
> Through flesh and bone worn to translucency,
> And all his face shone like Sir Galahad's.

Having passed through the crucible of suffering, Lancelot realizes
the smallness of his frame and

[11] Scudder, V. D., *Sir Thomas Malory's Morte Darthur*, p. 407.

That time is a shadow of eternity.

For God has many ways of drawing to Himself the hearts of men. . . .

> Some as Sir Galahad through innocence
> Whose white flower blossomed from his cradled years

others through disappointment in creatures, others like Lancelot through the dolorous way of penance, prayer, and fasting. But all of these elect must sooner or later come to realize, as did Lancelot, not with bitterness but with rapturous love, the *vanitas vanitatum* of which the wisest of kings sang. The wisdom which Galahad attained early in life, Lancelot learns in his declining years. And as keenly as of old he sought for human fame, Lancelot, remembering Galahad's courage,

> Strove mightily in prayerful contemplation
> To win the flashing splendor and the height.

Before it is too late, both he and Guenevere receive from on high the grace to discover " the canker at the root of love which runneth not the course of God." By separate paths which lead at length to God and endless union they together resolve to

> . . . storm the cidatel
> Of His vast mercy, each in other's prayers
> Winning Christ's mercy for the other's wound.

Here, as in Malory and Tennyson, we have that high hope and confidence in God's mercy which characterize His repentant saints. Thoroughly medieval in his philosophy, the author shows how the Church, as the mystical Body of Christ, lays hold of man's body and senses and passions, redeeming them by sanctifying grace, and how in the process of winning them back to God she at the same time ennobles and deepens them. In acute and prolonged conflicts with Gnostics, Manicheans, Albigenses, Bogomili, the Church has ever maintained an attitude of love and understanding towards man's nature, his bodily and sensitive structure, as well as his intellectual and spiritual powers. " As man came from the hand of God, in the beauty of his body, in the ardour of his sense life, in the storm and stress of his passions, with keen intellect and mighty will, even so does the Church affirm him and even so would she have him be. She would mould this man of ardent, stormy passions and clear-sighted strength so that he may belong to God, and that he may by union with the original basis of his life bring all the greatness and the glory of his natural gifts into inward harmony and perfection." [12] This is the truth which Dr. Pallen's poem conveys; this it is which gives to the religious element in the Arthurian story its comprehensive power of attraction. Galahad, though not actually present, is a vital force motivating the poem, and his spiritual relation to Lancelot's life of penitence must be understood if one wishes properly to appreciate the true significance of the work.

In the same year with C. B. Pallen's *Death of Sir Launcelot* came the first prose work of the twentieth century in which Galahad appears, namely, *The Book of Romance,* a juvenile work published in 1902 by Andrew Lang. Dr. Lang treats the world of romance much as a world of faery, for in his opinion "romances are only fairy tales grown up," and with him, " The whole mass of the plot and incident of romance was invented by nobody knows who, nobody knows when, nobody knows where." [13]

Dr. Lang's version is based mainly upon Malory's compilation, but the opening of the Grail story is adapted from Sebastian Evans' *High History of the Holy Graal.* In his introduction to the section dealing with the Holy Graal, the editor gives a brief history of the literary origins of the legend. " We must remember," he says, " that parts of these stories are very old; they were invented by the heathen Welsh, or by the ancient Britons, from whom the Welsh are descended, and by the old pagan Irish, who spoke Gaelic, a language not very unlike Welsh. Then these ancient stories were translated by the French . . . and Christian beliefs and chivalrous customs were added in the French romances, and, finally, the French was translated into English about the time of Edward IV by Sir Thomas Malory, who altered as he pleased. . . . The Graal is the holy vessel used by our Lord, and brought to Britain by Joseph of Arimathea. But in the older heathen Irish stories there

---

[12] Adam, Karl, *The Spirit of Catholicism,* p. 154.
[13] Preface to *The Book of Romance,* p. v.

is a mysterious vessel of a magical sort, full of miraculous food, and probably the French writers of the romances confused this with the sacred vessel brought from the Holy lands." [14]

The opening episode of the Graal story describes King Arthur's pilgrimage to the shrine of St. Augustine, and of the dream of his squire Chaus. The story then turns abruptly to the great gathering for the feast of Pentecost, but strangely enough it omits altogether the spectacular entrance of Galahad led by Joseph of Arimathea, and his achievement of the Siege Perilous. Galahad is already present among the knights when the Grail appears, and there is no apparent connection, as in Malory and the *Queste,* between the presence of the Promised Knight and the appearance of the Grail. This seems to be a rather serious omission as far as the artistic value of the story is concerned, since even children can appreciate the connection between these mysterious foreshadowings and Galahad's later successes. Moreover, since the esoteric and unearthly have an especial appeal for youthful minds, the incident of the Siege Perilous as well as that of the marvelous sword which Galahad drew from the floating stone (and which *The Book of Romance* neglects) would have greatly enhanced the story's worth and helped not a little towards the final resolution of events.

The second chapter recounts the story of Evelac's shield as related in Malory, as also the episode of the tombs, the Castle of the Maidens, and Galahad's successful encounter with Sir Lancelot and Sir Perceval. The manliness and courage of Galahad are especially stressed, and Galahad is presented as a hero worthy of any red-blooded youth's emulation. When, for example, the cavernous voice from the tombs warns him not to approach any farther, and the monks persuade him he is about to encounter a fiend, Galahad, nothing daunted, draws near the tomb, lifts the stone, and when out of it leaps "the foulest figure that was ever seen in the likeness of a man," Galahad does not flinch. Even the spirits of darkness must weaken before the power of the elect, and the fiend addressing Galahad says, "I see about thee so many angels that my power dare not touch thee." At the Castle of Maidens he overcomes single-handed seven knights, and even the great Sir Lance-

[14] *Ibid.*, p. 64.

lot is forced to admit the youth's superior prowess. When Galahad unhorses both Lancelot and Perceval, a nun in a nearby hermitage exclaims, " God be with thee, Galahad, thou best knight in the world."

The separate adventures of Lancelot, Perceval, Gawaine, and Bors, in the quest of the Graal, all follow Malory. The final episodes, likewise, are condensations of the earlier compilation adapted to juvenile intelligence. Galahad anoints the Maimed King and heals him, but nothing is said of the origin of the wound. The story of Galahad's parentage is likewise carefully avoided, and although he is everywhere alluded to as Lancelot's son, no explanation is given as to this relation. The filial devotion which characterizes the Galahad of Malory is even more noticeable here, and on the whole Dr. Lang has succeeded in depicting Galahad as the worthy exemplar of youth.[15]

[15] Many other juvenile works based upon Malory's *Morte Darthur* have given prominence and popularity to the Galahad character, but it would be out of the range of a study of this kind to examine each in detail. We might mention in passing a few of the best:

The Boy's King Arthur by Sidney Lanier. (1880, 1924). " Every word in this book," says Lanier, "except those which occur in brackets is Malory's, unchanged except that the spelling is modernized." (p. xxv). Lanier changed Caxton's " wholly unreasonable arrangement of twenty-one books " to six. Galahad's story occupies Book V.

The Story of King Arthur and the Knights of the Round Table by Dr. Edward Brooks, A. M. (1900). "Youth," says Dr. Brooks, "is a time for hero worship, and nowhere in literature can be found nobler examples of lofty heroism than in this story." (p. 3). Only the leading events have been taken, and these have been divested of unimportant and uninteresting details often found in the original. The author retains Malory's quaint language, but divides the story into eight books, the seventh of which treats of Galahad and the Grail.

The Age of Chivalry by Thomas Bulfinch. (1900). The editor states that he has drawn directly from Malory, especially in connection with the adventures of certain knights among whom he mentions Galahad.

King Arthur and His Noble Knights by Mary Macleod. (1902). The book is divided into seven parts, the sixth of which treats of Galahad. It is based entirely upon Malory.

King Arthur and His Knights by Maude R. Warren. (1902). This version follows Tennyson more closely than Malory, in that the author has Perceval relate the story of Galahad's adventures in pursuit of the

Far less effectively, though more closely than Dr. Lang, does Thomas de Beverley follow Malory in his portrayal of Galahad. Two of the seven Arthurian poems in his *Youth of Sir Arthour*

Grail. Instead of relating them to a monk, however, here he tells them to the king and the knights of the Round Table.

Stories of King Arthur and His Knights by U. Waldo Cutler. (1904). This version attempts to preserve, as far as may be, the language and spirit of Malory. The author says that he chose the stories best representing the whole, and modified them only to clarify the thought. Chapters XXV to XXXIV treat of Galahad.

Hamilton Wright Mabie includes Tennyson's lyric *Sir Galahad* in his *Legends Every Child Should Know.* (1906).

The Story of Sir Launcelot and *The Story of the Grail* (1910), by Howard Pyle. The two books are part of a series of four books pertaining to Arthur. The author identifies Elaine of Corbin with Elaine of Astolat. This noble lady dies giving birth to Galahad, and she commits her child to the care of Bors. Galahad is brought up by the nuns, and it is the abbess who tells Lancelot that Galahad is his son.

The Story of King Arthur by Winona C. Martin (1915). The present version, the author states, " grew out of a library hour," and is an attempt " to hold before the children of a materialistic age that vision without which the people perish." (p. iv). For obvious reasons, says the author, the versions of the masters have not always proved practicable in dealing with young children. Though her intention is good, the author fails to adhere to the simple style, and neither her choice of words nor her treatment of the story is particularly attractive.

King Arthur and the Knights of the Round Table edited by Clifton Johnson (1916). Whatever is unnecessary or morally doubtful in the original has been omitted, and in minor ways some recasting has been done, says the editor, but nothing essential has been sacrificed. One notable exception to this statement occurs, however, in the fact that the lady whom Lancelot frees from the scalding bath is Elaine of Corbin, who could not be relieved from the punishment Morgan le Fay had inflicted upon her until the best knight of the world had taken her by the hand. The castle in which he finds her is Corbin. Lancelot marries Elaine and Galahad is their child.

King Arthur and His Knights by Philip S. Allen. (1924). This is a greatly condensed version of Malory, divided into eight books. The story of Galahad and the Grail fills the eighth book.

King Arthur and His Knights by Elizabeth Merchant. (1927). This book based on Malory is a series of episodes in the story of the Grail. The story of Galahad's knighting and his appearance at the Round Table

(1925) [16] treat of Galahad; but these poems are for the most part only metrical transcriptions of Malory. *The Birth of Galahad* relates in one hundred and sixty-five lines of blank verse the story of Lancelot's visit to Corbenic, of his meeting with King Pelles and Elaine, and of Dame Brisen's sorcery in bringing Lancelot and Elaine together, in order to fulfill the prophecy concerning the

is a slight variant of the original. Nothing further is said of Galahad after his entrance into Arthur's court.

The Splendid Quest by Basil Matthews. (1929). This book is made up of stories designed to instill a spirit of leadership and bravery into the hearts of the young. There is no organic or chronological sequence in the arrangement, the story of Galahad, "The Knight of the Quest," appearing directly after the story of Abraham Lincoln. The facts are drawn from Malory, but they are too condensed for beauty, and the story has no climactic appeal.

Galahad Knight Errant by May E. Southworth. (1907). This is a brief idyllic prose sketch of Galahad's life, following Malory, and based for the most part on the episodes featured in Abbey's famous paintings in the Boston Public Library and in the House of Commons, London. In the Preface, which the author calls the Allegory, she briefly states Galahad's rôle and function in the world. "Galahad," she says, "seems best to typify the struggles of the human heart in seeking the Great Treasure, and reveals best how by a life of purity, a purity with a full knowledge of both good and evil, it is possible to have strength to overcome the bad and the grace to remain unsullied."

The book is divided into three parts: the Allegory, the Legend, and the Quest. The author describes the knighting of Galahad, his mysterious appearance at the Round Table, his departure for the Quest, his experiences at the Castle of the Grail, and his meeting with the loathely damsel; his conquest of the seven deadly knights outside the Castle of the Maidens, his freeing of the maidens, and his renunciation of Blanchefleur. She describes how he heals the wounded King Amfortas, and then departs in Solomon's ship for the city of Sarras, where after a year of spiritual kingship he is granted a vision of the Holy Grail and the Golden Tree, the symbol of his perfected works on earth.

Like Charles F. Bradley's *The Quest of the Holy Grail* (1896), and Sylvester Baxter's *Holy Grail: An Explanation* (1904), Miss Southworth's little book is a help toward a proper appreciation of the outstanding episodes in Galahad's life, and an aid to the correct interpretation of Abbey's magnificent paintings. While not claiming a place in the regular body of classical Arthurian literature, these three works admirably perform the service for which they were intended.

[16] Thomas de Beverley is the pseudonym of Thomas Newcomen.

Promised Knight. The incidents related are identical with those found in Book XI of Malory's *Morte Darthur,* and the poem ends with the visit of Bors to the Grail castle where he sees for the first time the infant Galahad. Although following Malory closely, de Beverley's prosaic verse borrows none of the charm and naïvete of Malory's quaint prose.

The Achievement of the Sangreale and the Death of Sir Galahad opens with the meeting of the three questers Bors, Perceval, and Galahad, at King Pelles' castle. Eleazar, Pelles' son, brings forth the marvelous sword with which Joseph of Arimathea had been wounded, and Bors and Perceval each attempt to piece the broken weapon and fail, but Galahad succeeds. The next day the three questers put out to sea, and although their various adventures are not related, they finally arrive at Sarras where after some time Galahad is crowned king.

> But little cared he for an earthly crown,
> For soon should he achieve the Holy Greale;
> Then would he die and gain a crown in Heaven.

A year from the day on which Galahad is proclaimed king, while assisting at Mass, he receives a summons to come forth to see what his soul has long desired to see. He is communicated at the hands of Joseph of Arimathea, and, after bidding farewell to his companions Bors and Perceval, he kneels a short while in prayer, and presently he sees a great multitude of angels come to bear his soul to heaven. At the same time the golden vessel and the spear are taken up to heaven by a " radiant hand."

There is nothing of outstanding importance in either of these two poems, nor is there any distinctive development of the character of Galahad. The works show, however, that in spite of this age of boasted materialism, interest in the Galahad material persisted. Indeed, at no period in our literary history has this interest in Galahad manifested itself with such startling contrasts as at the present decade. No two writers offer more diametrically opposed interpretations of Galahad than do Edwin Arlington Robinson and John Erskine. Before examining his rôle in the works of these two Amercan writers, we shall consider his treatment in the hands of Lord Hamilton.

Richard Hovey endeavored to legitimize Galahad's birth by placing Lancelot and Guenevere on a plane outside the moral order; after the first quarter of the twentieth century, an Englishman, Ernest Lord Hamilton, attempted a similar solution in that he completely destroyed the original story by making Galahad the lawful son of Lancelot by his much worshipped wife Elaine of Corbin, and Guenevere the scheming and unscrupulous courtesan striving however unsuccessfully for Lancelot's love. In thus exonerating Lancelot from his traditional rôle of illicit lover, Hamilton does not add to the dramatic value of the old story, a great part of which owed its appeal to the moral conflict in Lancelot's soul.

In the *Launcelot* of Lord Hamilton, Galahad enjoys a social dignity heretofore never accorded him, in that he is for the first time the offspring of a lawfully wedded pair.[17] Although such a change might affect the character of Galahad in the attitude of the modern mind, the fact remains that the Galahad of Hamilton is not basically different from the Galahad of Malory.

The romance consists of three parts: the first part deals with Lancelot's marriage to Elaine the daughter of King Pelles; the second part narrates Lancelot's experiences after he is called back to the court; and the third part (in which Galahad figures prominently), deals with the events related in the final chapters of Malory's *Morte Darthur.*

While his famous father is away fighting King Arthur's wars the child Galahad is carefully guarded and tended by his gentle mother Elaine, whose affection is divided between her infant son and her devoted husband. In the *Queste,* Bors is the first knight to visit Corbin and bring back to court the news of Lancelot's child; in Hamilton's version, it is Gawaine who first sees Galahad, with " a face like unto the angels of God and eyes that shone like stars." In the older romances, Lancelot is scarcely aware of Galahad's existence until the latter comes to claim the Siege Perilous and undertake the marvels of the quest; in the present romance Lancelot's mind is continually filled with thoughts of his wife and son, and no messenger is more welcome than one who brings news of them.

[17] Tennyson, it is true, never questions Galahad's legitimacy, but he does not give his genealogy.

The third part of the romance relates the story of Galahad's arrival at Camelot and his adventures in the quest of the Grail.

Galahad at sixteen, "grown tall and broad of shoulders and straight as the stem of a young sycamore tree," rides into Camelot dressed in red armour and bearing on his shoulder a white shield with a red cross. Launcelot leads him into the great hall where the Queen enlists him among her White Knights. That evening, when all are seated at the Round Table, Galahad, Perceval, and Bors, have a vision of the Holy Grail, whereupon Gawaine and the other knights vow to search for the Grail until they too have seen it.

After many months of fruitless questing, Lancelot arrives at Sarras where he finds Galahad dying. Not recognizing Lancelot, the nuns in attendance upon Galahad tell the strange knight that the boy is wasting away from the penances inflicted upon himself in atonement for his father's sins. Grief-stricken, Lancelot flings himself upon his knees before Galahad, asking him why he has done this, but Galahad gently replies that it was for the chastisement of the flesh. Lancelot knows that because of his sins, his guiltless son is dying.

At the same hour in which Galahad dies, his mother Elaine dies also, and Lancelot has them buried side by side in the nave of the chapel at Joyous Garde. Over their graves he gives vent to his grief, saying:

"Here lieth the sweetest lady and the fairest that ever drew breath in this sorrowful world, and with her lieth her most noble son, and because that they were dearer to me than any that ever bore life, I hereby make a vow before all that are here assembled that, in what part of the world soever I may die, my body shall be brought hither, if it be within the compass of my kin, and laid beside these two, my wife and my son, there to lie till the day when Christ shall summon us to rise." [18]

Thus in the matter of Galahad's death, as in many minor incidents of his life, Hamilton has recast and altered the original story, without however losing sight of that strictly spiritual atmosphere which everywhere surrounds the traditional Grail hero. Perhaps the most distinctive contribution which Hamilton makes to the development of the Galahad character is the definitely sacrificial rôle he assigns him in allowing him to offer his life for his father's salvation. For although Malory and Tennyson and other noted Arthurians have implied such a sacrifice, none of them give to this supreme act of love the prominence and pathos accorded it by Hamilton.

In noticeable contrast to the quiet dignity and moral tone of

[18] Hamilton, Ernest Lord, *Launcelot*, p. 239.

Hamilton's *Launcelot* is John Erskine's flippant, cleverly told novel, *Galahad.* Published in the same year, these two novels, closely allied in theme, but widely different in character, illustrate how diametrically opposed contemporary authors can be in their evaluation of legendary lore.

The year 1926 found John Erskine one of the most widely read interpreters of the character of the Grail hero. His *Galahad,* a modernization of the old romance, is a true book of our age in that it is a psychological prying into motives rather than a recital of objective facts. Though it presupposes the main episodes of the old romance, it utterly changes them to such a degree that when one finishes Mr. Erskine's very clever book, there is not any Galahad, or if there is, it does not matter much.

For if the truth be told, the book is not Galahad's but Guinevere's story, and her mission in life of " inspiring " three men in turn, Arthur, Lancelot, and Galahad, which ends in her " masterpiece " in the last instance, is an admirable analysis of a great woman. But the " masterpiece " itself is a thing of bitter irony, and Galahad, at the climax of the story, rides off on a negative quest, " to find a world with a new kind of men and women in it," an ungrateful, ungenerous, unlovable, and unloving prig.

There are nuances which give this version a new interest. Arthur, for instance, knows of the love of Lancelot and Guinevere, and decides " there was something to be said for the arrangement." The novel is divided into five parts, each of which is named for the character or episode dominating it. Part One deals with Elaine, Galahad's mother; Part Two: Elaine and Guinevere; Part Three: Guinevere and Galahad; Part Four: Galahad and the Quest; and Part Five: The White Elaine.

" The story begins," says the author,[19] " when Arthur, Guinevere, and Lancelot were young, four years after Arthur's wedding."

Elaine of Corbin goes to Camelot to ask Lancelot's advice concerning the rearing of their illegitimate son Galahad, and Lancelot, though deeply interested in the boy, does not wish to incur the queen's displeasure by too frequent meetings with Elaine. One day, however, the queen accidentally discovers him kissing Elaine, and seized with jealousy she banishes him

---

[19] *Galahad,* p. 16.

from her presence in spite of his protestations that he entertains toward Elaine only sympathy and pity. Soon after Lancelot's banishment the court hears that he has gone mad.

Seven years pass, and Lancelot's name ceases to be mentioned at Camelot. Meanwhile Elaine, having discovered the identity of the " madman," brings him to her castle and tenderly nurses him back to health and sanity. Then one bright day in spring the queen takes a fancy to go Maying as she had often done in her girlhood. Unaccompanied by any of her knights she and her two maids are seized by Sir Meliagrance and held captive in his castle. Sir Meliagrance calls for a champion to defend the queen knowing that there is not in Camelot a knight who is a match for him in prowess. The queen implores Bors to go in search of Lancelot and to tell him she asks his forgiveness. Bors carries the message to Corbin, and Lancelot rides back to Camelot.

Galahad at seventeen comes to Camelot to ask to be admitted to the order of knighthood. Lancelot, proud of the boy " with the build and carriage of an older man," shows great emotion as he touches the youthful shoulders with his sword and prays God to make the new knight good as he is beautiful. His chief concern is how to employ Galahad now that all of Arthur's wars are fought. But Galahad soon solves that problem for himself. " Like his father before him, Galahad found his way across the terrace to the door of the queen's tower." (p. 188). From the moment Guinevere lays eyes on Galahad, she begins to " inspire " him. She sees for him a new way of being a knight, a way different from his father's way, and Arthur's. His father and the king had created a state and a government. Galahad too must create. . . . Guinevere does not know just what he shall create, but she " feels the idea coming." She cautions him against falling in love, and especially against being made love to. " It distracts your attention," she says. Lancelot is slightly envious of the attention Guinevere lavishes on Galahad, and more than slightly annoyed at her manner of " inspiring " him. He resolves to save Galahad from having his life wrecked completely.

The king, not unmindful of what is transpiring, sends Galahad on a visit to Elaine, but Galahad remains at Corbin only a day. Returning to Camelot he meets Gawain who throws the first suspicions across his mind regarding his birth. Galahad confides his trouble to the queen, but finds her strangely tolerant of what to him is unpardonable sin. Unable to understand the queen's attitude, he tells her that if he finds it difficult to forgive his father, it is because of the ideals she herself has taught him. " I owe to you the vision I have of cleanness and strength," he says. And he asks whether she wishes him to unlearn it now. But Guinevere only evades his question and makes him promise that if ever he should have reason to be disappointed in her, he will give her up abruptly and cling to his ideals. If he does this, she tells him, he will be a greater man than his father.

Arthur resolves to send Galahad on a second and more hazardous errand. Meanwhile the boy hears Ettard, one of the queen's ladies, speak of Lancelot's " great love." Not knowing who it is his father loves, Galahad is more than ever perplexed and disgusted with Lancelot. He departs on his journey to the Duke of Lianors' Castle. When he returns eager and successful from his quest, the queen tells him the truth about Lancelot and herself. Galahad flees from the court, and is heard of no more.

Lancelot meets a second Elaine, who, like her namesake of Corbin, loves him at first sight, and persuades him to wear her token in the tournament at Winchester. The queen's jealousy is once more aroused until she discovers that the maid whose token Lancelot wore was not Galahad's mother, but Elaine of Astolat.

Lancelot enters the religious life and tells Brother Martin his story.

Such, then, is Erskine's *Galahad*. Perhaps the book has its intrinsic merits. As a story of a man of our times squaring high ideals with the shocking shortcomings of those whom he had idealized, it is an artistic piece of work. But it is not a story of Galahad, but rather a piece of insidious iconoclasm. One has only to look at the book's sub-title, *Enough of His Life to Explain His Reputation*, to realize that had Malory conceived of Galahad so cheaply, his story would not have lived these centuries to be explained.

The fault lies not in the fact that Galahad is permitted to think about his father and his mother, and Guinevere; he must have thought about them a great deal. It is rather in the utter lack of spirituality which makes him infinitely less than Lancelot and Arthur. His inspiration is an abstract ideal of Guinevere's, so limited in its perfection that it is unable to distinguish hatred of sin from hatred of sinner. His quest, which in the old romances was a seeking of God, because of love of God, becomes a running away at the suggestion of men and women who love him more than he deserves, for fear that this proud cocksure boy will fall terribly and disappoint those who have so guarded him.

It is another proof of the impossibility of basing purity on negation—on anything short of a positive love, and having a real man left. Erskine's offense, however, is not that he leaves much unsaid, nor that he writes in the spirit of his times, nor even that he tells a fascinating flippant story; it lies rather in the fact that he is unjust enough to call the book and the hero " Galahad."

Far different from Erskine's superficial exploitation of the old

romances is the sympathetic and understanding treatment accorded
them by that prince of present day American poets, Edwin Arlington Robinson. No other writer since Tennyson seems to have
grasped so readily the hidden mystery of the legends as a whole,
or to have possessed a clearer insight into the lives of these shadowy
Arthurian knights and ladies. Perhaps it is because he himself
" missed the medieval grace of iron clothing " that Robinson, the
romanticist, understands his characters so well There is this difference between Malory's version and Robinson's, however, that
whereas " Malory created a romantic though essentially objective
picture of obsolescent chivalry, the twentieth century poet has
retold this story not merely as a tale of love and almost universal
empire, but as the basis for an interpretation of life." [20]

Galahad finds place in two of the three lengthy blank verse
poems Robinson has constructed from the Arthurian story,[21] The
theme of these two poems, *Merlin* and *Lancelot,* is found in the
final chapters of Malory's tale of Arthur. As in the older Merlin
romances, Galahad himself never actually appears, but he remains
a vital force motivating the entire poem. When the grief-
stricken king foresees in Lancelot and Guenevere's guilty love the
wreckage of his kingdom, Merlin holds out to him the hope of a
better world to come, where the spirit will regain its ascendancy
over the flesh; when he for whom Merlin founded the Siege Perilous will come and find the Holy Grail, and restore all things to
perfect peace. And, though Galahad himself.

> . . . shall be too much a living part
> Of what he brings. . . .
> To be for long a vexed inhabitant
> Of this mad realm of stains and lower trials

still, his coming will bring light and healing to the wounded world.
The king draws comfort from Merlin's dark words, and says:

> ". . . I'll not ask for more. I have enough
> Until my new knight comes to prove and find
> The promise and the glory of the Grail."

---

[20] Beebe, Lucius, *Edwin Arlington Robinson and the Arthurian Legend,*
p. 8.
[21] *Merlin* (1917); *Lancelot* (1920); *Tristram* (1927).

Robinson's *Merlin* does not confine itself to any one version of the story, as the lesson it teaches is unlimited by person or period. Since, as Mr. Drinkwater observes,[22] every poet of importance from Aeschylus down to Mr. Robinson is fearless in making the essentialness of moral purpose the principle of his art, we may conclude that Robinson offers his own solution of life's baffling problems when he says through the lips of the aged Merlin that, if the world is to be saved, it is to be saved through the twofold medium of faith in God and faith in womankind, through

> ". . . the torch of women
> And the light that Galahad found."

In Robinson's poem, Merlin refers to Galahad as " Lancelot's undying son," and nowhere does this epithet apply to him more truly than in the poet's second Arthurian work, *Lancelot.* Lancelot, returned from the quest, has caught a glimpse of the Light that Galahad found, and can never more be satisfied. Even Guenevere's face is unable to extinguish the fire of divine discontent that burns within his breast. Gawaine notices the change and asks for an explanation, but Lancelot can only reply:

> " When I came back from seeing what I saw,
> I saw no place for me in Camelot.
> There is no place for me in Camelot.
> There is no place for me save where the Light
> May lead me, and to that place I shall go."

Galahad's example is a constant challenge to his father. What Lancelot needs is courage to fling away the baser things of sense and, like Galahad, to follow the way of the spirit; but still he demurs and dallies with the inspiration of grace until the crucial moment arrives—and then it is too late. Guenevere has asked for one last meeting before she and Lancelot go their separate ways, and Lancelot, knowing what his answer should be, sees beyond the golden head of Guenevere

> The triumph and the sadness in the face
> Of Galahad, for whom the Light was waiting

---

[22] John Drinkwater's *Preface to Robinson's Collected Poems* (English Edition).

. . . and his flickering will adjured him
To follow it and be free.

But the moment of grace passes; Lancelot succumbs to the promptings of his heart; and when for the first time he and the queen are guiltless, they are surprised by Modred in the queen's apartments; the king is informed; Guenevere is condemned to be burned at the stake, and Arthur's ideal realm suddenly collapses in utter ruin. The queen, saved by Lancelot, flees to Almesbury, and Lancelot, after one more mightly conflict of soul, realizes that Galahad's way is, after all, the only way to happiness and peace. For Lancelot, too, has seen the Light and

Where the Light falls, death falls;
And in the darkness comes the Light.

When a word stronger than his wills him away from Almesbury, Lancelot knows that a world has died for him that a world may live.

. . . He turned
Again; and he rode on, under the stars,
Out of the world, into he knew not what,
Until a vision chilled him and he saw,
Now as in Camelot, long ago in the garden,
The face of Galahad who had seen and died,
And was alive, now in a mist of gold.
He rode on into the dark, under the stars
. . . He rode on
Alone; and in the darkness came the Light.

Robinson's Galahad is perhaps the nearest approach to an abstract ideal of any Galahad of English literature. Through the darkest passes of sin, cynicism, and despair, he holds aloft the blazing torch of man's high spiritual destiny, standing before the world as the concrete embodiment of all that is best and finest in man's fallen nature, reflecting in himself that Light which is the life of the world, and which shineth in darkness though the darkness does not comprehend it.[23] Unlike Hovey's Galahad, Robinson's does not show " how light can look on darkness and forgive," but rather how the children of darkness can be transformed by grace into children of Light.

[23] *St. John*, I, 5.

Robinson's Galahad is permeated with that deep Christian philosophy which sees all truth in the light of Eternal Truth, and whose watchword is: *In tua lumine, videbimus lumen.* Like the Galahad of the *Queste,* he is concerned with one reality, the reality of the Eternal, and although he does not destroy the natural in man—since he knows that every natural thing, every natural passion is from God and therefore good—still his function is to elevate the natural, to transform it by the power of grace into the Divine. He is ever a challenge to his struggling father, a living reminder that " We have not here a lasting city, but we seek one that is to come." [24] He is ever pointing out to Lancelot that the pleasures of time are meagre and transitory; that man's heart will never rest until it rests in the Infinite Good. Galahad's aloofness and detachment from things terrestrial has nothing in it of Kant's " moral autonomy "; it shows rather an unbounded trust in a loving God, a childlike simplicity and humility, which turns the wayward father's feet from the dark paths of sin and despair into the bright way of eternal Light.

Finally, Robinson shows that the idea of Galahad is as vital today in the twentieth century as it was in the Middle Ages; that he is as essential to the modern world as he was to the medieval; that he is as necessary to Christianity as the entire idea of supernaturalized virtue. Without Galahad there would be no ideal of manhood, no knight without blemish, no model in whose footsteps men might walk. Without Galahad no man would be completely master of himself—physical strength, mere brute force, would govern the world; reverence for women and consideration for the afflicted would be ruled by passing whims. Without Galahad that " greatest lover of the world," Lancelot, would never have had a struggle or twinge of conscience, for there would have been no ideal to place upon the pedestal which every man erects within his inmost heart. Without Galahad, the Lancelots of the world, marred and scarred by many battles, would throw down their arms and surrender in despair; *with* him, however, they can not forget that deep in every human soul there is a crucible out of which, if each so wills, by the grace of God, may come a noble, unscarred, stainless knight, whose name is Galahad.

[24] *Hebr.,* xiii, 14.

CONCLUSION

Having followed Galahad through centuries of English literature, having touched here and there upon the historical and philosophical backgrounds of the authors in whose works his influence prevailed, we shall conclude with a summary and a brief speculation on the contribution which the character of Galahad has made to the history of English thought, and attempt to answer the question as to whether his character may be taken as an exponent of the thought of the times in which he appears. But first we shall offer a word in review concerning the reasons for Galahad's coming into being, and add a brief resumé of his literary history.

That Galahad's coming was an influence for good can hardly be denied, if literature is allowed to have any influence over the minds and hearts of men. That his coming satisfied a twofold purpose—desire on the part of his creators to urge men to lead better lives, and desire, from an artistic point of view, to complete an unfinished story—seems to be the accepted opinion of scholars. M. Albert Pauphilet, in an exhaustive study of the medieval *Queste*, the work in which Galahad first appears, undertakes to point out the dominant Cistercian influence in the creation of the Galahad character, and he lays great stress on the moralizing contained therein. Jessie L. Weston, on the other hand, insists that Galahad's coming was an artistic and psychological necessity capping the entire Arthurian cycle. The present writer, having carefully examined both sides of the question, attempted to prove a theory which acknowledges the didactic character of the Galahad-Grail story, and at the same time stresses its psychological and artistic necessity. She endeavored to show that her theory—the Original Sin and Grace Theory—is the only satisfactory solution to the question of Galahad's origin; it premises the fact that Galahad, in the mind of the Cistercian, represented not Christ but a mortal man who, clothed in grace, walked undaunted to his goal. This theory, moreover, denies the proposition that the Galahad elaboration is an incongruous grafting, having a few accidental beauties, but rather holds that the elaboration is the cycle's only

171

12

logical conclusion,—an artistic necessity having many accidental defects.

Turning now to Galahad's rôle in English literature, we find that the earliest English Arthurian works, beginning with Layamon's *Brut* in the early thirteenth century, made no mention of Galahad. The tendency of these earliest pieces was to stress the national rather than the religious elements in the cycle, and Galahad belonged essentially to the latter. In the last quarter of the fourteenth century, however, when interest in religious poetry prevailed, the Galahad tradition gained ground. The Joseph of Arimathea prelude to the Grail story (with which the Galahad character was definitely identified) acquired popularity, and England began to look to its buried literary traditions. Political conditions in the fifteenth century checked the cultivation of artistic expression, however, and Lovelich's *Holy Grail,* the first English work in which Galahad is explicitly mentioned, failed because of its tedious style to popularize the Grail hero. Malory's *Morte Darthur,* based largely upon the Old French *Queste,* gave in the latter fifteenth century the first complete picture in English of Galahad. After Malory, Galahad suddenly disappeared, and for three hundred years our literature was silent concerning him. This protracted silence is traceable chiefly to two causes: the skeptical attitude of the Renaissance towards medieval romances generally, and the cordial dislike which the reformers and humanists entertained for medieval philosophy and medieval literature, whose exponent Galahad was. Moreover, the spirit of rationalism, which began to expand in the fifteenth century and which reached its climax in the classicism of the seventeenth century, was also a vital force in preventing Galahad's reappearance in English literature. The Puritan Age had little sympathy with the medieval mystic, and the writers of the Restoration were for the most part scoffers of those very ideals which Galahad came to uphold. Not until the rebirth of medievalism in the latter eighteenth century did Galahad again attain to his full stature, and not until then did men begin to understand the purpose for which Galahad came into existence. Endowed with keen spiritual vision, Tennyson and his contemporaries sensed the meaning behind the allegory of the Grail, and each, according to his light, interpreted the Grail hero

as he saw him best. No period, however, approached so close or
wandered so far from the Cistercian conception of Galahad than the
early twentieth century—a period of shifting moral standards and
conflicting literary ideals.

In the history of every literature an individual character, like
Galahad, appears and reappears under varying motifs and treatments; and the *stoff,* or character material, may, with its modifications, be taken as indicative of the spiritual and intellectual life of
the period.[1] In German literature, for example, we have the Ideal
Man type appearing in the simple, God-fearing, very human Parzifal of Wolfram, of the years around 1200; again, in the rigid and
uncompromising ascetic Simplicissimus of Grimmelshausen, of the
seventeenth; later, in the avowed agnostic Agathon of Wieland, of
the eighteenth; and finally, in the confirmed rationalist Wilhelm
Meister of Goethe, of the beginning of the nineteenth century. In
English literature, the Lancelot material has gone through numerous treatments of all possible forms and conceptions, ranging
from the earliest metrical romances to Masefield's *Midsummer
Night* of the present decade.

It is to be noted, however, that practically always the fundamental idea and form is not accident, but is the expression of the
inner disposition of the age. The material is, so to speak, a " constant " through which a nation's mental life and its feelings of
form are manifest.

Now, the curious fact which presents itself in tracing Galahad's
path down the centuries of English literature is the constancy with
which, in spite of the various psychological and sociological forces
at play upon his character, he practically preserves those qualities
and characteristics peculiar to him in the Old French *Queste* and
in Malory. This constancy appears well-nigh phenomenal when
one compares the history of the *stoff* of the Parsifal, Gawain, Merlin,
Tristram, and Lancelot romances, to mention only Arthurian material. Whether the form of expression be drama, epic, lyric, or
novel, the character of Galahad remains essentially the same. In
this respect Galahad can not be taken as the exponent of the mind

---

[1] Cf. Paul Merker and Wolfgang Stammler, *Reallexikon der Deutschen
Literaturgeschichte*, Vol. 3, p. 309.

of the English people in the same sense as Wolfram's Parzifal can be taken as an exponent or *" Träger "* of the German mind in the late twelfth, Grimmelshausen's Simplicissimus in the seventeenth, Wieland's Agathon in the eighteenth, and Goethe's Wilhelm Meister in the beginning of the nineteenth century. For although the Galahad of Malory and of Lovelich may be said to reflect the mysticism of the medievalist; the Galahad of Tennyson and of Wordsworth, the moralizing mind of the Victorian; the Galahad of Morris, the emotional fervor of the Pre-Raphaelite romanticist; the Galahad of Erskine, the cynicism of the twentieth century pragmatist; and the Galahad of Robinson, the clear visioning of the twentieth century psychologist; still, through all the play and counterplay of philosophic thought, he remains fundamentally and essentially the same. The Galahad of English literature has a certain character of immutability which precludes the modifications proper to his analogue in German literature. Whether the nineteenth century Pre-Raphaelite adds a dash of color by portraying him smarting under the lash of fleshly temptations, or the twentieth century caricaturist depicts him as a selfish, unlovable prig, he remains unmistakably Galahad. He is ever the Quester of the Ideal, the Searcher for the Divine. The Galahad of Malory is the Galahad of Tennyson, of Hawker, of Davidson, of Robinson, —the Galahad who for five centuries has been a fixed ideal in the minds and hearts of the English people. *Why* this is so, the philosophy of literature must decide; the present writer merely ventures the suggestion that this constancy of the Galahad character is the result of a twofold cause: one, the subconscious annexing of Galahad to Christ; the other, an instinctive reverence for the integrity of the ideals rooted in the national literature. Possibly, too, the conservative Anglo-Saxon mind may be somewhat reluctant to accept and embrace new currents of thought coming to the peaceful island of England from a restless Continent.

Galahad, though purely literary in origin, represents in English literature the incarnation of an ideal so closely allied to the Divine Ideal that he shares the attribute of divine immutability. The perfect seeker after God, he stands witness to the yearnings of men's hearts towards that ultimate Ideal, that divine destiny which cannot be fulfilled in the plane of the natural order. Man, constantly reaching out after the unattainable, ever grasping but never seizing ideals of goodness and beauty, gropes blindly towards his supernatural end only because the finite is everywhere present to divert him from the infinite. Galahad solves the relation between the finite and the infinite, he gives meaning to the yearning of men's souls by spanning the bridge between sense and spirit, and showing man that the only way to lasting happiness is in the Quest of the Grail—in following Him Who is both God and Perfect Man, the Alpha and Omega of all being. This is the important message which Galahad has contributed to English literature, a message which derives its force from the stupendous fact of the Incarnation, in which God, by becoming Man, has lifted man up to God, and united man generically with his Maker. By the Incarnation man is raised above the purely natural order into a higher, diviner grade of existence; and it is only in that higher plane he can work out his destiny. Only in the sphere of the Grail can he attain to eternal life: for in the Grail is the secret of life, the solution to the mystery of life, the answer to the unsatisfied yearnings of man for an Infinite Love.

BIBLIOGRAPHY

A. CRITICAL WORKS (SELECTED).

Adams, Karl, *The Spirit of Catholicism.* New York, 1930.

Anitchkof, E., " Le Galaad du Lancelot-Graal et les Galaads de la Bible,"
Romania, LIII (1927), p. 388.

———— " Le Saint Graal et les Rites Eucharistiques," *Romania,* LV (1930),
p. 174.

App, August J., *Lancelot in English Literature.* Washington, 1929.

Balaguer, Bohigas P., " El Lanzarote " espanol del manuscritio 9611 de la
Bibl. Nacional, *Rev. de fil. esp.* 11 (1924), p. 282.

Baxter, Sylvester, *The Holy Grail: An Explanation.* Boston, 1904.

Becker, E. J., *A Contribution to the Comparative Study of the Medieval
Visions of Heaven and Hell.* Baltimore, 1899.

Bedier, J., *Preface to Boulenger's Merlin l'Enchanteur. Les de Lancelot.*
Paris, 1922.

Beebe, Lucius, *Edwin Alington Robinson and the Arthurian Legend.* (Privately printed.) Cambridge, Mass., 1921.

Billings, A. H., " A Guide to the Middle English Metrical Romances,"
Yale Studies in English, IX (1901).

Birch–Hirschfeld, *Die Sage vom Gral.* Leipzig, 1877.

Bonilla y San Martín, *Las Leyendas de Wagner en la Literatura Española.*
Madrid, 1913.

Borodine, M. Lot, *La femme et l'amour au XIIe siècle.* Paris, 1909.

———— " Tristam et Lancelot," *Medieval Studies in Memory of Gertrude
Schoepperle Loomis,* 21 (1927).

———— " Les deux conquerants du Graal: Perceval et Galaad," *Romania,*
XLVII (1921), p. 41 ff.

Bradley, Charles F., *The Quest of the Holy Grail.* Boston, 1896.

Brown, A. C. L., " The Grail and the English Sir Perceval," *Modern
Philology* XVI (1919), p. 559 ff. *Ibid.,* XVII (1919), p. 361.

———— " The Bleeding Lance," *Publications of the Modern Language Association,* XXV (1910), p. 1 ff.

———— " The Round Table Before Wace," *(Harvard) Studies and Notes in
Philology and Literature,* VII (1900), p. 183 ff.

———— " From Caldron of Plenty to the Grail," *Modern Philology,* XIV
(1916), p. 385 ff.

———— " Welsh Traditions in Layamon's Brut," *Modern Philology,* I (1903),
pp. 95-103.

Bruce, James Douglas, *The Evolution of Arthurian Romance from the
Beginnings Down to the Year 1300.* (2 vols.) Baltimore, 1923.

Bruce, James Douglas, "Modrain, Corbenic, and the Vulgate Grail Romances," *Modern Language Notes*, XXXIV (1919), p. 385.

———— "Did Chrétien Identify the Grail with the Mass," *Modern Language Notes*, 41 (1926), p. 226.

———— "Galahad, Nascien and Some Other Names in the Grail Romances," *Modern Language Notes*, XXXIII (1918), p. 129 ff.

Brugger, E., *The Illuminated Tree in Two Arthurian Romances*. New York, 1929.

Cambridge History of English Literature. Vol. I. *From the Beginnings to the Cycles of Romances*. London and New York, 1907.

Carmen, Bliss, *Introduction to Richard Hovey's Holy Grail*. New York, 1907.

Chambers, E. H., *Arthur of Britain*. London, 1927.

Chesterton, G. K., *Tennyson*. London, 1903.

Cohen, Gustave, *Chrétien de Troyes et son œuvre*. Paris, 1931.

Coulton, G. G., *Medieval Studies*. London, 1907-1924.

Cross, Tom Peete and William A. Nitze, *Lancelot and Guinevere: A Study on the Origins of Courtly Love*. Chicago, 1930.

Dickinson, W. H., *King Arthur in Cornwall*. London, 1900.

Dunlop, John C., *History of Prose Fiction*. Vol. I. London, 1896.

Dunbar, H. F., *Symbolism in Medieval Thought and Its Consummation in the Divine Comedy*. New Haven, 1929.

Faral, E., *Recherches sur les sources latines des contes et romans courtois du moyen âge*. Paris, 1913.

Fisher, Lizette Andrews, *The Mystic Vision in the Grail Legend and in the Divine Comedy*. Columbia University, New York, 1917.

Fletcher, R. H., *The Arthurian Material in the Chronicles especially Those of Great Britain and France*. Boston, 1906.

———— "Some Arthurian Fragments," *Publications of the Modern Language Association*, XVIII (1903), p. 84 ff.

Frazer, Sir James G., *The Golden Bough*. London, 1900.

Gardner, Edmund G., *The Arthurian Legend in Italian Literature*. New York, 1930.

Gilson, E., "La mystique de la grâce dans la Queste del Saint Graal," *Romania*, LI (1925), p. 321.

Golther, Wolfgang, *Parzival und der Graal*. Stuttgart, 1925.

———— *Parzival in der deutschen Literatur*. Berlin, 1929.

Gourvitch, J., "Drayton's Debt to Geoffrey of Monmouth," *The Review of English Studies*, IV, No. 16 (1928), p. 394 ff.

Grenlich, Emil, *Die Arthursage in der Historia regum Brittanniae des Golfred vom Monmouth*. Diss. Halle, 1916.

Griscom, Acton, *The Historia Regum Brittaniae of Geoffrey of Monmouth*. New York, 1929.

Gurteen, S. Humphrey, *The Arthurian Epic. A Comparative Study of the*

Cambrian, Breton, and Anglo-Norman Versions of the Story and Tennyson's Idylls of the King. New York, 1895.

Hallam, Lord Tennyson, *Alfred Tennyson: Memoir by His Son.* (2 Vols.) New York, 1897.

Hamblin, Frank Russell, *Development of Allegory in Classical Pastoral.* Chicago, 1922.

Harper, Carrie Anna, *The Sources of the British Chronicle in Spenser's " Faerie Queen."* Philadelphia, 1910.

Harper, George McLean, *The Legend of the Holy Grail.* Baltimore, 1893.

Heffner, Ray, " Spenser"s Allegory in Book I of the Faerie Queene,"' *Speculum,* XXVII (1930), p. 142-161.

Heinzel, R., " Über die französischen Gralromane," *Denkschriften der Kais. akad. der Wiss. Philo. Hist. Klasse,* XL. Vienna (1892).

Henderson, G., *Arthurian Motifs in Ghadelic Literature.* Halle, 1912.

Hertz, W., *Die Sage von Parzival und dem Gral.* Breslau, 1882.

Hibbard, Laura, *Medieval Romance in England.* New York, 1924.

——— " Arthur's Round Table," *Publications of the Modern Language Association,* 41 (1916), p. 771.

Hodghin, Thomas, *Cornwall and Brittany.* 38th Annual Report of the Royal Cornwall Polytecnic Society, New Series. Vol. 1, Part 3. Penryn, (1911), p. 434-468.

Hopkins, Annette B., *The Influence of Wace on the Arthurian Romances of Crestien de Troies.* Diss. University of Chicago, 1913.

Jaffrey, Robert, *King Arthur and the Holy Grail,* New York, 1928.

——— *The Two Knights of the Swan, Lohengrin and Helyas.* London and New York, 1910.

Jewett, Sophie, *Introduction to Tennyson's Holy Grail.* New York, 1901.

Jones, Richard, *The Growth of the Idylls of the King.* Philadelphia, 1895.

Jones, T. Gwynn, *Some Arthurian Material in Keltic Awerystwyth Studies.* VIII, 1926.

Jones, W. L. *King Arthur in History and Legend.* Boston, 1914.

Jubainville, H. D. Arbois de, *L'Epopée Celtique en Irlande.* Paris, 1892. Tome I. *In Cours de Littérature Celtique.* Tome V.

Kempe, Dorothy, *The Legend of the Holy Grail, Its Sources, Character and Development.* London, 1905.

Kittredge, George Lyman, *Sir Thomas Malory.* (Privately Printed.) Barnstable, 1925.

Kurz, Johann Baptist, *Wolfram von Eschenbach.* Ansbach, 1930.

Legouis, Emile, and Louis Cazamian, *A History of English Literature.* (2 Vols.) London and Toronto, 1926 and 1927.

——— *Edmund Spenser.* Paris, 1923.

Liss, Oskar, *Die Arthurepen des Sir Richard Blackmore.* Diss. Strassburg, 1911.

Litchfield, Mary E., *Edmund Spenser.* New York, 1906.

Loomis, Roger Sherman, " Some Names in Arthurian Romances," *Publica-*

cations of the Modern Language Association, XLV (1930), p. 416-443.

Loomis, Roger Sherman, *Celtic Myth and Arthurian Romance.* New York, 1927.

—— " Geoffrey of Monmouth and Arthurian Origins," *Speculum,* January, 1928.

—— " Studies and Notes," *Philology and Literature,* X, (1906).

—— *Medieval Studies in Memory of Gertrude Schoepperle Loomis.* Paris and New York, 1927.

—— " Medieval Iconography and the Question of Arthurian Origins," *Modern Language Notes,* 40 (1925), p. 105.

—— " The Story of the Modena Archivolt and Its Mythological Roots," *RR.* 15 (1924), p. 266.

—— " The Date, Source, and Subject of the Arthurian Sculpture at Modena," *Medieval Studies in Memory of Gertrude Schoepperle Loomis,* Paris and New York, 1927, p. 209.

Lot, Mme. Myrrha, *La femme et l'amour au XIIe siècle, d'après les poèmes de Chrétien de Troyes.* Paris, 1909.

Lot-Borodine M., et Gertrude Schoepperle, *Lancelot el Galaad mis en nouveau langage, avec une introduction par* Roger S. Loomis. New York, 1926.

Lot, Ferdinand, *Etude sur le Launcelot en prose.* Paris, 1918.

—— " Les Sources de la Vita Merlini de Gaufrei de Monmouth," *Annales de Bretagne,* XV (1899-1900), p. 325-347 and p. 555-569.

—— " Nouvelles Etudes sur la Provenance du Cycle Arthurian," *Romania,* XXVII (1898-1899), p. 529-573. Vol. XXVIII, p. 321 ff.

—— " Celtics," Notes on Arthurian Subjects. *Romania,* XXIV (1895), p. 321-338.

—— " Glastonbury et Avalon," *Romania,* XXVII (1898), p. 529 ff.

Loth, Joseph, *Contributions à l'étude des romans de la Table Ronde.* Paris, 1912.

—— " Des Nouvelles Théories sur l'Origine des Romans Arthuriens," *Revue Celtique,* XIII, p. 475-503.

McCallum, W. M. *Tennyson's Idylls of the King and Arthurian Story from the Sixteenth Century.* Glasgow, 1894.

Malone, Kemp, " Artorius," *Modern Philology,* XXII (1925), 367-374.

Maynadier, Howard, *The Arthur of the English Poets.* Cambridge, Mass., 1907.

Mead, W. E., *Chinon of England.* E. E. T. S. London, 1925.

Millican, Charles, " Spenser and the Arthurian Legend," *Review of English Studies,* VI (1930), p. 167-174.

Newell, William Wells, *King Arthur and the Table Round.* (2 Vols.) Boston, 1897.

—— *The Legend of the Holy Grail and the Perceval of Crestien of Troyes.* Cambridge, Mass., 1902.

Nitze, William A., " On the Chronology of the Grail Romances," *Language and Literature*, Chicago, 1923.

———" Glastonbury and the Holy Grail," *Modern Philology* (1903), p. 247 ff.

———" The Fisher King in the Grail Romances," *Publications of the Modern Language Association*, XXIV (1909), p. 365 ff.

———" The Sister's Son and the Conte del Graal," *Modern Philology*, IX (1912), p. 291 ff.

———" Concerning the word *Graal, Greal*," *Modern Philology*, XIII (1916), p. 681.

———" The date of Robert de Borron's 'Metrical Joseph' ", *The Manly Anniversary Studies in Language and Literature*. Chicago, 1923.

———" The Identity of Brons in Robert de Borron's 'Metrical Joseph'," *Medieval Studies in Memory of Gertrude Schoepperle Loomis*. Paris and New York, 1927.

Nutt, Alfred T., *Stuudies on the Legend of the Holy Grail*. London, 1888.

———*Popular Studies in Mythology, Romance and Folklore*. London, 1902.

Pallen, Conde B., *The Meaning of the Idylls of the King*. New York, 1904.

Paris, Gaston, " Etudes sur les romans de la Table Ronde," *Romania*, X (1881), p. 465 ff. XII (1883), p. 459 ff.

———" Les romans en vers du cycle de la Table Ronde," *Histoire Littéraire de la France*, XXX (1888), p. 1 ff.

———*Medieval French Literature*. Translated by Hannah Lynch. London, 1903.

Parry, John J., Arthurian Bibliography. 1931.

Paton, Lucy Allen, *Studies in the Fairy Mythology of Arthurian Romance*. Boston, 1903.

Pauphilet, Albert, " La Queste del Saint Graal du MS. Bibl. Nat. Fr. 343," *Romania*, XXXVI (1907) p. 591-609.

———*Études sur la Queste del Saint Graal Attribuée à Gautier Map*. Paris, 1921.

Peebles, Rose J., *The Legend of Longinus in Ecclesiastical Tradition and English Literature and Its Connection with the Grail*. Baltimore, 1911.

Pierce, Grace A., *The Red Cross Knight and the Legend of Britomart (The Lady Knight) from Spenser's "Faerie Queene."* New York, 1924.

Pietsch, Karl, " The Madrid Manuscripts of the Spanish Grail Fragments," *Modern Philology*, 18 (1920) (1921), p. 147-591.

———*Spanish Grail Fragments. (El Libro de Josef Abarimatia; la Estoria de Merlin, Lancarote.)* University of Chicago, 1924.

Power, Eileen, *Medieval English Nunneries*. Cambridge, Mass., 1922.

Redman, B., *Edwin Arlington Robinson*. New York, 1927.

Rhys, John, *Studies in the Arthurian Legend*. Oxford, 1891.

Robinson, J. A., *Two Glastonbury Legends: King Arthur and St. Joseph of Arimathea.* Cambridge, Mass., 1926.

Routh, James E., *Two Studies on the Ballad Theory.* Baltimore, 1905.

Schiller, Meir, *Sir Thomas Malory's " Le Morte D'Arthur " und die Englische Arthurdichtung des XIX Jahrhunderts.* Strassburg, 1900.

Schlauch, Margaret, *Medieval Narrative.* New York, 1928.

Schröder, Franz Rolf, *Die Parzivalfrage.* München, 1928.

Schofield, W. H., *English Literature from Norman Conquest to Chaucer.* New York, 1906.

——— *Chivalry in English Literature.* Boston, 1895.

Scudder, Vida D., *Morte Darthur of Sir Thomas Malory and Its Sources.* New York, 1917.

Singer, S., *Die Arthursage.* Bern und Leipzig, 1926.

Slover, Clark, H., *Early Literary Channels Between Britain and Ireland.* Diss. University of Texas, 1929.

Sommer, O. H., *Introduction to Le Morte Darthur by Syr Thomas Malory.* London, 1891.

——— " Galahad and Perceval," *Modern Philology.* July 1907, January 1908, Vol. V, p. 55 ff. and 181 ff.

Strachey, Sir Edward, *Introduction to Malory's Le Morte Darthur.* New York, 1901.

Taylor, A. B., *An Introduction to Medieval Romance.* London, 1930.

Titchener, F. H., " The Romances of Chretien de Troyes," *RR.* 16 (1925), p. 165.

Van Doren, Mark, *Edwin Arlington Robinson*, New York, 1927.

Van Dyke, Henry, *The Poetry of Tennyson.* New York, 1898.

Ven-ten Bensel, Elise van der, *The Character of King Arthur in English Literature.* Amsterdam, 1925.

Vinaver, Eugene, *Malory.* New York, 1929.

Waddell, H. A., *The British Edda.* London, 1929.

Waite, A. E., *The Hidden Church of the Holy Grail.* London, 1909.

Walther, Marie, *Malory's Einfluss auf Spensers Faerie Queene.* Eisleben, 1890.

Wechssler, Edward, *Die Sage vom heiligen Gral in ihrer Entwicklung bis auf Richard Wagners Parsifal.* Halle, 1898.

Weston, Jessie L., *The Legend of Sir Lancelot Du Lac.* London, 1901.

——— *The Legend of Sir Gawain.* London, 1897.

——— *The Legend of Sir Perceval. Studies upon its Origin, Development, and Position in the Arthurian Cycle.* (2 Vols.) London, 1906.

——— *King Arthur and His Knights. A Survey of Arthurian Romance.* London, 1899.

——— *Sir Gawain at the Grail Castle.* London, 1903.

——— *The Quest of the Holy Grail.* London, 1913.

——— *From Ritual to Romance.* London, 1920.

Weston, Jessie L., " The Relative Position of ' Perceval ' and ' Galahad '
    Romances," *Modern Language Review*, XXI (1926), p. 385.
———— " The Relation of the Perlesvaus and the Cyclic Romances," *Romania*, XLI (1925), p. 348.
———— "Notes on the Grail Romances: Caput Johannis, Caput Christi,"
    Romania, 49 (1923), p. 273.
Wilmotte, M., " La Part de Chrétien de Troyes dans la Composition du plus
    ancien Poème sur le Gral," *Academie Royal de Belgique*, XVI (1930),
    p. 46-60 and 97-119; 378-393.
———— " L'état actuel des études sur la legende du gral," *Academie Royal
    de Belgique*, XV (1929), p. 100-122.
———— *Le poème du Gral et ses auteurs.* Paris, 1930.
Wülker, Richard, "Über die Quellen Layamon's Brut," *PBB*, III (1876).
Wright, Thomas, *Introduction to Malory's Morte Darthur.* London, 1889.
Zarncke, F., " Zur Geschichte der Gralsage," *Paul and Braune's Beiträge*,
    III (1876).

B. Literary Works.

Ancient English Metrical Romances. (3 Vols.)   Joseph Ritson.   London,
    1802.
Arnold, Matthew, *Tristam and Iseult, Poetical Works.*   New York, 1897.
Arthur: A Short Sketch of His Life and History in English Verse of the
    First Half of the Fifteenth Century.   Ed. by Frederick Furnivall.
    London, E. E. T. S., 1864.
Austin, Martha W., *Tristram and Isoult.*   Boston, 1905.
Amours, T. J. (ed.), *Awyntyrs of Arthure* in *Scottish Alliterative Poems.*
    Edinburgh and London, 1897.
Beverly, Rhomas de, (Newcomen, Thomas), *The Youth of Sir Arthur and
    Other Poems.*   London, 1925.
Binyon, Laurence, *Arthur: A Tragedy.*   Boston, 1923.
Blackmore, Richard, *Prince Arthur, an Heroick Poem.*   London, 1695.
Boron, Robert de, *Le roman de l'estoire du Graal.*   Ed. by W. A. Nitze,
    Paris, 1927.
Bulwer-Lytton, *King Arthur.*   Poetical Works.   London, 1695.
Carr, J. Comyns, *Tristram and Iseult.*   A Drama in Four Acts.   London,
    1906.
———— *King Arthur.*   London, 1895.
Child, F. J., *English and Scottish Ballads.*   Ed. by Francis J. Child, Boston, 1898.
Coffin, Robert P., " Tristram.   The Ballad of San Graal."   *Poet Lore*
    XXXIII (1922), p. 464-468.
Comfort, William Wistar, *The Quest of the Holy Grail.*   London, 1926.
Davidson, John, *The Last Ballad and Other Poems.*   London and New
    York, 1899.
Dillon, Arthur, *King Arthur Pendragon.*   London, 1906.

Drayton, Michael, *Polyolbion, The Complete Works*, Vol. I. London, 1906.

Dryden, John, *King Arthur or the British Worthy.* London, 1691.

Ellis, Sir Henry, *Hardyng's Chronicle.* London, 1812.

Erskine, John, *Galahad.* Indianapolis, 1926.

Evans, Sebastian, *The High History of the Holy Grail.* London, 1899.

Fabyan, Robert, *New Chronicles of England and France. Two Parts.* Ed. by Henry Ellis. London, 1811.

Furnivall, F. J., *La Queste del Saint Graal.* London, 1864.

✓ *Gawaine, The Marriage of Sir,* Ed. by I. Gollancz in *The Percy Folio of Old English Ballads and Romances.* Vol. I, p. 59-67. The De La More Press. Folio, n. d.

Gordon, Adam Lindsay, *The Rhyme of Joyous Garde.* London, 1912.

Graal, Les Adventures au la Queste del Saint. Ed. by Oskar H. Sommer in *Vulgate Version of Arthurian Romances*, Vol. VI. Washington, D. C., 1913.

Grafton's Chronicle: or History of England. London, 1809.

Y Seint Greal, originally written about 1200. Ed. with a translation and glossary from a copy preserved among the Hengwrt MSS. in the Peniarth Library by Robert Williams. London, 1876.

Gruffydd, W. J., *The Mabinogion.* Transactions of the Hon. Society of Cymmrodorion. Session 1912-1913.

Guest, Charlotte, *The Mabinogion.* English Translation. Everyman's Library, 1919.

Guthrie, Kenneth Sylvan, *Perronik the 'Innocent.'* New York, 1915.

Hamilton, Lord Ernest William, *Lancelot: A Romance of the Court of King Arthur.* London, 1926.

Hawker, Robert Stephen, *Quest of the Sangraal.* Poetical Works. New York, 1899.

Heber, Reginald, *Morte D'Arthur: A Fragment.* Poetical Works. London, 1841.

Heywood, Thomas, *The Life of Merlin,* London, 1641.

Hicks, Edward, *Sir Thomas Malory, His Turbulent Career.* Boston, 1928

Hilton, William, *Arthur, Monarch of the Britains. A Tragedy.* Newcastle upon-Tyne, 1776.

Hole, Richard, *Arthur: or the Northern Enchantment. A Poetical Romance in Seven Books.* London, 1789.

Hooker, Brian, *Morven and Grail.* Yale University Press, 1915.

Horton, Douglas, *A Legend of the Grail.* Boston and Chicago, 1925.

Hovey, Richard, *Launcelot and Guenevere: A Poem in Dramas.* Boston, 1898-1907. (This includes: *The Quest of Merlin; The Marriage of Guenevere; The Birth of Galahad; Taliesin,* and a fragment—*The Holy Graal*).

Hucher, Eugene, *Le Saint Graal.* (3 Vols.) Paris, 1875-1878.

Joseph of Arimathie: Otherwise Called the Romance of the Seint Grall, or

Holy Grail. Edited with notes and glossarial index, by W. W. Skeat. London, E. E. T. S. (1871). No. 44.

Knowles, James, *The Legends of King Arthur and His Knights.* London, New York, 1923.

Launfal, Ed. by Joseph Ritson in *Ancient English Metrical Romances.* Vol. I. London, 1802.

Layamon's Brut, Ed. with Introduction, Notes and Glossary by Joseph Hall. Oxford, 1924.

Layamon's Brut or Chronicle of Britain, Ed. by Frederick Madden. London, 1847.

LeGallienne, Richard, " On Rereading *Le Morte d'Arthur.*" Poem. *Bookman* L (1920), p. 417-420.

Leland, John, *Assertio Inclytissimi Arturii.* Ed. by William E. Mead, E. E. T. S., Original Series No. 165. London, 1925.

Libius Disconus. Ed. by I. Gollancz in *The Percy Folio of Old English Ballads and Romances,* Vol. III p. 58 ff. The De La More Press Folio. n.d.

Lord, Daniel A., *The Vision of Sir Launfal,* Chicago, 1918.

Lot, Mme. Myrrha, *Lancelot et Galaad* mis en nouveau langage par Myrrha Lot-Borodine et Gertrude Schoepperle, avec une Introduction par Roger Loomis. New York, 1926.

Lovelich, Henry, *The History of the Holy Grail.* Ed. by F. J. Furnivall. E. E. T. S., Extra Series, Vol. I (1874); Vol. II (1877).

Masefield, John, *Midsummer Night.* New York, 1928.

Merlin, A Transcript from MS No. 159 in Lincoln's Inn Library made by George Ellis. Specimens of Early English Metrical Romances, (1848), London, p. 77-143.

Mead, William E., *Chinon of England.* E. E. T. S., London, 1925.

Middleton, Christopher, *Chinon of England.* Ed. by William E. Mead, E. E. T. S. Original Series, No. 165, London, 1925.

Milton, John, *Complete Works.* New York, 1930.

Moore, J. S., *Ancient Ballad Poetry of Great Britain.* London, 1860.

Morris, William, *The Defence of Guenevere. Early Romances.* New York, 1910.

—— *King Arthur's Tomb. Early Romances.* New York, 1910.

—— *Sir Galahad, a Christmas Mystery. Early Romances.* New York, 1910.

—— *A Good Knight in Prison. Early Romances.* New York, 1910.

Newbolt, Henry, *Modred: A Tragedy.* London, 1895.

Pallen, Conde B., *The Death of Sir Launcelot and Other Poems.* Boston, 1902.

Paris, Paulin, *Les romans de la Table Ronde mis en nouveau Langage.* (Vols. III, IV, V.) 1872-1877.

Pauphilet, Albert, *La Queste del Saint Graal roman du XIIIe siècle.* Paris, 1923.

Peacock, Thomas Love, *The Misfortunes of Elphin.* The World Classics, 1924.

Percy Folio of Old English Ballads and Romances, The Ed. by I. Gollancz. The De La More Press. Folio.

Percy, Thomas, *Reliques of Ancient Poetry,* Ed. by J. V. Prichard (2 Vols.) London, 1892. Edited with Notes, Glossary, etc., by Henry B. Wheatley. (3 Vols.) London, 1886.

Rhys, Ernest, *Lays of the Round Table and Lyric Romances.* London, 1918.

———— *The Masque of the Grail.* London, 1908.

———— *Welsh Ballads and Other Poems.* London, 1898.

Robinson, Edwin Arlington, *Lancelot,* New York, 1920.

———— *Merlin.* New York, 1917.

———— *Tristram.* New York, 1927.

Robinson, Richard, *Translation of John Leland's Assertion of King Arthure.* Ed. by William E. Mead. E. E. T. S. London, 1925.

Rowley, William, *The Birth of Merlin..* Edited by A. F. Hopkinson. London, 1901.

Scott, Sir Walter, *The Bridal of Triermain.* Complete Poetical and Dramatic Works. London and New York, 1883.

———— *Preface to Dryden's King Arthur,* revised and corrected by George Saintsbury. Edinburgh, 1884. Vol. VIII.

Scottish Alliterative Poems. Edited by F. J. Amours with Notes and Glossary. Edinburgh and London, 1897.

Sir Gawayne and the Green Knight. Ed. by Richard Morris. London, E. E. T. S. 1864. Second Edition Revised 1869.

Skene, William F., *The Four Ancient Books of Wales.* (Vols I and II.) Edinburgh, 1868.

Sommer, O. H., *The Vulgate Version of the Arthurian Romances.* (7 Vols.) Washington, D. C., Vol. I, L'Estoire del Saint Graal (1909) ; Vol. II, L'Estoire de Merlin (1908) ; Vol. III (1910), Vol. IV (1911), V (1912), *Le Livre de Lancelot del Lac;* Vol. VI, *Les Aventures ou La Queste del Saint Graal, La Mort le Roi Artus.* (1913).

Southworth, May E., *Galahad, Knight Errant.* Boston, 1907.

Spence, Walter, *Idylls of the King: A Spiritual Interpretation.* New York, 1909.

Spenser, Edmund, *Faerie Queene.* Complete Works. Boston and New York, 1908.

Swinburne, Algernon C., *Tristram of Lyonesse.* Poems, Vol. I. London, 1911.

———— *The Tale of Balen.* Poems. Vol. IV. London, 1911.

Taft, Linwood, *Galahad: A Pageant of the Holy Grail.* New York, 1924.

Tennyson, Alfred, *The Lady of Shalott; Morte d'Arthur; Sir Galahad; Sir Launcelot and Queen Guinevere; Merlin and the Gleam.* Complete Works. New York, 1891.

Tennyson, Alfred, *Tennyson's Coming of Arthur, Gareth and Lynette.* With Notes by Willie Boughton. New York, 1913.

———— *Idylls of the King.* With Introduction and Notes by William T. Vlymen. New York, 1901.

———— *Idylls of the King.* With Introduction and Notes by W. D. Lewis. New York, 1911.

Thornton, Robert, *King Arthur.* Ed. from Robert Thornton's MS. E.E.T.S. Original Series No. 8.

Tristrem, Sir, ed. by George P. McNeil. Edinburgh and London, 1886.

Trevelyan, Robert C., *The Birth of Parsival: A Drama.* New York, 1905.

———— *The New Parsival: An Operatic Fable.* London, 1914.

Warton, Thomas, *The Grave of King Arthur.* Poems. Vol. LXVIII. Cheswick, 1822.

Westwood, Thomas, *The Quest of the Sangreal.* London, 1885.

Whiton, Helen Isabel, *Parsifal and Galahad: the Quest of the Ideal.* New York, 1904.

Williams, Robert, *Y Seint Greal.* Translated from Hengwrt MSS. preserved in Peniarth Library. London, 1876-1892.

Wilmotte, Maurice, *Le Roman du Gral, d'après les versions les plus anciennes.* Paris (1930).

Wordsworth, William, *The Egyptian Maid.* Complete Works. New York, 1888.